BIBLIOGRAPHIES IN AMERICAN MUSIC

Editors J. Bunker Clark and Marilyn S. Clark
University of Kansas

THE COLLEGE MUSIC SOCIETY

President Arthur R. Tollefson
University of Arkansas

PUBLICATIONS COMMITTEE

Chairman Daniel T. Politoske
University of Kansas

Theodore Albrecht
Park College

J. Bunker Clark
University of Kansas

Marilyn S. Clark
University of Kansas

Robby D. Gunstream *ex officio*
The College Music Society

AMERICAN MUSIC STUDIES
A CLASSIFIED BIBLIOGRAPHY OF MASTER'S THESES

JAMES R. HEINTZE

BIBLIOGRAPHIES IN AMERICAN MUSIC   NUMBER EIGHT
PUBLISHED FOR THE COLLEGE MUSIC SOCIETY
INFORMATION COORDINATORS, INC.   1984   DETROIT

On the endsheets "Halleluja" from the *Paradisches Wunder-Spiel,* 1751,
Ephrata Cloister, Pennsylvania.
COURTESY OF THE MUSIC DIVISION OF THE LIBRARY OF CONGRESS.
SEE PAGE 124.

Copyright © 1984 *The College Music Society*
Printed and bound in the United States of America
Publisher *Information Coordinators, Inc.*
1435-37 Randolph Street, Detroit, Michigan 48226
Editing *J.Bunker Clark, University of Kansas*
Book design *Vincent Kibildis*
Photocomposition *Elaine Gorzelski*

Library of Congress *Cataloging in Publication Data*
Heintze, James R.
American Music Studies
(Bibliographies in American music, no. 8)
"Sources cited": p.
Includes indexes.
1. Music—United States—History and criticism—Bibliography.
2. Dissertations, Academic—United States—Bibliography.
I. Title.   II. Series.
ML128.M8H44   016.78'0973   84-9103
ISBN 0-89990-021-6

In Memory of My Brother

RICHARD G. HEINTZE

Musician, 1939-1981

*C*ontents

AMERICAN MUSIC STUDIES
A CLASSIFIED BIBLIOGRAPHY OF MASTER'S THESES

Acknowledgements

THERE ARE MANY PERSONS who deserve special thanks for helping to make this book possible. Timothy Lenk visited a number of college libraries in Colorado and reported their thesis holdings to me; Gillian Anderson and Wayne Shirley of the Music Division, Library of Congress, Judith Lehman Proffitt of the Historical Society of Frederick County, Frederick, Maryland, and Jane Katz of the John Work Garrett Library of Johns Hopkins University, cheerfully spent time assisting me with their libraries' holdings; Francine Krasowska and Joe Moriarty assisted me in typing the several drafts of this work; Donald D. Dennis, University Librarian at the American University, without whose support this project could not have been completed; the staff of the Reference Division of the American University Library who procured numerous studies through interlibrary loan; a word of gratitude is certainly due to both Dominique René de Lerma, who, having read my pilot study, offered his support, and to H. Wiley Hitchcock, whose continuing interest in all of my projects has meant a great deal to me; special appreciation to J. Bunker and Marilyn S. Clark who patiently read my drafts and offered many excellent and useful suggestions; to all of the many librarians who cheerfully found time in their busy schedules to photocopy the enormous amount of data utilized in this study; and, most of all, to my son Terry, who brings a special joy to my life.

JAMES R. HEINTZE

The American University
Washington, D.C.
May, 1984

*I*ntroduction

THE IDEA FOR COMPILING a list of master's theses in American music studies was conceived in 1979 while advising a graduate student regarding his interest in selecting a thesis topic in American music. I had no way of determining with reasonable certainty the extent to which specific topics had been researched, or if a given subject had ever been examined.

The two "official" sources for theses, *Masters Abstracts* and *RILM Abstracts of Music Literature* were of limited use in that only a small number of theses written each year were cited in them. Moreover, since many studies which deal with American music have been completed in disciplines other than music, the problem was compounded.

In order to identify theses not listed in the above sources, we were faced with the prospect of searching through an unusually diverse array of published sources, a chore which most students and researchers would usually, but understandably, not undertake. And in addition to this, it was considered likely that a significant number of studies were not included in any published source.

The purpose of my undertaking this project, therefore, was to help prevent students from duplicating previous research and to provide a stimulus for research yet untouched. Further, because the master's thesis is considered a valuable source for the study of American music, in that much of the exploratory work in the discipline has been done in this medium, it seemed a useful endeavor to bring together in one source as many of these studies as possible.

Before undertaking the project on a national scale, I decided to test its feasibility at a local level, using Washington, D.C. as my test area. The results of this initial study were presented both in the form of a paper entitled "Theses and Dissertations in Washington, D.C. Metropolitan Area Music Studies," at a meeting of the American Musicological Society, Capital Chapter, held at the Library of Congress on May 12, 1979, and a bibliography which is cited below. Because of the favorable response to this initial study, I decided to proceed further.

Scope and Methodology

The present study is based on both published and unpublished lists of master's theses, responses to requests for titles of theses sent to schools throughout the United States, and an examination of a number of college and university card catalogs. In order to insure accurate and comprehensive coverage, it was important to formulate an effective search strategy. Identifying bibliographies of theses in music and related disciplines was the first important step.

A number of lists of bibliographies were cited in various published sources. Michael M. Reynolds' *A Guide to Theses and Dissertations: An Annotated International Bibliography of Bibliographies* (Detroit, 1975) was useful for identifying both published and unpublished compilations through 1973. For published lists after 1973, I used the *Bibliographic Index: A Cumulative Bibliography of Bibliographies* (New York, 1937-) and the Library of Congress's *Subject Catalog* for the years 1974-80. Other lists were located by using the Ohio College Library Center (OCLC) on-line computer. Because of the lack of subject access to OCLC, I had to formulate a key-word title search tactic based on certain words one would expect to see in a title of a bibliography of master's theses.

The result of this first step was an extensive list of bibliographies representing the following disciplines: anthropology, communications, dance, education, folklore, history, library science, music, religion, and sociology. Included in this list were a few compilations of theses written in foreign universities. Some of these bibliographies were available for examination in Washington, D.C. area libraries; others were obtained through interlibrary loan. It took several months to read systematically and select appropriate works from the more than seventy thousand thesis titles contained in these bibliographies.

The next step consisted of contacting various colleges and universities throughout the United States. By referring to *The Musician's Guide* (New York, 1972), I was able to compile a list of schools known to offer graduate programs in music. A letter which explained the nature of the project was sent to the library of each school. Because accuracy in reporting data was of prime importance, each library was required to photocopy thesis cards as they appeared in their catalogs. This also provided an opportunity for me to correct entries which appeared in error in the published bibliographies I examined. In all, ninety-two schools responded to the letter. Of these, seventy-two schools reported over eight hundred theses. Twenty schools reported that they had no relevant studies.

For the final step, card catalogs in an additional twelve colleges and universities were examined personally: American University, Catholic University of

America, George Washington University, Howard University, Johns Hopkins University, University of Maryland, Morgan State University, Peabody Conservatory of Music, University of Pennsylvania, Rutgers University, University of Virginia, and Virginia Commonwealth University.

During the process of selecting theses for this study, I decided to include not only annotations for works which I had in hand, but also to contact certain schools in order to obtain annotations for theses whose titles needed clarification.

Included in the present guide are theses whose subject matter pertains to American music in an historical, sociological, or analytical manner. Because of the vast number of music education theses written over the years, only those studies which are historically oriented are cited. Not listed, for example, are theses which deal with instrumental or vocal programs in individual schools. Studies on individuals include those of native-born Americans and immigrant musicians who achieved recognition in this country.

A significant number of studies which pertain to American music, but written in disciplines other than music, are cited. For example, theater and music have been closely related arts in America's music history. For this reason, I have included a number of studies concerning theater of various localities, individual theaters, and various other topics because it is likely that most, if not all, of these works refer to music.

Arrangement

Citations in this bibliography are arranged alphabetically by author under appropriate topics. Due to their subject matter, a number of theses could have been listed under more than one classification. It is recommended, therefore, that topics being examined be cross-checked using the Subject Index.

Information on each thesis includes: author, title, degree awarded, discipline or subject other than music mentioned in the sources used, university, date completed, and (if known) number of pages, illustrations, photographs, and plates.

Following is a bibliographic entry number which refers to the source(s) consulted for this information, the volume number of that source, in parentheses, the number assigned to that thesis in the source, and the page number. Following this is additional contents information for various theses.

A few variations in the manner in which certain studies are cited deserve mention. For instance, if a specific degree such as an M.A. or M.M., etc., is not provided in the published source(s), then the entry is designated simply "Master's thesis." If the completion date of a thesis varies in the sources consulted, then the earliest date is cited. Theses reported to me by colleges and universities are cited with asterisks. Published sources for these works are, however, also cited.

Biographical information concerning various individuals was verified in the following sources: Ruth E. Anderson's *Contemporary American Composers: A Biographical Dictionary* (Boston, 1976); *Baker's Biographical Dictionary of Musicians,* 6th ed., rev. Nicolas Slonimsky (New York, 1978); and *The New Grove Dictionary of Music and Musicians,* ed. Stanley Sadie (London, 1980).

S*ources Cited*

A1   *Masters Abstracts: A Catalog of Selected Masters Theses on Microfilm.* Ann Arbor, Michigan: University Microfilms International, 1962-December, 1983.

A2   SILVEY, Herbert M. Master's Theses in the Arts and Social Sciences in the United States and Canada. Cedar Falls, Iowa: Bureau of Research, University of Northern Iowa, 1976-82. 6 vols.

MUSIC

B1   ANDERSON, Donna K. *Charles T. Griffes: An Annotated Bibliography-Discography.* Bibliographies in American Music, 3. Detroit: Information Coordinators, 1977.

Annotated.

B2   BORG, Earl Ronald. "A Codified Bibliography of Music Education Research at the Master's Level in Selected Institutions of the North Central Association." 2 vols. Ph.D. dissertation, Northwestern University, 1964.

Vol. 2: Bibliography and Appendixes with Supplement.

B3   "Brass Bibliography: 1946-1950." *Brass Quarterly* 1/3 (March 1958): 168-81.

B4   CIPOLLA, Frank J. "Annotated Guide for the Study and Performance of Nineteenth Century Band Music in the United States," *Journal of Band Research* 14 (Fall 1978): 22-40.

B5   "Current Bibliography and Discography: Dissertations and Theses" [title varies]. Compiled by Frank J. GILLIS, Joseph C. HICKERSON, Don L. ROBERTS, and Neil ROSENBERG. *Ethnomusicology* 12 (Jan 1968): 138-39; (May 1968): 276; (Sept 1968): 440; 13 (May 1969): 348; 14 (May 1970): 350-51; (Sept 1970): 496-97; 19 (Jan 1975): 134-36; 20 (Sept 1976): 588-89; 21 (Sept 1977): 495-96; 22 (Sept 1978): 512-13; 23 (May 1979): 324-25; (Sept 1979): 457; 24 (Jan 1980): 103-04; 24 (May 1980): 284-85.

B6   De LERMA, Dominique René. *A Selective List of Masters' Theses in Musicology.* Bloomington, Indiana: Denia Press, 1970.

B7   GILLIS, Frank J., and Alan P. MERRIAM. *Ethnomusicology and Folk Music: An International Bibliography of Dissertations and Theses.* Special Series in Ethnomusicology, 1. Middletown, Connecticut: Wesleyan University Press, 1966.
       Annotated.

B8   HARTLEY, Kenneth R. *Bibliography of Theses and Dissertations in Sacred Music.* Detroit Studies in Music Bibliography, 9. Detroit: Information Coordinators, 1967.

B9   HEINTZE, James R. "Theses and Dissertations in Washington, D.C. Metropolitan Area Music Studies: A Bibliography." Typescript. Washington, D.C.: American University, 1980.
       Annotated.

B10   HINSON, Maurice. *The Piano Teacher's Source Book: An Annotated Bibliography of Books Related to the Piano and Piano Music.* Melville, New York: Belwin-Mills, 1974.

B11   KEFFER, Constance. "University of Arizona: Current Research by Graduate Students," *Current Musicology* 22 (1976): 7-10.
       Annotated.

B12   LARSON, William S. "Bibliography of Research Studies in Music Education, 1949-1956," *Journal of Research in Music Education* 5/2 (Fall 1957): 63-225.

B13 "Masters' Theses in Musicology, First [and] Second Installment[s]." Compiled by D. Jay RAHN and Douglass SEATON, respectively. *Current Musicology* 12 (1971): 7-37; 17 (1974): 69-76.

B14 MERRIAN, Alan. "Annotated Bibliography of Theses and Dissertations in Ethnomusicology and Folk Music Accepted at American Universities," *Ethnomusicology* 4 (Jan 1960): 21-39.

B15 MORGAN, Hazel B. *Bibliography of Research, School of Music, Northwestern University.* Evanston, Illinois: Northwestern University, 1958.

B16 POWELL, Martha C. *A Selected Bibliography of Church Music and Music Reference Materials.* Louisville: Southern Baptist Theological Seminary, 1977.
Annotated.

B17 *RILM Abstracts of Music Literature.* New York: International RILM Center, 1967-August, 1978.

B18 Texas Music Educators Association. *A Bibliography of Master's Theses and Doctoral Dissertations in Music Completed at Texas Colleges and Universities, 1919-1972.* Houston, 1974.

RELATED ARTS
Dance

C1 IREY, Charlotte. *Research in Dance II.* Washington, D.C.: American Association for Health, Physical Education and Recreation, 1973.

C2 PEASE, Esther E. *Compilation of Dance Research, 1901-1964.* Washington, D.C.: American Association for Health, Physical Education and Recreation, 1964.

Theater

D1 KNOWER, Franklin H. "Graduate Theses: An Index of Graduate Research in Speech and Cognate Fields," *Speech Monographs* 35 (Aug 1968): 348-99.

D2   KNOWER, Franklin H. "Graduate Theses - An Index of Graduate Work in Theatre," *Educational Theatre Journal* 3 (1951): 143-55; 4 (1952): 146-57; 5 (1953): 166-77; 6 (1954): 153-63; 7 (1955): 154-62; 8 (1956): 143-53; 9 (1957): 141-50; 10 (1958): 139-49; 11 (1959): 143-52; 12 (1960): 128-38; 13 (1961): 121-30; 14 (1962): 158-68; 15 (1963): 166-77.

D3   LARSON, Carl F. W. *American Regional Theatre History to 1900: A Bibliography.* Metuchen, New Jersey: Scarecrow Press, 1979.

RELATED DISCIPLINES
Communications

E1   CHEYDLEUR, Raymond D. *A Compilation of Radio Theses in American Colleges and Universities, 1918-1950.* Huntington, West Virginia: Marshall College, 1950.

E2   FIELDING, Raymond. *A Bibliography of Theses and Dissertations on the Subject of Film: 1916-1979.* University Film Association Monographs, 3. Houston: University Film Association, 1979.

Education

F1   SILVEY, Herbert M. *Master's Theses in Education, 1951-1981.* 30 vols. Cedar Falls, Iowa: Research Publications.

Library Science

G1   HARRIS, Michael, and Donald G. DAVIS, Jr. *American Library History: A Bibliography.* Austin: University of Texas, 1978.

G2   MAGNOTTI, Shirley. *Master's Theses in Library Science, 1960-1969.* Troy, New York: Whitston, 1975.

G3   MAGNOTTI, Shirley. *Master's Theses in Library Science, 1970-1974.* New York: Whitston, 1976.

G4   "Theses and Dissertations Accepted by Graduate Library Schools" [title varies]. Compiled by Richard A. DAVIS, E. J. HUMESTON, Jr., and Howard W. WINGER. *Library Quarterly* 36 (Jan 1966): 38-47; 38 (Oct 1968): 442-52; 40 (Oct 1970): 423-33; 43 (Jan 1973): 53-64.

Literature

H1 EMERSON, O. B., and Marion C. MICHAEL. *Southern Literary Culture: A Bibliography of Masters' and Doctors' Theses.* University of Alabama Press, 1979.

Contains some annotations.

H2 HOWARD, Patsy C. *Theses in American Literature, 1896-1971.* Ann Arbor: Pierian Press, 1973.

H3 WAGES, Jack D., and William L. ANDREWS. "Southern Literary Culture. 1969-1975." *Mississippi Quarterly* 32 (Winter 1978-79): 13-215.

Minority Groups, Folklore, and Anthropology

I1 DOCKSTADER, Frederick J., and Alice W. DOCKSTADER. *The American Indian in Graduate Studies: A Bibliography of Theses and Dissertations.* 2 vols. New York: Museum of the American Indian Heye Foundation, 1973-74.

Vol. 1, nos. 1-3659; vol. 2, nos. 3660-7446.

I2 DUNDES, Alan. *Folklore Theses and Dissertations in the United States.* Publications of the American Folklore Society, Bibliographical and Special Series, 27. Austin: Published for the American Folklore Society by the University of Texas Press, 1976.

I3 HAYWOOD, Terry S. *A Bibliography of Master Theses on Blacks Accepted in the Ohio State University, 1915-1974.* Columbus, Ohio: author, 1976.

I4 McDONALD, David R. *Masters' Theses in Anthropology: A Bibliography of Theses from United States Colleges and Universities.* New Haven, Connecticut: Human Relations Area Files, 1977.

Religion

J1 Moravian Music Foundation. Research Supported by the Moravian Music Foundation. Typescript. Winston-Salem, no date.

J2 SAPPINGTON, Roger E. *A Bibliography of Theses on the Church of the Brethren.* Elgin, Illinois: Christian Education Commission, Church of the Brethren, 195[?].

J3   Southern Baptist Convention, Historical Commission. *Index of Graduate Theses in Baptist Theological Seminaries, 1894-1962*. Nashville, 1963.

J4   WILLIAMS, Ethel L., and Clifton F. BROWN. *The Howard University Bibliography of African and Afro-American Religious Studies*. Wilmington, Delaware: Scholarly Resources, 1977.

COLLEGES AND UNIVERSITIES

K1   *Abstracts of Theses and Dissertations [awarded at Bowling Green State University] 1970-1977*. Bowling Green State University, 1977.

K2   California State University. *Masters Theses, 1964-1978*. Hayward: State University Library, 1978.

K3   Catholic University of America. *Theses and Dissertations: Cumulation, 1961-1967*. Washington, D.C.: Catholic University of America, 1970.

K4   DOMITZ, Gary. *Theses and Dissertations Accepted by Idaho State University, 1957-1976*. Pocatello: Idaho State University, 1977.

K5   North Carolina University Libraries, Humanities Division. *The Graduate School Dissertations and Theses. First Supplement: 1946-1959*. Chapel Hill: University of North Carolina Libraries, 1960.

K6   OETTING, Edward C. *Master's Theses, State University of New York at Albany: A Bibliography, 1914-1978*. Albany: State University Libraries, Special Services Division, 1980.

K7   *Theses and Dissertations Accepted in Partial Fulfillment of Requirements for Advanced Degrees at the College of the Pacific, 1913-1956*. Stockton, California: College of the Pacific Library, 1957.

K8   WILDER, Bessie E. *University of Kansas Graduate School Theses, 1948-1958*. Lawrence: University of Kansas Libraries, 1961.

K9   WILLIAMS, Evan W. *Author and Subject Indices to Kansas State University Doctoral Dissertations, Masters' Theses and Masters' Reports. First Supplement 1969-1973*. 2 vols. Manhattan: Kansas State University Library, 1975.

STATE AND LOCAL

L1   ADRIAN, Frederick W. "Theses and Dissertations Dealing with Nebraska and Nebraskans," University of Nebraska Studies, New Series, 49 (June 1975). Annotated.

L2   BLEICH, Pamela A. "A Study of Graduate Research in California History in California Colleges and Universities," *California Historical Society Quarterly* 44 (Dec 1965): 333-48; 45 (June 1966): 149-61.

L3   DUNCAN, Richard R., and Dorothy M. BROWN. *Master's Theses and Doctoral Dissertations on Maryland History.* Baltimore: Maryland Historical Society, 1970.

L4   DUNCAN, Richard R., and Dorothy M. BROWN. "Theses and Dissertations in Virginia History: A Bibliography," *Virginia Magazine of History and Biography* 79 (1971): 55-109.

L5   DUNN, James T. "Masters' Theses and Doctoral Dissertations on New York History," *New York History* 36 (April 1955): 233-51.

L6   DUNN, James T. *Masters' Theses and Doctoral Dissertations on New York History, 1870-1954.* No place, 1955.

L7   ELLIS, L. Tuffly, and Barbara J. STOCKLEY. "A Checklist of Theses and Dissertations in Texas Studies, 1964-1974," *Southwestern Historical Quarterly* 78 (Oct 1974): 183-98; 78 (Jan 1975): 313-24; 78 (April 1975): 447-63; 79 (July 1975): 69-90; 79 (Oct 1975): 205-19; 79 (Jan 1976): 317-32; 79 (April 1976): 441-60; 80 (July 1976): 79-94; 80 (Oct 1976): 201-14; 80 (Jan 1977): 302-22; 80 (April 1977): 417-24; 81 (Jan 1978): 299-322; 81 (April 1978): 427-50.

L8   "Graduate Theses Relating to Missouri History," *Missouri Historical Review* 59 (Jan 1965): 251-52; 66 (Jan 1972): 303.

L9   HATHAWAY, Richard J. *Dissertations and Theses in Michigan History.* Lansing: Michigan History Division, Michigan Department of State, 1974.

L10 LAWTON, Elizabeth, and Raymond S. SWEENEY. *Maryland History: A Selective Bibliography.* Rockville, Maryland: Montgomery County Historical Society, 1975.

L11 MOORE, Marie D. "Selected Bibliography of Completed Theses and Dissertations Related to North Carolina Subjects, 1974-1978," *North Carolina Historical Review* 56 (Jan 1979): 64-107.

L12 MORRIS, Mary E. *Bibliography of Theses on Oklahoma in the University of Oklahoma Library.* Norman: Institute of Community Development, University of Oklahoma, 1956.

L13 POSNER, Walter H. *A List of Master's Theses on the History of San Diego Written at San Diego State University.* 3rd ed. San Diego State University, 1975.

L14 SMITH, Sam B. *Tennessee History: A Bibliography.* Knoxville: University of Tennessee Press, 1974.

L15 SOCOLOFSKY, Homer. *Kansas History in Graduate Study: A Bibliography of Theses and Dissertations.* Manhattan: Kansas State University, 1959.

FOREIGN

M1 Institute of United States Studies, London. "Theses on American Topics in Progress and Completed at British Universities," *Journal of American Studies* 12 (Aug 1978): 271-87.

M2 PATERSON, Geoffrey M., and Joan E. HARDY. *Index to Theses Accepted for Higher Degrees by the Universities of Great Britain and Ireland and the Council for National Academic Awards.* 26 vols. London: Aslib, 1950-74.

*D*egrees

A.M.L.S.	Master of Arts in Library Science
M.A.; A.M.	Master of Arts
M.C.M.	Master of Church Music
M.E.; M.Ed.; Ed.M.	Master of Education
M.F.A.	Master of Fine Arts
M.H.T.	Master of Hebraic Theology
M.L.S.; M.S. in L.S.	Master of Library Science; Master of Science in Library Science
M.M.; M.Mus.	Master of Music
M.M.E.; M.M.Ed.; M.Mus.Ed.	Master of Music Education
M.R.E.	Master of Religious Education
M.S.	Master of Science
M.S.M.; S.M.M.	Master of Sacred Music
M.S.T.; S.T.M.	Master of Sacred Theology
Th.M.	Master of Theology

AMERICAN MUSIC STUDIES
A CLASSIFIED BIBLIOGRAPHY OF MASTER'S THESES

THESES 1 *Research and Reference Materials*

1 BEISWANGER, Barbara Page. A Selected List of Music Especially Written for Dance by Composers in America. M.A., New York University, 1943. C2 39, p. 8.

2 BLANCHARD, Marguerite S. Index for the *California Music Educators News,* 1948-55. Master's thesis, University of California at Los Angeles, 1955. F1 1123, p. 53.

3 *BLANDING, Mary Catherine. A Catalogue of the Eva Jessye Afro-American Music Collection as of May 1, 1974. Master's thesis, University of Michigan, 1974.

4 CHIASERA, Dorothy Crocher. Early American Vocal Sheet Music: A Descriptive Catalog of Items in Special Collections, San Diego State University Library. M.A., San Diego State University, 1976. 100 pp. B17 (10/3) 4563, p. 285.
There are 359 song entries covering the period 1810-99.

5 COOK, Jeannette L. Documents on Music Issued by the United States Government: An Annotated Bibliography. Master's thesis, University of Nebraska, 1978. A2 3406, p. 145.

6 *CORBO, Angelo. George Gershwin: A Thematic Catalogue of His Published Songs. M.A., Brooklyn College of the City University of New York, 1975. 86 pp.

Contains a list of 257 published songs. Unpublished songs or songs published only in an original full score version of a musical or opera are not included. Each entry includes one or more musical incipits, publication data, and the title of the show, movie, or occasion for which the song was written.

7 *CROSMAN, Max W. Bibliographic Materials for the Study of Folk Music in the United States. Master's thesis, University of Michigan, 1946. B7 156, p. 22; J2, p. 186.

8 DEMPSEY, Karen. Music and Books about Music in Roorbach's *Bibliotheca America,* 1820-61. M.A., Kent State University, 1972. 84 pp. B17 (6/1) 35, p. 5.

9 DOWD, Aelred. A Descriptive Catalog of the Loeffler Collection of the Library of Congress Music Division. M.S. in L.S., Catholic University of America, 1960.

There are 1333 entries of music, letters, and other papers. Included is an "Index of Correspondents."

10 ELSASS, David. Music in Kelly's *American Catalogue of Books,* 1861-71. M.A., Kent State University, 1972. 39 pp. B17 (6/1) 44, p. 6.

11 EPSTEIN, Lena. An Annotated Bibliography of the Dances of the Indians of the United States of America. M.A., New York University, 1936. C2 186, p. 18.

12 *FASTHOFF, Henry J. A Catalogue of Ensemble Music for Woodwind, Brass, and Percussion Instruments Written by Composers in the United States. M.Mus.Ed., Florida State University, 1949. 266 pp. B3 302, p. 171; B12, p. 83.

13 FISHER, Suzanne M. An Index to Biographical Information on Rock Musicians. M.L.S., Library Science, Kent State University, 1973. 57 pp. B17 (9/1-2) 84, p. 7.

Biographical writings published since 1965 in 27 books and six magazines are indexed. Reviews and critical studies are omitted.

14 *GIBSON, Gerald Don. An Annotated, Indexed Discography of Scholarly Anthologies of Western Art Music in Series Issued and Generally Commercially Available in the Continental United States within the Period 1900 thru 1970, Excluding Performer Oriented Sets. M.A., Eastman School of Music of the University of Rochester, 1975. B17 (9/1-2) 231, p. 14.

Includes 1552 separate recordings in 99 different series.

15 GILLIS, Frank James. Minnesota Music in the Nineteenth Century: A Guide to Sources and Resources. M.A., Library Science, University of Minnesota, 1958. 91 p. B7 254, p. 34; I2, p. 274.

Indian musical sources are also discussed.

16 HALPERN, Kathryn D. A Preliminary Checklist of Allentown and Bethlehem, Pennsylvania Imprints, 1813-1876, with a Historical Introduction. M.S. in L.S., Catholic University of America, 1964. 89 pp. G2, p. 89.

Includes lists of books, serials, periodicals, newspapers, printers, and publishers. The hymn and song books listed are arranged chronologically. A typical entry includes the imprint, number of pages, size of book, and library location(s).

17 HEARD, Priscilla S. An Annotated Bibliography of Music and Reference to Music Published in the United States before 1801. M.M., Baylor University, 1969. B18 BU-1969-3, p. 4.

Published under the title *American Music, 1698-1800: An Annotated Bibliography* (Waco, Texas: Baylor University Press, 1975).

18 HICKERSON, Joseph Charles. Annotated Bibliography of North American Indian Music North of Mexico. M.A., Indiana University, 1961. 464 pp. B7 320, p. 42; I1 5187, p. 150; I2, p. 293.

Includes about 1300 items and a Tribal Index.

19 *HITCHCOCK, Hugh Wiley. Lectures and Bibliographical Materials for a Course in the History of American Music. Master's thesis, University of Michigan, 1948.

20 ISEMINGER, George. A Compilation and Annotation of American Folksong Literature and Its Use in the Public School. M.M., University of South Dakota, 1951. 82 pp. B12, p. 137; I2, p. 224.

21 JASEN, David. The Ragtime Discography, 1897-1958. Master's thesis, Library Science, Long Island University, 1972. G3, p. 32.

Published under the title *Recorded Ragtime, 1897-1958* (Hamden, Conn.: Archon, 1973).

22   JEFFREY, Valeta. Index to Articles of the Yearbooks of the Music Supervisor's National Conference (1910, 1912-1934). M.M., Northwestern University, 1935. B15 370, p. 16.

23   JOHNSON, Ellen Louise. The Unpublished Mountain Folk Songs Collected by Dorothy Scarborough. M.A., English, Baylor University, 1941. 2 vols. 736 pp. H1, p. 232; H2 5375, p. 199; I2, p. 160.

   Collected in Virginia, North Carolina, and some allied mountain regions of South Carolina, Tennessee, and Georgia.

24   KACZMAREK, Regina A. A Catalog of Selected Piano Rolls from the Library of Congress Collection. M.S. in L.S., Catholic University of America, 1960. 322 pp. G2, p. 115.

   Includes a descriptive catalog, title and performer indexes, and a check list of piano roll manufacturers. American performers represented include Richard Buhlig, Austin Conradi, John Duke, John Powell, and Artur Rubinstein. American composers represented include John Carpenter, R. Nathaniel Dett, Louis Moreau Gottschalk, Edward MacDowell, John Philip Sousa, and Septimus Winner.

25   KELLER, Dean Howard. The Selection of Phonograph Records for the Library. Master's thesis, Library Science, Kent State University, 1958. 62 pp.

   Includes a history of phonograph record libraries. The following public libraries are mentioned: Cleveland Public Library, Detroit Public Library, Free Public Library, Free Public Library in Philadelphia, Minneapolis Public Library, Springfield Public Library in Massachusetts, and St. Paul Public Library. The university libraries discussed include: Brown University, University of California, Columbia University, Harvard University, and University of Illinois. There is also an annotated bibliography consisting of 1) books that are intended to be aids for the selection of phonograph records; 2) reviewing periodicals of reviews about phonograph records; 3) books to aid the librarian in locating information about music, musicians, and composers; 4) record dealers and library supplies; and 5) record companies.

26   McCORMICK, Elizabeth Marie. An Index to *The Caecilia* from 1925-1934: Volume 52 to Volume 61. M.A., Catholic University of America, 1967. 234 pp.

   This Catholic publication was begun in Saint Francis, Wisconsin.

27   MEILANDER, Margery A. A Discography of the Bassoon. M.L.S., Library Science, Kent State University, 1972. 80 pp. B17 (9/1-2) 236, p. 14.

   Sources for the recordings listed include both American and British catalogs. The period covered is from January 1953 through August 1972. Included is an index of performers.

28 MERRITT, Nancy Gertrude. Negro Spirituals in American Collections (A Handbook for Students Studying Negro Spirituals). M.A., English, Howard University, 1940. 59 pp. H1, p. 233; J2, p. 152.

A comprehensive listing of Negro spirituals with a comparison of southern white and southern Negro spirituals.

29 *PEBWORTH, James R. A Directory of 132 Arkansas Composers. M.M., University of Arkansas at Fayetteville, 1979. 89 pp.

30 RAPHAEL, Miriam. A Listing of Available Recorded Music for Teaching Folk Dance, American Country Dancing, and Simple Compositions in Modern Dance. M.A., New York University, 1947. C2 530, p. 40.

31 REUSS, Richard A. An Annotated Field Collection of Songs from the American College Oral Tradition. M.A., Folklore, Indiana University, 1965. 355 pp. B5 12, p. 276; I2, p. 324.

Texts and annotations for 64 college songs. Includes an excellent introduction to this type of song, its definition, and the particular problems which pertain to it.

32 SCHROEDER, Pollyanna Tribouillier. Miguel Sandoval: Guatemalan-American Composer — A Chronological Catalogue of His Collected Works. M.A., American University, 1976. 103 pp. A1 (15/1) 13-08889, p. 44.

33 SIEVERT, John Louis. A Classified Annotated Bibliography of Materials Contained in Issues of *The Diapason* from 1934 to 1954. M.M., Northwestern University, 1955. B12, p. 92; B15 746, p. 27.

34 SPOTTSWOOD, Richard Keith. A Catalog of American Folk Music on Commercial Recordings at the Library of Congress, 1923-1940. M.S., Library Science, Catholic University of America, 1962. 440 pp. B9 29, p. 4; G2, p. 210; K3, p. 105.

35 STANLEY, Jonathan J. A Critical and Annotated Bibliography of Negro Minstrelsy in America. M.A., English, University of Maryland, 1972. 112 pp.

Almost every aspect of the subject is covered. The organization is in three parts: a critical essay evaluating sources about minstrelsy and describing minstrel collections; a bibliographical listing of minstrel show books, anthologies, jokebooks, music books, and catalogued collections of several libraries; and an annotated bibliographical listing of sources about minstrelsy. Also lists an additional 26 theses which touch on the subject of minstrelsy.

36 STORCK, John W. P. Boys' Choirs: A Discography. M.L.S., Library Science, Kent State University, 1974. 149 pp. B17 (9/1-2) 242, p. 15.

Choirs in both the U.S. and Europe are indexed alphabetically. Composers are indexed. There are 538 entries spanning the period 1949-73.

37 STRAUSS, Barbara. A Register of Music Performed in Concert, Nazareth, Pennsylvania from 1796 to 1845: An Annotated Edition of an American Moravian Document. M.A., University of Arizona, 1976. B11, p. 9; B17 (10/2) 2780, p. 174.

Based on a translation of the "Register" which contains 1093 entries for 351 concerts.

38 *TIPTON, Patricia Gray. An Index to References to Music in Thomas Jefferson's Paris Letters. M.Mus., Memphis State University, 1972. 79 pp.

39 *VOORHEES, Anna Tipton. An Annotated, Indexed Guide to Symphonic Program Notes in a Selected Group of Books. Master's thesis, Library Science, Kent State University, 1964. 135 pp.

Most of the 48 books listed were published in the United States. No specific symphony orchestras are treated.

40 WAGNER, Marjorie K. Music Librarianship in the United States: An Annotated Classified Bibliography. M.S. in L.S., Catholic University of America, 1957. 77 pp.

Almost every aspect of the field is treated. Included is a list of 37 additional master's theses on music librarianship.

41 WALTER, Vincent P., Jr. An Author and Subject Index of the Periodical *MUSART,* September 1962 through June 1972. M.M.Ed., Catholic University of America, 1972. 91 pp.

The official publication of the National Catholic Music Educators Association. Includes author-subject indexes and indexes to book reviews and record reviews.

42 WASHBURN, Alice. A Descriptive Catalogue of Confederate Music in the Duke University Collection. Master's thesis, History, Duke University, 1937. H1, p. 370.

43 WILGUS, Donald Knight. A Catalog of American Folk Songs on Commercial Records. M.A., Ohio State University, 1947. B7 843, p. 104; I2, p. 196.

44   WILLIAMS, Philip Lynn. Music by John Powell in the John Powell Music Collection at the University of Virginia: A Descriptive Bibliography. M.A., University of Virginia, 1968. 99 pp.

45   WILLIFORD, Doxie K. A Discography of Mississippi Negro Vocal Blues, Gospel, and Folk Music. Master's thesis, University of Mississippi, 1968. G4, p. 431.

46   *WONG, Mary Ruth. A Survey of References to Folk and Traditional Music in the *National Geographic Magazine*. M.A., University of North Carolina at Chapel Hill, 1969. 130 pp. illus.

THESES 2 *Historical Studies*

SOCIO-CULTURAL

47 ANTIN, Arthur P., and Jean P. ANTIN. Take This Hammer (An Approach to Understanding America at Work through Song and Dance). M.A., New York University, 1950. C2 16, p. 7.

48 APICELLA, Anthony. A Survey of Music Activities in the Penal Institutions of the Northeastern United States. M.M.Ed., Boston University, 1952. B12, p. 1092.

49 *BORGMAN, George Allan. Nationalism in Contemporary American Music. M.M., Indiana University, 1953. 83 pp. B7 73, p. 12.

50 BOY, Charles Alexander. A Survey of the Uses of Music in the Industries of the Greater Boston Area. M.M.Ed., Boston University, 1952. B12, p. 102.

51 *BRITTON, Vera Dorothea. Music in the Present World War. Master's thesis, University of Illinois at Urbana-Champaign, 1943. 96 pp.

52 BROWN, Jean W. A Study of the American Civil War as Reflected in the Music of the Period and the Application of That Music to a Junior High School Choral Production. Master's thesis, Texas Woman's University, 1962. B18 TWU-1962-1, p. 62; F1 1243, p. 57.

53 BULLINGTON, Ailcy Josephine. Twentieth Century American Music. M.M., Northwestern University, 1945. B2, p. 120; B15 107, p. 8.

54 *BURDICK, Virginia. Influences of European Music throughout the History of American Music. M.Mus., Syracuse University, 1934. 46 pp. illus.

55 CAVALLERO, Joseph. Reflections on a Little War: The Vietnam Conflict as Portrayed in Selected Examples of Art, Literature, Film, and Popular Music. Master's thesis, Northeast Missouri State University, 1980. A2 3514, p. 158.

56 CHARLES, Norman. Social Values in American Popular Songs. M.A., Sociology, University of Pennsylvania, 1958.

57 *CONNOR, Daniel Emmett. Music in Colonial America, 1770-1778. M.M., DePaul University, 1947. 82 pp. B2, p. 27.

58 *COOPER, Jack A. An Analysis of the Area Affected by the National Music Camp and the Economic Impacts that Exist. M.A., Eastern Michigan University, 1966. 37 pp. illus.

59 *COTTER, John Cleophus. The Negro in Music in St. Louis. A.M., Washington University, 1959. 503 pp. B6 C847, p. 11.

60 CULLINS, Ella Webb. Origin of American Negro Folkways. M.A., Boston University, 1942. 83 pp. B7 159, p. 23; B14 40, p. 24.

61 DAVIS, Audrey Hennen. Americanization of the American Symphony. M.M., Northwestern University, 1930. B15 173, p. 10.

62 *DAVIS, Harvey Owen. Wagner's Music in America, 1870-1890. M.A., University of Kentucky, 1968. 101 pp. B17 (10/2) 2849, p. 178.

63 DILLON, Clarissa F. "And Raise Our Voices High": Some Twentieth Century American Folk Songs of Protest and Propaganda as an Aspect of Social History. M.A., History, University of Chicago, 1960. 97 p. I2, p. 284.

64 *EAKLOR, Vicki Lynn. Music in the American Antislavery Movement, 1830-1860. Master's thesis, Washington University, 1979. 89 pp. A2 3107, p. 135.

See also the author's Ph.D. dissertation "Music in American Society, 1815-1860: An Intellectual History" (Washington University, 1982).

65 EDWARDS, D. Robert. The American Mind as Expressed in Music. M.A., Education, University of Maryland, 1935. 85 pp. I2, p. 108.

The period covered is 1620-1800; this is a general study of music in colonial America.

66 *ENGELHARDT, Helen Louise. Music in Mental Institutions. M.A., University of Kansas, 1941.

67 *EWING, Roberta Louise. The Development of Music Therapy in the United States. Master's thesis, University of Michigan, 1963.

68 GARDNER, Arthur E. Early American Life as Expressed in Certain Songs. M.A., Arizona State University, 1952. F1 858, p. 45; I2, p. 231.

69 GUTOWSKI, Lynda Diane. George Gershwin's Relationship to the Search for an American Culture during the Nineteen-Twenties. M.A., English, University of Maryland, 1967. 124 pp.

70 HENRY, Betty Park. The Story of America Told in Song. M.Ed., Alfred University, 1949. 133 pp. I2, p. 207.

71 HOLMES, Annette Cecile. Prominent Amateur Musicians of the Revolutionary Period. M.A., Catholic University of America, 1966. 94 pp. illus. B13, p. 18; K3, p. 55.

Discusses Francis Hopkinson, Thomas Jefferson, and Benjamin Franklin.

72 *HOWARD, Lucinda Elizabeth. The Unitas Fratrum in Bethlehem, 1741-1800: The Relationship between Music and Culture in a Stable Religious Community. M.A., Crane School of Music, 1976. 68 pp. B17 (10/2) 2711, p. 171.

73 *JAMES, Hobert Lee. The Social Value, Meaning, and Significance of Black Music to the Black Community. M.A., DePaul University, 1973. 131 pp.

74 *JOHNSON, Guy B. Study of the Musical Talent of the American Negro. M.A., Sociology, University of North Carolina at Chapel Hill, 1927.

75 JOHNSON, Lillian. The Significance of Negro Music to America. M.M.E., Texas Southern University, 1944. B18 TSU-1944-1, p. 55; I2, p. 178.

76 JONES, Sara Ellen. Music Appreciation in America: Its History and Typical Units of Study. M.M., Northwestern University, 1946. B15 387, p. 16.

77 KELLY, Jacquelin Joan. The Muse Dons Khaki: American Songs and Music of World War I. M.A., History, University of Maryland, 1963. 175 pp. illus. I2, p. 307.
Includes complete texts and some music for 40 songs.

78 KINNEY, Mary Gene. Public Concert Life in Boston 1852-1857, as Seen through Dwight's *Journal of Music*. Master's thesis, University of Southern California, 1972. B13, p. 73.

79 *KOOI, Ray C. Music in Employee Recreation. M.A., Wayne State University, 1950. 59 pp.

80 KRUPSKY, Shannon Harry. Singing Americana: A Study of Democracy in Song. M.M.Ed., DePaul University, 1943. 169 pp. I2, p. 173.

81 *LANGSFORD, Harry M. Music in Industry. M.A., Wayne State University, 1943. 82 pp.

82 LEIDMAN, Mary Beth. At the Crossroads: A Study of the American Musical Theatre and Its Relationship to the Society of the 1960's. M.S., Emerson College, 1976. 614 pp.

83 *LITTELL, William J. A Survey of the Uses of Music in Correctional Institutions in the United States. M.M.Ed., University of Kansas, 1961. 54 pp.

84   MALTBY, Marc S. American Popular Music and Social Change, 1960-79. Master's thesis, Niagara University, 1981. A2 2360, p. 110.

85   MEEKS, Judith A. The Social Function of Protest Music in America from 1960 to 1970. Master's thesis, Indiana Central College, 1970. F1 1468, p. 70.

86   *MIDDLETON, James Wesley. Early Americans and Their Music. M.A., Ohio State University, 1950. 207 pp. B12, p. 128.

87   *MOLLAHAN, Elizabeth T. Gad's Hill: An Experiment in Socialized Music. M.A., DePaul University, 1946. 62 pp. illus.
      Gad's Hill Center, Chicago, Illinois.

88   MORIN, Margaret Fleming. America's Interest in Chopin, 1830-1879. M.A., Catholic University of America, 1936.

89   NOLAN, Carolyn Galbraith. Thomas Jefferson: Gentleman Musician. M.A., University of Virginia, 1967. 126 pp. H1, p. 96.

90   *OJA, Carol Jean. Musical Subjects in the Paintings of William Michael Harnett. M.A., University of Iowa, 1976. 127 pp. B17 (10/1) 133, p. 9.
      Discusses the musical instruments and scores. Also includes a discussion of the "musical subjects in the still-life paintings by the followers of Harnett."

91   *PETZ, Weldon. Music and Abraham Lincoln. M.A., Wayne State University, 1951. 167 pp. B6 P513, p. 25.

92   *POWELL, Clifford Elizabeth. A Music Survey Conducted in a Few Alabama State Institutions. M.Mus., Syracuse University, 1943. 54 pp. illus.

93   RABB, Tamar M. Music Therapy in the United States and Great Britain. M.E., Rutgers University, 1974. 108 pp.
      A study, based on available literature and visits to therapists' sessions, of historical origins, development, theories, clinical findings, applications, and prospects of musical therapy in America and England.

94 REDMAN, Vesper M. A Survey of Music during World War II: Effect upon Music Education. M.A., Catholic University of America, 1968. 56 pp.

Discusses popular, band, and service music as well as "music activities for defense," the role of the musician during the war, and to a lesser extent, music education during the war.

95 *RUSSELL, Clyde. The Interpretation of Social Values as Found in Folk Songs and Ballads. M.A., Sociology, University of North Carolina at Chapel Hill, 1926. H1, p. 235.

96 SALMONS, Lee Allen. The Relationship between Artist, Audience, and Music and the Emergence of a New Musical Form. M.A., Communications, University of Pennsylvania, 1978. 65 pp. illus.

97 *SHAWHAN, H. R. American Musical Life, 1930-1940. Master's thesis, Columbia University, 1949. 154 pp.

Includes a list of composers, pp. 138-44, a list of the names and location of "Federal orchestras," pp. 145-46, and organizations, pp. 147-49.

98 SIMONS, Carolyn Wood. H. L. Mencken: Music from a Layman's Point of View. M.M., Baylor University, 1971. B9 63, p. 8; B17 (10/4) 16580, p. 859; B18 BU-1971-9, p. 5.

99 SORENSON, G. N. Influence of American Life on the Rhythms of the Decorative Arts, Music, and Dancing. M.A., Fine Arts, University of Southern California, 1946. 171 pp. B14 148, p. 33.

100 SOULES, Lillian Lohmeyer. Music at the White House during the Administration of Theodore Roosevelt. M.M., Catholic University of America, 1968. 92 pp. B9 28, p. 4; B13, p. 26.

Covers the years 1901-09.

101 STEWART, Johnathan. The Writing of Music History in America: The First Fifty Years. Master's thesis, Baylor University, 1979. A2 3194, p. 138.

102 THOMPSON, Wilma. Thomas Jefferson: Lifelong Musician. Master's thesis, Southern Illinois University at Edwardsville, 1973. H3 1156, p. 83.

103 *TORGE, Herman. Patriotic and Military Music of the American Revolutionary War. M.M., University of Cincinnati, 1951. 63 pp.

104 TRONE, Dolly G. The Influence of the World War (1917) on the Art of Music in America. M.M., Northwestern University, 1940. B2, p. 158; B7 797, p. 98; B15 848, p. 30.

105 WAKELAND, Myrtle. Walt Whitman and Music. M.S., Texas A & M University, 1950. B18 TA & I-1950-2, p. 47.

106 *WHITE, Edith Lee. Knowing Americans through Their Music. M.A., Ohio State University, 1946.

107 WILLIAMS, Charlotte F. American Issues (1865-1900) as Expressed in the Songs of the People. Master's thesis, History, Columbia University, 1942. H1, p. 237.

Texas cowboy songs, southern farmer songs, spirituals, and Civil War songs are discussed.

108 WILSON, John E. Music Composed in Honor of George Washington. M.M., Baylor University, 1971. B18 BU-1971-10, p. 5.

109 *WINCENCIAK, Sue Lockhart. An Investigation of the Persuasive Impact of Popular Music during the Civil War. Master's thesis, Speech, Kent State University, 1971. 91 pp.

110 WRAGG, Eleanor Newton. The American Civil War as Reflected in the Religious Song of the Age. M.A., Boston University, 1935. B8 436, p. 32; H1, p. 237.

Discusses Sidney Lanier and Henry Timrod.

111 YU, Grace Shui-Chi. Trends and Development of Music in the United States and China. M.A., Texas Woman's University, 1967. B18 TWU-1967-5, p. 63.

AREAS. REGIONAL

112 *GACH, Christine. American Summer Music Festivals. M.A., Eastern Michigan University, 1979. 89 pp. illus.

Discusses growth and development of selected festivals with an emphasis on Meadow Brook. Includes an appendix of summer music festivals in North America.

113 *HICKMAN, Felton. A History of Music on the Comstock, 1860-1875. M.A., Brigham Young University, 1954. 168 pp.

114 KULTTI, Karl R. Development of Summer Music Camps in the Western United States. M.M., University of Southern California, 1951. B12, p. 77.

115 *MASAILO, Michael Peter. Summer Music Camps in New England. M.Mus.Ed., Hartt College of Music of the University of Hartford, 1956. 65 pp.

116 SOUTHWICK, Lynda Meredith Miller. The Symphony Tradition in New England, 1880-1930. M.M., University of Texas at Austin, 1970. B18 UT-1970-31, p. 95.

117 *WARGELIN, Carol Grace. Musical Activity in the Eastern United States, 1750-1800. Master's thesis, University of Michigan, 1970.

AREAS. STATES AND COUNTIES

118 ASBAUGH, Harold B. A History of the Music Contest in South Dakota. M.M., University of South Dakota, 1950. B12, p. 137.

119 BAADER, Mary Lenore. The Music of Early Wisconsin. M.M., Catholic University of America, 1967. 115 pp. illus. B13, p. 31.

Discusses the music of Indian tribes, French "Voyageurs," and lumberjack songs.

120 *BECK, Emily Johnson. The Musical Heritage of Hawaii. Master's thesis, University of Michigan, 1969.

121 *BLANTON, Mary Jacqueline. Percy Grainger in Missouri. Master's thesis, University of Missouri-Columbia, 1978. 126 pp.

122   BOYD, Jarritus. The Golden Age of Maryland Culture, 1750-1770. M.A., University of Maryland, 1967. B9 39, p. 5; B17 (10/4) 9339, p. 581; L10, p. 10.
Brief discussion of the Tuesday Club of Annapolis and theater.

123   BURNHAM, Ray G. The History of Music Festivals in Louisiana. Master's thesis, Northwestern State College, 1966. F1 1621, p. 68.

124   BURT, George W. The Organization and Management of Music Festivals in California. M.S., University of Southern California, 1950. B12, p. 74.

125   CARROW, Catherine Ikard. The Amusements of Texas from 1880-1890. M.A., University of Texas at Austin, 1943. B18 UT-1943-1, p. 68.

126   *DICKEY, Judy Ruth. The Music of a Louisiana Plantation Family, 1814-1874. M.A., Louisiana State University, 1968. 111 pp. illus.
Thomas Butler (born 1785) family.

127   EWING, Crystal. A Survey of Community Music in New York State. M.Mus., Eastman School of Music of the University of Rochester, 1948. 181 pp.

128   FORBES, Kenneth V. A. A Chapter from the Story of Early Vermont Music. M.A., University of Iowa, 1927. 186 pp. B7 229, p. 31; I2, p. 50.
Discusses the music of 19th-century Franklin County, Vermont.

129   FOSTER, (Mrs.) Henry. A Study of the Development of Music in Hall County, Texas. M.A., Hardin-Simmons University, 1942. B18 HSU-1942-1, p. 7.

130   GASTHOFF, Patricia Ann. An Analytical Investigation of Historical Pageantry in the State of Illinois. M.M., Northwestern University, 1955. B12, p. 90.

131   GERTJEJANSEN, Kenneth. Music in Minnesota's History. Master's thesis, Minnesota State Teachers College at Mankato, 1956. F1 1087, p. 51.

132   GIBBONS, Rendol. A History of the Growth and Development of the Northern Arizona Music Festival. Master's thesis, Arizona State College at Flagstaff, 1952. F1 1293, p. 59.

19

133 *GILLUM, Lawrence Joseph. Ohio Musicians, Composers and Their Compositions. M.A., Ohio State University, 1953. 49 pp.

134 HANSEN, Harald Alvin. Ancient Music of Hawaii. M.Mus., Catholic University of America, 1960. 121 pp. I2, p. 285; K3, p. 51.

135 HARBISON, David. A Study in the Song Tradition of Metcalfe County,
Kentucky. M.M., Southern Illinois University, 1971. 290 pp.

136 *LEBAR, Elaine E. Lebowitz. History of Musical Development in Missouri. M.A.,
University of Missouri-Columbia, 1950. 249 pp.

137 LEWIS, Eileen. The Origin and Development of Music Festivals in Kentucky.
M.M., Northwestern University, 1943. 100 pp. B15 458, p. 18; I2, p. 173.

138 LINCOLN, Jean. Music in Michigan before 1860. M.A., Michigan State
University, 1939. L9 618, p. 48.

139 *MANOR, Harold Carl. A History of Music in Parke County, Indiana. M.A.,
Indiana University, 1938.

140 MITCHELL, Josephine Gray. Creative Music in Texas and Some of Its
Significant Composers during 1950-1970. M.A., Texas Woman's University,
1971. B18 TWU-1971-3, p. 63; F1 1470, p. 70; L7 80, p. 320.

141 MORAN, John E. History and Development of the Music Festival in New
Hampshire up to 1951. M.M.Ed., Boston University, 1951. B12, p. 106.

142 MORRIS, Arthur Corwin, Jr. Music in Rhode Island 1630-1820. M.A., Brown
University, 1956. 78 pp. B7 554, p. 70; F1 1262, p. 58; I2, p. 287.

143 *NELSON, J. Andrew. A Study of Music Competition-Festivals in the State of
Kansas. M.A., University of Missouri-Kansas City, 1960. 171 pp.

144 PINE, Mary Louise. A History of Music Contests in Iowa. M.M., Northwestern
University, 1941. B15 629, p. 23.

145   ROLLER, Bert A. Tennessee in Poetry and Song. M.A., English, George Peabody College for Teachers, 1923. 125 pp. I2, p. 37.

146   SEELENBINDER, Ray Lee. A Study of the Franklin County Music Festival. M.A., Ohio State University, 1955. B12, p. 129.

147   THEIS, Cecelia M. A Survey of the Development of Some of the Outstanding Music Organizations in Kansas. M.A., Kansas State College of Pittsburg, 1938. 50 pp. L15 656, p. 42.

148   THOMAS, Marjorie C. Music in the Protestant Settlements of Pennsylvania: 1637-1810. Master's thesis, University of Miami at Coral Gables, 1978. A2 3520, p. 149.

149   WINTER, Elizabeth Harrell. Music in Texas since 1920. M.A., Sul Ross State College, 1940. 43 pp. B7 850, p. 105; B14 178, p. 35; I1 3571, p. 353; I2, p. 156.

       Also includes a chapter on "The Texas Indian and Music."

150   WOLZ, Larry R. A Survey of Concert Life in Texas during the Nineteenth Century. Master's thesis, Texas Christian University, 1976. A2 4889, p. 200.

151   ZELLER, Frederick R. A Survey and Evaluation of Music Contests and Music Festivals in Pennsylvania. M.Mus., Eastman School of Music of the University of Rochester, 1939. 116 pp.

AREAS. CITIES

152   ALLEN, Larry Steven. Musical Life in Old Town Alexandria, Virginia, 1749-1814. M.A., American University, 1979. 146 pp. photos. A1 (17/4) 1312965, p. 277; B9 69, p. 9.

       This documentary is based on court and church records, diaries, family papers, and more than 6000 issues of the *Alexandria Gazette* and other newspapers that were published during those years. Included are directories of music and dancing instructors, music instructors' advertisements, photographs of instruments, and a discussion of John J. Frobel, John Constantine Générès, and Charles Leonard.

"A Favorite Minuet, by Mr. Laonard."
Likely Charles Leonard, violinist and composer in Alexandria, Virginia.
From the larger Thomas Schley Manuscript, c. 1780, Marshall L. Etchison Collection.

153 *BITTNER, Robert E. The Concert Life and the Musical Stage in New Orleans up to the Construction of the French Opera House. M.M., Louisiana State University, 1953. 177 pp.

154 BROWN, Lilla Jean. Music in the History of Dallas, Texas, 1841-1900. M.M., University of Texas at Austin, 1947. B12, p. 143; B18 UT-1947-2, p. 69.

155 *CARDEN, Joy C. Lexington's Music, 1775-1840. M.M., University of Kentucky, 1975. 260 pp. illus.

This study has been published under the title *Music in Lexington before 1840* (Lexington: Lexington-Fayette County Historic Commission, 1980).

156 CARROLL, Elizabeth Woodruff. The Bethlehem Bach Festivals. S.M.M., Union Theological Seminary, 1954. B8 860, p. 61.

Bethlehem, Pennsylvania.

157 *COKER, John W. Charleston, South Carolina, a Century of Music, 1732-1833. M.M., University of Cincinnati, 1955. 55 pp.

158 *DAUGHERTY, Edward B. Presentational Entertainments in Opelousas, Louisiana, from 1886 through 1900. M.A., Speech, Louisiana State University, 1953. D2 (7) 1261, p. 156.

159 DiBIASE, Mildred. A Survey of Music Composed and Published in Buffalo Prior to 1900. Master's thesis, Canisius College, 1952. F1 1282, p. 59.

160 *DUNAWAY, Cynthia Williams. A Historical Study of Musical Development in Cedar City, Utah, from 1851 to 1931. M.A., Brigham Young University, 1969. 259 pp. photos. B13, p. 74.

161 *ENGEL, Kathlyn. Musical Life in Boston and New York, 1849-1854. Master's thesis, University of Michigan, 1947.

162 FALCONE, Patricia Jane. Secular Music in Worcester, Massachusetts from the Turn of the 18th Century to the Onset of the Civil War (1800-1863). M.M., University of Lowell, 1980. 99 pp. A1 (19/2) 1315487, p. 176.

Discusses various music teachers and music instrument firms.

163 *FULLER, Marion Kendall. Vienna and Hartford in 1850; Being a Musical, Social and Educational Picture of the Two Cities at Mid-Century. M.Mus.Ed., Hartt College of Music of the University of Hartford, 1958. 48 pp.

164 HALL, Vilvin Susan Buckholts. A Cultural and Recreational History of Corpus Christi, Texas. M.A., University of Texas at Austin, 1959. B18 UT-1959-8, p. 82.

165 *HARRISON, Doris. A Survey of Musical Conditions in Montgomery, Louisiana, and the Surrounding Community. Master's thesis, Louisiana State University, 1936.

166 HASKINS, John C. Music in the District of Columbia, 1800 to 1814. M.A., Catholic University of America, 1952. B9 18, p. 3.

This documentary based on the subjects discussed include in this order: concert life, opera, music education, dealers in music, and community music.

167 *HAWKINS, Richard L. A Study of Community Music Activities in Selected Florida Communities. M.Mus.Ed., Florida State University, 1955. 105 pp. B12, p. 83.

168 HEINTZE, James Rudolph. Music in Colonial Annapolis. M.A., American University, 1969. 79 pp. A1 (8/2) M-2152, p. 81; B6 H471, p. 17; B9 51, p. 7; B17 (3/1-2) 1080, p. 81.

This documentary is based on church records, colonial inventories, and more than 1600 issues of *The Maryland Gazette*. Includes a directory of music tutors and a discussion of Alexander Malcolm, Charles Leonard, Daniel Thompson, and John Schneider.

169 *HIRTZEL, Robert Louis. A History of Music in Fort Vancouver and the City of Vancouver, Washington, 1824 to 1950. M.A., Portland University, 1953. 86 pp. illus.

170 JACKSON, Frances Helen. The German Swiss Settlement at Gruetli, Tennessee. Master's thesis, Vanderbilt University, 1933. 70 pp.

Discusses, in part, music and the community life of the settlers.

171 JONES, Martha Howard. Show Business in the Bootheel — A History of the Performing Arts in Cape Girardeau, Missouri, 1868-1963. M.S., Southern Illinois University, 1963. D3 730, p. 82.

The earliest extant piece of chamber music composed in America.
The first page of the "Anniversary Ode of the Tuesday Club" of Annapolis, Maryland,
written for two violins, violoncello, and small chorus, 1750,
by Thomas Bacon (Club name, Signior Lardini).
From the *Tuesday Club Record Book.*

172 *KOZLOWSKI, Marianne Clare. Music in Chicago, 1830 to 1850. Master's thesis, University of Illinois at Urbana-Champaign, 1977. 2 vols. 631 pp.

173 LARSON, Esther. The History of Music in Los Angeles. Master's thesis, University of Southern California, 1930. L2 2294, p. 346.

174 *LEAHY, Eugene Joseph. Music, the Settlement, and the Community: A Study of Social Music at Gads Hill Center. Master's thesis, DePaul University, 1949. 51 pp.

Gads Hill Center, Chicago, Illinois.

175 McGILVRAY, Byron Wendell. A Brief History of the Development of Music in Fort Worth, Texas, 1848-1972. M.M.E., Texas Christian University, 1972. B18 TCU-1972-3, p. 55.

176 *MYRACLE, Kay Ferree. Music in Memphis, 1880-1900. M.M., Memphis State University, 1975. 188 pp.

Based to a large extent on primary sources (20 newspapers & periodicals). Includes a survey of social-cultural life in Memphis prior to 1880, minstrel shows, opera, concerts, bands, clubs including the Mozart Society, Mendelssohn Society, Casino Club, the *Maennorchor,* the Philharmonic Orchestral Association, and the Beethoven Club. American musicians discussed include John Philip Sousa, Jacob Bloom, and MacKenzie Gordon, among others.

177 *NELSON, Sandra Lee. The Harlem Renaissance, 1920-1932. M.A., Eastern Michigan University, 1973. 137 pp. illus. B17 (8/1) 830, p. 55.

A documentation of "the black American's cultural attainments within the fine arts — music, literature, poetry, art, theater and drama." Various appendices list musicals, record companies, a discography of black recording artists, and black composers of serious music.

178 OTT, Pamela Worley. A Comparative Study of Drama, Art, Music, and Dance in Highland, Illinois. M.S., Southern Illinois University, 1971. D3 325, p. 37.

179 POHLY, Linda L. Music in Wichita, 1870-1906. M.Mus., Wichita State University, 1978. 168 pp. illus.

180 POINT, Phil. The History and Development of Music in Temple, Texas. M.M., University of Texas at Austin, 1961. B18 UT-1961-11, p. 85.

181 PRESTON, Katherine K. John Prosperi and Friends: Professional Musicians in Washington, D.C., 1877-1900. M.M., University of Maryland at College Park, 1981. 270 pp. illus.; photos.

This study examines the variety and numbers of performing jobs available to musicians, the role played by the Marine Band apprenticeship program, the comparative economic standing of musicians in the community, and the repertory performed at events ranging in diversity from theatrical performances and steamboat excursions to academic commencements, dedication ceremonies and parades, and bicycle races. The author includes an appendix of "Seasons in Three Washington Theatres": National Theatre/Ford's Grand Opera House, 1883-84; Herzog's Ninth Street Opera House, 1885-86; Kernan's Lyceum, 1892-93.

182 RAUCHLE, Bob Cyrus. The Social and Cultural Contributions of the German Population in Memphis, Tennessee, 1840-1880. Master's thesis, University of Tennessee, 1964.

Discusses the *Maennorchor,* a musical organization active in Memphis during the 1870s and 1880s, and various local music teachers.

183 *REHM, Barbara Ann Masters. A Study of the Cape Verdean Morna in New Bedford, Massachusetts. M.A., Brown University, 1975.

184 *ROBERTSON, Reba. Musical History of Cincinnati. M.M., Cincinnati Conservatory of Music, 1941. 100 pp.

185 *ROBERTSON, Susanne M. Scott. Musical Activity in Lowell, Massachusetts from 1825 to 1900. M.M., Indiana University, 1973. 126 pp. illus. B17 (8/2-3) 2607, p. 194.

186 *ROGERS, Delmer Dalzell. Nineteenth Century Music in New York City as Reflected in the Career of George Frederick Bristow. Master's thesis, University of Michigan, 1967. B13, p. 32.

187 *SCHROEDER, Vernon Paul. Cincinnati's Musical Growth, 1870-1875. M.M., University of Cincinnati, 1971. 167 pp. illus.

188 SEYMOUR, Margaret R. Music in Lincoln, Nebraska in the Nineteenth Century: A Study of the Musical Culture of a Frontier Society. M.A., University of Nebraska, 1968. B5 (14), p. 497; L1 2519, p. 255.

189   SHIFFLET, Anne Louise. Church Music and Musical Life in Frederick, Maryland, 1745-1845. M.A., American University, 1971. 130 pp. A1 (10/1) M-2954, p. 104; B9 62, p. 8; B17 (10/4) 10199, p. 592; L10, p. 57.

Shifflet lists the contents of the Thomas Schley music manuscripts which contain over 400 pieces and are located in the Marshall L. Etchison Collection, Historical Society of Frederick County, Frederick, Maryland. The contents are also listed in James J. Fuld and Mary Wallace Davidson, *18th-Century American Secular Music Manuscripts: An Inventory* (Philadelphia: Music Library Association, 1980), pp. 53-61. Also included is an appendix of music and dancing teachers advertising in Frederick during the years 1802-45.

190   *SHUMWAY, Lenn M. A Collection of Ballads, Folk Songs, Dance Tunes and Marches from Taylor, Arizona. M.A., Brigham Young University, 1957. 106 pp. I2, p. 271.

Includes music on sound recording tape in back of volume.

191   STAATER, H. Ray. The First Quarter Century of Music in Chicago (1835-1860). M.A., DePaul University, 1940. B2, p. 35.

192   STEELMAN, Gloria Geren. Musical Activity in Lampasas, Texas, 1880-1929: A Socio-Historical Study. M.Mus., University of Texas at Austin, 1971. B18 UT-1971-28, p. 96; L7 (81/4), p. 431.

193   *STOKES, Cloyce. The History of Music in Grand Junction to 1940. M.A., Brigham Young University, 1957. 117 pp. photos.

Grand Junction, Colorado.

194   *SUMMEY, Patricia Ann. A History of Musical Activities in Greenville, South Carolina, 1800-1900. M.Mus.Ed., Florida State University, 1960. 101 pp.

195   TARICANI, JoAnn. Music in Colonial Philadelphia and Michael Hillegas. M.A., University of Pennsylvania, 1977. 74 pp. illus.

Includes: "A Survey of Earlier Histories of Music in Colonial Philadelphia"; "Some Primary Sources Concerning Music in Eighteenth-Century Philadelphia"; a biography of Michael Hillegas, fiddle player and owner of a music store; and "Musical Connections Between Philadelphia and London." Included is an "Appendix of the correspondence of Hillegas pertaining to his music business."

196   *THOMPSON, Reed Paul. Eighty Years in Music in St. George, Utah, 1861-1941. M.A., Brigham Young University, 1952. 257 pp. photos.

197 *THOMPSON, Wilfred Zinow George. The Saginaw May Festival, 1901-1911. M.A., Wayne State University, 1962. 172 pp. illus.

198 TVRDY, Helen. A Century of Music in Omaha, 1854-1954. M.A., Creighton University, 1954. 162 pp. Ll 2520, p. 255.

199 *VAN COTT, Frank A. A Comparative Analysis of Music in the Homes of Provo and Springville. Master's thesis, Brigham Young University, 1934.

200 *VOSBURGH, Theodore. History of Vocal Music in Charleston, South Carolina from 1670-1800. Master's thesis, Eastman School of Music of the University of Rochester, 1937.

201 *WHITEHILL, Eleanor M. Adjunctive Studies in the Music History of Pittsburgh and Environs, 1758-1858. M.Mus.Ed., Florida State University, 1959. 48 pp. illus.

202 WILLIAMS, Gomer. An Outline of the History of Music in Emporia, Kansas (1865-1938). M.A., Kansas State Teachers College at Emporia, 1939. 170 pp. L15 657, p. 42.

203 WOLFE, A. D. Nineteenth Century New Orleans Composers. M.M., North Texas State University, 1968. B18 NTSU-1968-31, p. 27.

204 *WYRICK, Charles R. Concert and Criticism in Cincinnati, 1840-1850. M.M., University of Cincinnati, 1965. 163 pp. illus. B6 W993, p. 31.

AREAS. TERRITORIES

205 CASO, Fernando H. Héctor Campos Parsi in the History of Twentieth-Century Music of Puerto Rico. M.M., Indiana University, 1972. 125 pp. illus. B17 (6/2) 1903, p. 144.
Discusses the history of Puerto Rican music in 1898-1972.

206 VEGA, Hector. Some Musical Forms of African Descendants in Puerto Rico: Bomba, Pleua, and Rosario Francés. M.A., Hunter College of the City University of New York, 1969. B5, p. 325.

COMPOSERS. LIFE AND WORKS

207   ADAMS, Tina A. The Published Works of David Diamond. Master's thesis, Kansas State College, 1966. F1 1608, p. 67.

208   *ADAMSON, John. Leonard Bernstein and the Musical Stage. Master's thesis, University of Michigan, 1966.

209   ALEXANDER, Marianne Ellis. John Hill Hewitt—A Shadow on the Wall: A Study of the Reflections and Contributions of a Nineteenth Century Composer, Editor, and Poet. M.A., English, University of Maryland, 1964. B9 35, p. 5; L10, p. 82.

210   AMACKER, Marianne. A Study of the Organ Works of Leo Sowerby. M.M., Baylor University, 1970. B18 BU-1970-1, p. 5.

211   *ANDERS, Gerald R. The Keyboard Sonatas of Alexander Reinagle. M.A., Ohio State University, 1972. 201 pp.

212   *ANDERSEN, David Clive. William Claude Clive, His Life and Contribution to Music in Utah. M.S., Brigham Young University, 1963. 63 pp.

213   ANDERSON, Donna K. The Works of Charles T. Griffes. Master's thesis, Indiana University, 1966. B13, p. 27.

214   *APPELSTEIN, Aaron. Joseph Philbrick Webster: Nineteenth-Century American Songwriter. M.A., University of Wisconsin at Madison, 1975. 118 pp. illus.

215   AXSOM, Ronald B. The Orchestral Music of Charles Hommann. M.A., West Chester University, 1982. 96 pp.

216   *BACHELDER, Marilyn Meyers. Women in Music Composition: Ruth Crawford Seeger, Peggy Glanville-Hicks, Vivian Fine. M.A., Eastern Michigan University, 1973. 138 pp. B17 (8/1) 627, p. 43.

   The works discussed include: "Piano Study in Mixed Accents" and "Suite for Wind Quintet" by Seeger, "Sonata for Harp" and "The Transposed Heads" by Glanville-Hicks, and "Sinfonia and Fugato" and "Paean" by Fine. Included is a list of works for each of the composers, pp. 131-38.

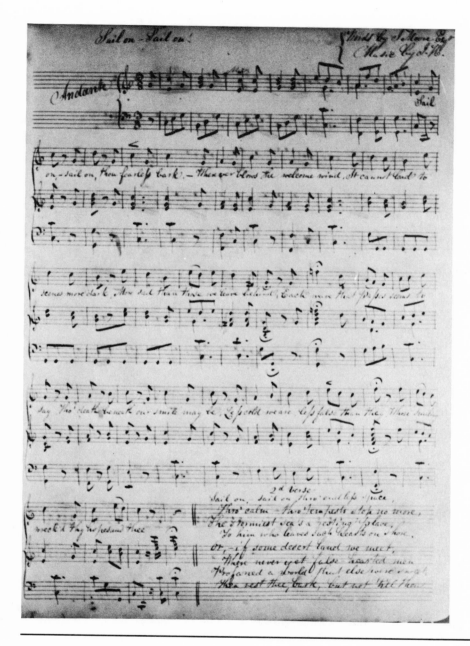

"Sail On—Sail On!" Music by John Hill Hewitt.
From the John Hill Hewitt Manuscript Book (ML 96.H486).

"Rondo" for pianoforte. Music by John Hill Hewitt.
From the John Hill Hewitt Manuscript Book (ML 96.H486).

217 BADING, David C. Leo Sowerby's Works for Organ with Orchestra or Ensemble. M.M., Musicology, University of Kansas, 1983. 135 pp.

A discussion of *Medieval Poem* (1926), Concerto in C (1937), *Classic Concerto* (1944), *Concert Piece* (1951), *Festival Musick* (1953), and *Triptych of Diversions* (1963).

218 BAER, Verna Lucile. The Concerto for Violin and Orchestra by Samuel Barber. M.Mus., Eastman School of Music of the University of Rochester, 1944. 70 pp.

219 BAGLEY, Sally Twedell. John Powell: Folk Musician. M.A., University of Virginia, 1970. 93 pp.

220 BAKER, Harold Vernon. Victor Herbert, the Man, His Music, and His Influence. M.M., Northwestern University, 1941. B15 27, p. 5.

221 *BALDRIDGE, Terry L. Louis Weber (1851-1931), Kansas City Composer and Publisher. M.M., Musicology, University of Kansas, 1980. 170 pp. illus.

222 BARNES, Carol A. John Alden Carpenter and Ned Rorem: Two American Composers of Art Song Recital. Master's thesis, Central Missouri State College, 1965. F1 1601, p. 71.

223 BARTHOLOMEW, Carolyn Ruth. The Contribution of Christian Ignatius Latrobe to Moravian Music. S.M.M., Union Theological Seminary, 1951. B8 809, p. 58.

224 *BASSE, Albert, Jr. The Songs and Larger Choral Works of Jules Jordan. M.A., Brown University, 1959. F1 987, p. 47.

225 *BATES, Carol Henry. The Piano Music of Henry Cowell. M.M., Indiana University, 1967. 106 pp. illus.

Also listed in B6 H521, p. 17, and B13, p. 27, under the name Carol Jennifer Henry.

226 *BEESLEY, Dorothy Hills. A Study of Some Texas Composers. M.A., Ohio State University, 1938. 107 pp.

33

227   BERMAN, Mitchell Alan. Gerald Strang: Composer, Educator, Acoustician. M.A., California State University at Long Beach, 1977. 79 pp. A1 (15/2) 13-09624, p. 108.

228   BILHARTZ, Patty A. The Piano Music of Norman Dello Joio. Master's thesis, Sam Houston State University, 1982. A2 2953, p. 143.

229   *BISSMEYER, Mary Carolyn. American Composers for the Piano. M.M., University of Cincinnati, 1948. 84 pp. illus.

230   *BLAHA, Pamela Jane. Aaron Copland since 1950. M.A., Ohio State University, 1975. 116 pp.

231   BLAND, Lewis Horace. James Allen Bland, Negro Composer: A Study of His Life and Works. M.M.E., Howard University, 1968. 93 pp. B9 8, p. 2; B17 (10/4) 10317, p. 598.
      Bland (1854-1911) wrote approximately 700 songs, of which 21 are discussed in this study.

232   *BLANKENSHIP, Adele Jean. Bernstein's *Lamentation* Compared to Classical Hebrew Musical Tradition. M.A., Central Washington University, 1971. 19 pp.

233   *BOEWE, John Frederick. The String Quartets of Johann Friedrich Peter. M.Mus., University of Illinois at Urbana-Champaign, 1957. 197 pp. B6 B673, p. 8; J1.
      Includes a list of the major hymnbooks of the Brethren from 1501 through the period of the "Hidden Seed," pp. 159-60.

234   *BORDERS, Barbara A. Elliott Carter's Double Concerto for Harpsichord and Piano with Two Chamber Orchestras (1961). M.M., Theory, University of Kansas, 1973. 116 pp.

235   *BOUNDS, Charles Evans. A Study of the Solo Songs of Charles Ives. M.M., North Texas State University, 1951. 111 pp. illus. B18 NTSU-1951-1, p. 17.

236   *BRANDLEY, Marian Proctor. The Art Songs of Charles Tomlinson Griffes. M.A., Brigham Young University, 1956. 152 pp.
      Includes tape recording bound on back cover.

237   BRIMHALL, Cleo Ann Larsen. The Life and Works of John Cage. M.M., University of Nebraska, 1976. 162 pp. B17 (10/4) 10849, p. 621.

238   *BROWN, Katherine Lydia. The Influence of John Cage on Contemporary Music: A Catalyst to the Growth and Development of a New Era. M.A., California State University at Hayward, 1970. 92 pp. K2 148, p. 18.

239   *BRYAN, James Kenneth. The Life and Works of Claude Marion Almand, with Analyses of Three Sacred Anthems: *Fanfare of Praise, Psalm 100, Dedication Anthem.* M.C.M., Southern Baptist Theological Seminary, 1973. 160 pp. illus.

240   BUCKLEY, Patricia M. Philip Paul Bliss, American Hymnist (1836-1876). M.A., Catholic University of America, 1967. 69 pp. B13, p. 21.

241   CALMER, Charles E. Philip Greeley Clapp: The Early Years (1888-1909). Master's thesis, University of Iowa, 1982. A2 2959, p. 143.

242   *CAMP, Virgil H. John Elliott Tullidge: The Influence of His Life and Works on the Musical Culture of Utah. M.A., Brigham Young University, 1957. 61 pp. plates. B8 1498, p. 105.

243   CARDULLO, Karen Mandeville. Ruth Crawford Seeger: Preserver of American Folk Music. M.A., George Washington University, 1980. 75 pp.

244   CARTER, Marva Griffin. Hall Johnson (1888-1970): Preserver of the Old Negro Spiritual. M.A., Boston University, 1975. B17 (9/1-2) 2206, p. 140.

245   *CEPIN, Caroline Coker. A Study of Samuel Barber's Piano Music. M.M., University of Alabama, 1970. 111 pp. illus.

246   CHAN, Wing-Chi. A Study on Chou Wen-Chung. M.M., Northern Illinois University, 1981. 99 pp. A2 2964, p.144.

247   *CHAPMAN, Mary Helen. The Piano Works of John Powell. M.M., Indiana University, 1968. 110 pp. B6 C466, p. 10; B13, p. 27.

248 CHESTER, Nancy Claire. The Piano Works of Wallingford Riegger. M.M., University of Texas at Austin, 1963. B18 UT-1963-5, p. 86.

249 *CHIARELLI, Nancy Carole Schoener. The Art Songs of George W. Chadwick. M.M., University of Cincinnati, 1972. 142 pp. illus.

250 CHOTOFF, Robert B. George Gershwin and American Music. Master's thesis, University of Buffalo, 1957. F1 932, p. 44.

251 *CHRISTIANSEN, Lyn May. The Songs of Arthur Shepherd. M.M., University of Utah, 1978. 75 pp. A2 3517, p. 158.

252 CIECIUCH, Helen Roberta. Wallingford Riegger: The Man and His Music. Catholic University of America, 1972. 78 pp.

The second part of this study is an analysis of Riegger's Trio for Piano, Cello, and Violin in G Minor, "New Dance," and Symphony No. 3. Included is a list of works and publishers and a discography.

253 *CLARKE, Mary Gray. Raynor Taylor, Musician in Federal America. M.A., University of North Carolina at Chapel Hill, 1955. 50 pp. B9 42, p. 6; K5, p. 203.

254 *CORBETT, Donald M. The Life and Works of Richard Purvis. M.A., California State University at Long Beach, 1969. 45 pp.

255 CORRIE, Shirley Polk. Gian Carlo Menotti: A Study of the Man and His Operas. M.M., Baylor University, 1965. B18 BU-1965-2, p. 3.

256 *COUSINS, Elaine B. The Music of Steve Reich: A Discussion of the Composer's Music and a Study of the Phasing Pieces, 1965-1971. M.A., Eastern Michigan University, 1971. 88 pp. illus.

257 CRAIN, Martha. John Alden Carpenter: American Art Music in the Early Twentieth Century with Emphasis on Gitanjali. M.M., Bowling Green State University, 1981. 45 pp. A2 2969, p. 144.

258 CROCKETT, Charlotte Gwen. Henry Cowell: The String Quartets. M.M., University of Texas at Austin, 1971. B18 UT-1971-11, p. 95.

259 CROOKS, Greta Lee Bardsley. Mittie Banks Howard: Her Songs and Stories. M.A., University of Texas, 1955. 256 pp. B18 UT-1955-6, p. 77; I2, p. 251.

260 *DARTER, Thomas Eugene. Elliott Carter's String Quartet No. 1. M.F.A., Cornell University, 1972.

261 *DAUM, John LaVern. Alexander Reinagle: *The Federal March,* a Study and Transcription for Band. M.M.Ed., Southern Illinois University, 1962. 2 vols.

Volume 2 contains a facsimile of *The Federal March,* composed in 1788, and transcriptions in manuscript.

262 *DAVIES, Katherine Currie. Charles Tomlinson Griffes and His Music. Master's thesis, Eastman School of Music of the University of Rochester, 1937.

263 *DAYS, Grace Eleanor. William Billings' Status in American Music. Master's thesis, University of Michigan, 1943.

264 *DEAN, Harry A. Adam Craig Smyth and His Influence on Choral Music of Central Utah. Master's thesis, Brigham Young University, 1938. B8 1501, p. 105.

265 *DeCHARMS, Desiree. The Musical Pioneer of the Western Country: Robert Patterson's Church Music. M.Mus., University of Illinois at Urbana-Champaign, 1972. 121 pp.

266 DEIBERT, William Edward Ellis. Thomas Bacon, Priest of the Establishment: The Life, Thought and World of a Maryland Clergyman. M.A., University of Maryland, 1966. B9 44, p. 6; H1, p. 4; L3, p. 11

Bacon was a significant 18th-century Maryland composer-musician.

267 *DEN, Marjorie Freilich. Joseph F. Lamb: A Ragtime Composer Recalled. M.A., Brooklyn College of the City University of New York, 1975. 71 pp.

An examination of Lamb's life based on personal letters and taped interviews of people who knew him. Lamb's music is not analyzed in this study.

268 *DEW, Phoebe Yan-Chee. Francis Hopkinson and His Music. M.A., University of California at Los Angeles, 1967. 112 pp. B13, p. 71; B17 (1/1) 183, p. 15.

Thomas Bacon (Club name, Signior Lardini),
eighteenth century Maryland composer and viola da gamba player.
Sketch by Alexander Hamilton, secretary of the Tuesday Club, 1751.
From the *Tuesday Club Record Book*.

269 *DOBBYN, Freddie Phyllis. The Instrumental Music of John Alden Carpenter. A.M., Indiana University, 1952. 94 pp.

270 *DOWDEN, Ralph Del. *Poems of Love and the Rain* by Ned Rorem. M.Mus., North Texas State University, 1969. 298 pp. illus. B18 NTSU-1969-4, p. 27.

271 *DRUMMOND, Robert Paul. The Life and Works of Merit N. Woodruff. M.M., Eastern New Mexico University, 1979. 93 pp. illus.

272 DWYER, Deborah. A Study of Selected Songs by John Duke. M.A., Smith College, 1982. 210 pp. A2 2977, p. 144.

273 EDWARDS, John Solomon. Sidney Lanier: His Life and Work in Music. M.A., University of Georgia, 1967. 103 pp. B6 E26, p. 13; B9 46, p. 6.

274 EDWARDS, Vernon Henry. The Life and Works of Clarence Cameron White. M.M., Catholic University of America, 1979. 70 pp.

Biography and analysis of selected compositions. Includes a list of his compositions.

275 *ELLIS, Mark C. Aaron Copland: Twelve Poems of Emily Dickinson. M.M., Mankato State University, 1975. 68 pp.

276 ETHERIDGE, Jane. Stephen Foster and the American Folk Ballad. M.A., Southern Methodist University, 1934. 146 pp. H1, p. 230; I2, p. 99.

277 *EVERETT, Donald Malin. Samuel Barber's Piano Sonata, Op. 26. M.M., Eastman School of Music of the University of Rochester, 1951. 108 pp. illus.

278 *FARBER, Daniel Lewis. Some Forgotten American Composers of the 20th Century. M.F.A., Brandeis University, 1970. B13, p. 26.

279 FERRIS, John Raymond. The Chorale Preludes of Three Contemporary American Composers. S.M.M., Union Theological Seminary, 1952. B8 911, p. 64.

280   FINALDI, Edmond T. Some Musical Ideas of Charles E. Ives, Connecticut's Pioneer in Contemporary Music. Master's thesis, Danbury State College, 1960. F1 1332, p. 61.

281   *FRIEDBERG, Ruth Crane. The Songs of John Duke. M.A., University of North Carolina at Chapel Hill, 1961. 136 pp.

282   *FRKOVICH, William Michael. The Published Songs of Charles T. Griffes. M.Mus., Arizona State University, 1976. 82 pp. illus. A2 2746, p. 113.

283   FRYE, Daniel W. *In Summer Fields* by Charles Ives. M.M., Bowling Green State University, 1974. K1 2565, p. 146.

284   FULKERSON, Noel W. The Lives and Works of Three Aleatoric Composers: John Cage, Morton Feldman, and Earle Brown. Master's thesis, Central Missouri State College, 1965. F1 1630, p. 72.

285   *FULTON, Alvin W. Ernest Bloch's Sacred Service. M.M., Eastman School of Music of the University of Rochester, 1953. 72 pp. illus. B8 629, p. 46.

286   *FURLAN, Kenneth R. The Aaron Copland Piano Variations. Master's thesis, Kent State University, 1969. 32 pp.

287   GAHIMER, Lora. Attitudes on Contemporary American Composition as Exemplified by Copland, Hanson, Harris, and Moore. M.Mus., Eastman School of Music of the University of Rochester, 1947. 68 pp.

288   *GALLAGHER, Jack B. Sonata for Piano: A Study of Miklós Rózsa's Violin Concerto, op. 24. M.F.A., Cornell University, 1975.

289   GALLIGAN, Ellen Marie. The Contributions of a Group of the New England Composers of the Nineteenth and Twentieth Centuries. M.A., Catholic University of America, 1956. 107 pp.

290   *GARRETT, Allen McCain. William Billings and the Fuguing Tune. M.A., University of North Carolina at Chapel Hill, 1949. 99 pp. B8 1275, p. 88; K5, p. 200.

291   GAYLE, Cecil M. Vocal and Instrumental Works of John Gambold. M.A., University of North Carolina, 1970. 2 vols. J1.

292   GIBSON, Gloria J. A Study of the Life of the Black American Composer Howard Swanson with an Analysis of His Work *Short Symphony*. Master's thesis, Southern Illinois University at Edwardsville, 1978. F1 1188, p. 70.

293   GRACE, Edwin A. Aaron Copland — A Study of His Life and Works. Master's thesis, Central Missouri State College, 1960. F1 1339, p. 61.

294   *GRACE, Richard. Charles Ives, American Song Writer. M.M., University of Cincinnati, 1952. 58 pp.

295   GRANT, James Stuart. The Works of Carl F. Mueller with Emphasis on His Anthems. M.A., American University, 1970. 64 pp. A1 (9/1) 13-02387, p. 32. Includes a list of the composer's works through May 1970.

296   *GREEN, Franklin Pasco. The Life and Works of Edwin Gerschefski, with Analysis of Two Choral Compositions: *The Lord's Controversy with His People* and *There Is a Man on the Cross*. M.C.M., Southern Baptist Theological Seminary, 1975. 133 pp. illus.

297   HAHN, Katherine. David Moritz Michael: Works for Wind Instrument Ensembles. Master's thesis, University of Missouri-Columbia, 1979.

298   HALBROOK, Mamie S. A Study of the Music of Sidney Lanier's Poetry. M.A., George Peabody College for Teachers, 1931. H2 3612, p. 134.
      For a bibliography of 73 theses on Sidney Lanier, poet, see Patsy C. Howard's *Theses in American Literature, 1896-1971* (Ann Arbor: Pierian Press, 1973).

299   *HALL, James Ramsey. The Vocal Music of Dudley Buck. M.A., University of North Carolina at Chapel Hill, 1951. 135 pp. B8 1279, p.88; K5, p. 202.

300   *HALLOCK, Norman Everett. A Study of Three Piano Sonatas by Norman Dello Joio. M.M., Eastman School of Music of the University of Rochester, 1953. 83 pp. illus.

301   HANKE, Arline Marie. A Study of the Gitanjali Songs by John Alden Carpenter. M.A., Eastman School of Music of the University of Rochester, 1942. 56 pp.

302 HARRIS, Charlene Diane. Margaret Bonds, Black Woman Composer. M.M., Bowling Green State University, 1976. 43 pp. A2 2755, p. 113; K1 3045, p. 220.

Includes a list of Bonds' published works.

303 *HARRISON, Daniel Chandler. Aaron Copland: *Piano Variations* (1930) and *Orchestral Variations* (1957). M.A. Brigham Young University, 1973. 91 pp.

304 HARVEY, Marion Bradley. The Songs of Charles T. Griffes. M.A., University of Pennsylvania, 1973. 2 vols. 145 pp. illus.

Volume 2 consists of facsimiles of the published songs.

305 *HAUSFELD, Susan Elizabeth. A Study of *Mass* by Leonard Bernstein. M.A., Ohio State University, 1977. 98 pp.

306 HAWKINS, Deborah A. Louise Crawford, 1890-1973: Her Life and Works. Master's thesis, University of Iowa, 1982. A2 2998, p. 145.

307 *HEBDA, Paul Thomas. Characteristics of Selected Twentieth Century Dance Suites. M.M., George Peabody College for Teachers, 1975. 93 pp. illus.

The American works discussed include four dance episodes from *Rodeo* by Aaron Copland, and *Pocahontas* by Elliott Carter.

308 *HEBERT, Rubye Nell. A Study of the Composition and Performance of Scott Joplin's Opera *Treemonisha*. Master's thesis, Ohio State University, 1976. 51 pp.

309 HENRICHS, William Lee. The Music of Ernest Bloch: A Critical Survey. M.M., Texas Christian University, 1958. 174 pp. B18 TCU-1958-2, p. 52.

310 HICKMAN, Charles Leroy, Jr. Andrew Law, Intellectual Musician. S.M.M., Union Theological Seminary, 1950. B8 984, p. 69.

311 *HIXON, Donald L. Bio-Bibliography of Early American Composers. M.A., California State University at Long Beach, 1968. 150 pp.

See also Hixon's *Music in Early America: A Bibliography of Music in Evans* (Metuchen, N.J.: Scarecrow, 1970).

312 HOBERG, John Louis. A Study of the *Four Roman Sketches* of Charles T. Griffes. Master's thesis, College of the Pacific, 1955. 17 pp. K7 419, p. 38.

313 HODGES, Sylvia Ray. A Study of Contemporary American Piano Literature for Children. M.M., University of Texas at Austin, 1964. B18 UT-1964-9, p. 87.

314 HOFFMAN, Timothy P. The Life and Works of John Barnes Chance. M.M., Bowling Green State University, 1981. 166 pp. A2 3004, p. 145.

315 HOLLMAN, Jenette H. Oklahoma Composers. M.M.Ed., University of Oklahoma, 1941. L12, p. 85.

316 *HORNER, Mary Katherine Hall. The Ballet Suites of Aaron Copland. Master's thesis, University of Michigan, 1964.

317 HOUCK, Elizabeth Stephenson. Johann Conrad Beissel, His Life and Music. S.M.M., Union Theological Seminary, 1956. B8 996, p. 70.

318 *HOWELL, Lillian Pope. Lowell Mason: Composer of Hymn-Tunes. M.S.M., Southern Baptist Theological Seminary, 1948. 86 pp. B8 334, p. 26; J3 1443, p. 85.

319 HOYLE, Stephen Edwin. The Songs of Aaron Copland. M.M., University of Houston, 1973. 164 pp. A1 (12/1) 13-05318, p. 48.

320 HRIBAR, Mary P. A Study of Two Songs from Ned Rorem's Cycle: Six Songs for High Voice and Orchestra. Master's thesis, Bowling Green State University, 1981. A2 2909, p. 138.

321 HUHN, Robert Erwin. William Billings. S.M.M., Union Theological Seminary, 1952. B8 998, p. 70.

322 JARRETT, Alfred Roosevelt. "New Music" in the U.S.A., 1960-1966. M.M., Howard University, 1967. 86 pp. B17 (1/1) 271, p. 22.

  Composers discussed include in this order: Charles Ives, Edgard Varèse, Henry Cowell, George Antheil, John Cage, Morton Feldman, Christian Wolff, Earle Brown, Vladimir Ussachevsky, Otto Luening, Halim El-Dabh, and Lukas Foss.

323   JOHNSTON, Linda Carol. The Piano Sonatas of Vincent Persichetti. M.M., University of Texas at Austin, 1970. B18 UT-1970-9, p. 94.

324   *JOHNSTON, William R. Choral Settings of Walt Whitman by Norman Dello Joio. Master's thesis, Louisiana State University, 1970.

325   *JONES, Milton Sylvester. Three Symphonic Band Compositions of Vincent Persichetti. M.S., Southern Illinois University, 1971. 113 pp.

326   JONES, Richard Lawrence. The Mason Dynasty in American Music. M.A., University of California at Los Angeles, 1959. 130 pp.

327   *JONES, Steven Donald. The Twelve Bagatelles of George Rochberg. M.M., Indiana University, 1974. 101 pp.

328   JONES, Velma. The Life and Works of Mark Oakland Fax. M.A., Morgan State University, 1978. 108 pp. illus. B9 20, p. 3.
       Fax (1911-74) was born in Baltimore, taught at Howard University, and composed no less than 129 compositions.

329   KACHMAN, Myra. Jerry Herman: A Composer-Lyricist and His First Five Musicals. Master's thesis, Northeastern Illinois University, 1976. A2 2777, p. 114.

330   *KANE, Arthur Matthew, Jr. The Piano Music of Charles Grobe. M.M., Ohio State University, 1973. 94 pp. plates.

331   KEENAN, Joseph John. The Catholic Church Music of Benjamin Carr. M.M., Catholic University of America, 1970. 96 pp. illus. B9 54, p. 7; B17 (10/4) 10063, p. 586.

332   *KEFALAS, Elinor. The Role of the Contemporary American Woman Composer. M.A., San Diego State University, 1977. 213 pp.

333   *KELLY, Earl E. The Piano Music of Peter Mennin. Master's thesis, Kent State University, 1964. 32 pp.

334 KESSON, Jane Haines. Four Contemporary American Composers. M.A., University of Pennsylvania, 1950. 114 pp. illus.

> The four composers discussed are Charles E. Ives, Henry Cowell, Aaron Copland, and Roy Harris.

335 *KEYTON, Robert. Griffes: Two Coloristic Works. M.M., Eastman School of Music of the University of Rochester, 1952. 94 pp. illus.

336 KIERMAN, Marilois Ditto. The Compositions of Leo Sowerby for Organ Solo. M.A., American University, 1967. 130 pp. A1 (5/3) 13-01098, p. 15.

337 KINSEY, Mary Etta. North Carolina Composers. M.M., Northwestern University, 1951. B15 412, p. 17.

338 *KUSHNER, David Z. Ernest Bloch and His Piano Music. M.M., University of Cincinnati, 1958. 70 pp.

339 *KUSHNER, David Zakeri. Ernest Bloch and His Symphonic Works. Master's thesis, University of Michigan, 1967.

340 *LANGOSCH, Marlene. The Published Works of Timothy Swan (1758-1842). M.M., Indiana University, 1968. 113 pp. illus. B6 L284, p. 21; B13, p. 23.

341 *LANSFORD, Julia Ann. The Hermit Songs of Samuel Barber. M.Mus., North Texas State University, 1964. 73 pp. illus. B18 NTSU-1964-11, p. 23.

342 *LANTZ, Russell Audley. American Composers and Their Works (1880-1934). M.A., Ohio State University, 1934. 200 pp.

343 LAUGHBAUM, Nancy. A Study of the Piano Quintet of Herbert Inch. M.Mus., Eastman School of Music of the University of Rochester, 1944. 113 pp.

344 *LENKE, Wayne Elden. James Hotchkiss Rogers, American Composer, Cleveland Critic. 67 pp. M.A., Ohio State University, 1960.

345 LEONARD, Effie Lou Graham. The Piano Works of Ernest Bloch. M.M., University of Texas at Austin, 1959. B18 UT-1959-12, p. 83.

346 *LOESSI, John. The Choral Works of Randall Thompson. M.M., University of Cincinnati, 1955. 41 pp.

347 *LOFTIS, Deborah Carlton. The Hymns of Georgia Harkness (1891-1974). M.C.M., Southern Baptist Theological Seminary, 1977. 106 pp. illus.

348 LOGANBILL, G. Bruce. Menottian Opera: A Synthesis of Drama and Music. M.A., Speech and Drama, University of Kansas, 1958. D2 (13) 2830, p. 124.

349 LONG, William R. Scott Joplin: The Piano Works. Master's thesis, Central Missouri State University, 1976. A2 2787, p. 114.

350 *McBEAN, Bruce Parker. Elliott Carter: *Variations for Orchestra.* Master's thesis, University of Michigan, 1963.

351 *McCANN, June. The Solo Songs of Charles Griffes and Samuel Barber. Master's thesis, Kent State University, 1960. 280 pp.

352 *McCLAIN, Charles Sharland. The Organ Chorale Preludes of Roger Sessions. A.M., Cornell University, 1957. 70 pp.

353 McCOY, Robert Charles. The Organ Works of Leo Sowerby. S.M.M., Union Theological Seminary, 1952. B8 1060, p. 74.

354 McDONALD, Ann. Contemporary Works for Two Pianos by Stravinsky, Bowles, Poulenc, and Milhaud. M.M., Southern Methodist University, 1953. B18 SMU-1953-4, p. 37.

355 McDONALD, Gail Faber. The Piano Music of Daniel Gregory Mason: A Performance Tape and Study of His Original Works for Piano Solo and Two Pianos. Master's thesis, University of Maryland, 1977. 32 pp.

356 MACKOWITZ, Phyllis Ruth. A Preliminary Investigation of American Women Song Composers of the Nineteenth and Early Twentieth Centuries. M.A., Wesleyan University, 1977.

357 *MAGEE, Noel Howard. The Short Piano Works of Charles Ives. M.M., Indiana University, 1966. 143 pp. B10, p. 23; B13, p. 27.

358 *MANGLER, Joyce Ellen. Andrew Law, Music Reformer. M.A., Brown University, 1956.

359 *MARIK, Joseph Jerome. A Study of the Operas of Gian Carlo Menotti. Master's thesis, DePaul University, 1953. 140 pp. illus.

360 MARR, James Anita. Gian Carlo Menotti: The Fusion of Music and Drama. M.A., Catholic University of America, 1959. D2 (13) 2831, p. 124.

361 *MARTINEZ, Victoria Elena. The Piano Sonatas of Vincent Persichetti. M.A., Tulane University, 1964. 73 pp. illus.

362 MATHIAS, Michele A. Samuel Barber's Sonata for Piano, op. 26. M.M., Bowling Green State University, 1977. 31 pp. K1 3181, p. 155.

363 MEAHL, Mary Daniel. The Third Symphony of Paul Creston. M.M., Eastman School of Music of the University of Rochester, 1962. 94 pp. illus.
Contains a list of Creston's compositions, pp. 89-91.

364 *MEHRLING, Mary Lou. James Hotchkiss Rogers, Cleveland Organist, Composer, and Critic, 1857-1940. M.A., Wayne State University, 1963. 177 pp.

365 *MENDENHALL, Miriam Lucille. The Songs of John Alden Carpenter. M.M., North Texas State University, 1952. 158 pp. B18 NTSU-1952-10, p. 18.

366 *MILEY, Malcolm Wayne. A Study of the Life and Works of William Billings. M.C.M., Southwestern Baptist Theological Seminary, 1961. 128 pp. illus. B8 1467, p. 103; B18 SBS-1961-8, p. 43; J3 1484, p. 87.

367 MILLER, Elaine K. A Study of Samuel Barber's Piano Music. Master's thesis, Kent State University, 1960. 67 pp. illus.

368 *MILLER, Kay. Charles Edward Ives, Innovator. M.A., West Texas State University, 1973. 49 pp. illus.
The works discussed include: Second Pianoforte Sonata, Fourth Violin Sonata, *Lincoln, the Great Commoner,* Sonata No. 3 for Violin and Piano, Symphony Nos. 2 and 4, and a selection of songs.

369 *MILLER, Leland Glenn. Dane Rudhyar: His Life, Writings, and Music. M.A., Arizona State University, 1976. 126 pp.

Includes a chronological list of musical compositions, pp. 77-96.

370 *MINEAR, Carolyn Cockrum. The Works of Charles Wuorinen: An Annotated Bibliography. M.M., Florida State University, 1977. 52 pp.

371 MITCHELL, Margaret Penelope. Leo Sowerby's Solo Organ Compositions Based on Hymn Tunes. M.M., North Texas State University, 1966. B18 NTSU-1966-15, p. 25.

372 MONAGHAM, Francis Borgia. The Songs of George Frederick Root. M.A., Catholic University of America, 1957. 91 pp.

373 *MOON, Wallace G. Charles E. Ives: Two Works Explored. M.A., Eastern Illinois University, 1971. 68 pp.

374 MOORE, Alicia Y. A Study of Anthony Philip Heinrich, an American Composer. Master's thesis, University of North Carolina at Greensboro, 1963. F1 1459, p. 66.

375 MOORE, James Edward. Aspects of the Evolution of Music of the Black Church as Shown through Selected Works of Mrs. Undine S. Moore. M.M., Virginia Commonwealth University, 1975. 32 pp.

376 MORTENSEN, Randy. The Final Phase of Richard Rodgers' Career: A Historical Study of His Original Works for the Musical Stage, 1960-1979. Master's thesis, Northern Illinois University, 1981. A2 4693, p. 230.

377 *MUCCI, Ferdinand Rudolph. Songs for the Harpsichord by Francis Hopkinson: A Study and Selected Transcriptions for Wood-Wind Ensemble. M.M.E., Southern Illinois University, 1959. 38 pp. score (13 pp.)

378 MUILENBURG, Harley W. A Study of Selected Unpublished Choral Compositions of Leo Sowerby. M.S., University of Wisconsin at Eau Claire, 1976. 121 pp. A2 2809, p. 115.

379 MURASE, Natsuko. John Cage: The Music of Changes (1951). Master's thesis, University of Western Ontario, 1981. A2 2956, p. 140.

380 *MURRAY, Martha M. George Gershwin: Classical Composer. M.M., Mississippi College, 1971. 104 pp.

381 *MURRAY, Sterling E. The Life and Music of an Early American Composer, Timothy Swan (1758-1842). Master's thesis, University of Michigan, 1969. B13, p. 32.

382 MYERS, Betty Dustin. The Orchestral Music of Charles Ives. M.M., Indiana University, 1951. 85 pp.

383 MYERS, Howard Leo. The Music of Septimus Winner. M.A., University of North Carolina at Chapel Hill, 1951. 159 pp. K5, p. 202.

384 NELSON, Wayne A. Edgard Varèse and the Electronic Medium. Master's thesis, University of Montana, 1980. A2 3641, p. 163.

385 NYQUIST, Janet Eloise Brown. The Solo Piano Works of Aaron Copland. M.M., University of Texas at Austin, 1963. B18 UT-1963-14, p. 87.

386 O'ROURKE, Betty L. The Piano Music of John Knowles Paine. Master's thesis, University of California at Riverside, 1978. A2 3478, p. 147.

387 *OVERSON, Marion Peter. Joseph J. Daynes, First Tabernacle Organist: His Contributions to the Musical Culture of Utah and the Significance of His Life and Works. M.A., Brigham Young University, 1954. 155 pp. B8 1505, p. 105.

388 *PAULSON, John Charles. The History, Current Status and Possible Future of Electronic Music as Exemplified by the Works of Vladimir Ussachevsky. M.M., University of Utah, 1976. 292 pp. A2 2815, p. 115.

389 PEARCE, Eva F. The Influence of Music on the Literary Career of Sidney Lanier. M.A., Columbia University, 1913. H2 3633, p. 135.
An additional 73 theses on Sidney Lanier, poet, are listed in H2.

390 PERKINS, Laurence. The Sonatas for Violin and Piano by Charles Ives. M.Mus., Eastman School of Music of the University of Rochester, 1961. 188 pp.

391 *PETERS, Damaris Porter. An American Song Cycle: Twelve Poems of Emily Dickinson by Aaron Copland. Master's thesis, Kent State University, 1979. 73 pp.

392 *POOL, Evelyn Ivora. A Study of Ned Rorem and His Song Cycle, *Poems of Love and the Rain*. M.A., Ohio State University, 1966. 131 pp.

393 *POPE, Mary Bhame. The Sacred Choral Works of John S. Duss. M.C.M., Southern Baptist Theological Seminary, 1971. 147 pp. illus.

394 *PRUETT, James Worrell. Francis Florentine Hagen, American Moravian Musician. M.A., University of North Carolina at Chapel Hill, 1957. 89 pp. B8 1290, p. 88; J1; K5, p. 204.

395 *PURDY, William Earl. The Life and Works of Charles John Thomas: His Contribution to the Music History of Utah. M.A., Brigham Young University, 1949. 73 pp. B8 1506, p. 105.

396 *PUTNAM, Howard Hoggan. George Edward Percy Careless: His Contributions to the Musical Culture of Utah and the Significance of His Life and Works. M.A., Brigham Young University, 1957. 102 pp. plates. B8 1507, p. 105. Careless' dates are 1839-1932.

397 QUISTORFF, Lynda. Selected Piano Works by Four American Women. M.A., Central Missouri State University, 1982. 140 pp. A2 3049, p. 147.
The composers are Vivian Fine, Miriam Gideon, Julia Smith, and Louise Talma.

398 RAMSAY, Russell G. David Van Vactor: Composer, Musician and Educator. Master's thesis, University of Tennessee at Knoxville, 1970. F1 1477, p. 70.

399 REDDELL, Harlan West. Factors in Gian Carlo Menotti's Success as a Modern Opera Composer. M.M.Ed., Texas Tech University, 1968. B18 TTU-1968-6, p. 60.

400 *REED, Tracey L. Johann Christian Bechler, Moravian Minister and Composer: The American Years, 1806-1836. M.A., Indiana University of Pennsylvania, 1973. 96 pp.

401   RESTINE, James Harold. The Choral Idiom of Randall Thompson. M.A., West Texas State College, 1959. 83 pp.

Twelve pieces are discussed.

402   *REVICKI, Robert Kenneth. A Study of Recent Settings of the Mass by American Composers. Master's thesis, Brown University, 1960. F1 1275, p. 58.

403   REYNOLDS, Friede Berglind. The Music of Supply Belcher. M.M., Chicago Musical College of Roosevelt University, 1968. 87 pp. B6 R462, p. 26.

404   RICHARDSON, Cynthia S. Mary Carr Moore's *Narcissa:* A Unique American Opera. Master's thesis, University of Southern California, 1983.

405   *RILEY, Paul Jerome. The Piano Works of Norman Dello Joio. M.M., Indiana University, 1961. 163 pp. illus.

406   RITCHEY, Liane M. Sidney Lanier's Two Springs: Music and Poetry. M.A., Indiana University of Pennsylvania, 1965. 47 pp. H2 3637, p. 135.

407   *ROBERTS, Kenneth Creighton, Jr. John Knowles Paine. Master's thesis, University of Michigan, 1962.

408   ROBERTSON, Carol Beth Villarreal. The Woodwind Chamber Works of Walter Piston. M.M., University of Texas at Austin, 1960. B18 UT-1960-21, p. 84.

409   RODGERS, James William, Jr. A Study of Selected Lyrics by Oscar Hammerstein II. M.A., Bowling Green State University, 1961. D2 (15) 2452, p. 171.

410   *ROWE, Jack Calvin. William Billings: Father of the Fuguing Hymn-Tune. M.S.M., Southern Baptist Theological Seminary, 1949. 57 pp. B8 38, p. 26; J3 1457, p. 86.

411   *RUCKERT, George. Charles Ives' Four Violin Sonatas. 2 vols. M.A., Queens College of the City University of New York, 1967. illus.

412   RUFF, Edwin E. A Study of Five Songs of Charles Ives. M.Mus., Eastman School of Music of the University of Rochester, 1942. 44 pp.

413 RYAN, Jean F. George Crumb's Makrokosmos, Volume III. Master's thesis, College of St. Rose, 1980. F1 1235, p. 73.

414 SHANK, Carl Dean, Jr. The *Evocations* of Carl Ruggles. M.M., North Texas State University, 1971. B18 NTSU-1971-20, p. 30.

415 *SHERIDAN, Wilbur. Chamber Music of Walter Piston. M.M., Eastman School of Music of the University of Rochester, 1947. 178 pp. illus.

416 SHIEBER, Jeanne. The Piano Variations of Aaron Copland. M.Mus., Eastman School of Music of the University of Rochester, 1942. 59 pp.

417 SIMPSON, Mary Lou. William Grant Still: A Review of Literature, a Proposed Unit of Study. M.A., Texas Woman's University, 1972. B18 TWU-1972-6, p. 64; F1 1332, p. 66.

418 SLATTERY, Paul Harold. A Comparative Study of the First and Fourth Symphonies of William Grant Still. Master's thesis, San Jose College, 1969.

419 SMITH, Elizabeth Evelyn. A Study of *Canticum Fratris Solis* by Charles Martin Loeffler. M.M., Eastman School of Music of the University of Rochester, 1947. B8 723, p. 52.

420 *SMITH, James A. Charles Sanford Skilton (1868-1941), Kansas Composer. M.A., Musicology, University of Kansas, 1979. 176 pp. illus.
Includes a list of Skilton's works, pp. 163-72.

421 *SMITH, Lyneer Charles. Brigham Cecil Gates: Composer, Director, Teacher of Music. M.A., Brigham Young University, 1952. 63 pp. photos.

422 *SPARGER, A. Dennis. A Study of Selected Choral Works of Randall Thompson. M.A., Eastern Illinois University, 1965. 73 pp.

423 SPIELMAN, Earl V. Alexander Reinagle and His American Keyboard Sonatas. Master's thesis, University of Wisconsin, 1968. B10, p. 29; B12, p. 21.

424 *STALLINGS, Valdemar Lee. A Study of *Forsaken of Man,* a Sacred Cantata by Leo Sowerby. M.S.M., Southern Baptist Theological Seminary, 1956. 116 pp.

425 *STARKS, Laura Geralee. Anthony Philip Heinrich—Piano Music in Dance Forms. M.A., University of California at Los Angeles, 1976. 284 pp.

426 STEPHENSON, Mary Lee. The Life and Works of Edward MacDowell. Master's thesis, Catholic University of America, 1952. 89 pp.

Includes brief descriptions and some analyses of MacDowell's works.

427 *STEWART, Marilyn. The Life and Accomplishments of Lisle Bradford. M.A., Brigham Young University, 1957. 52 pp. plates.

Lisle Bradford, Utah musician, 1887-1953.

428 STOLL, Robert J. The Piano Music of Charles T. Griffes. M.M., University of Wisconsin, 1967. 108 pp. B1 479, p. 147; B10, p. 30; B13, p. 30.

429 STORK, George Frederick. Problems of the American Composer: A Study in Recognition. M.A., University of Pennsylvania, 1950. 121 pp.

Part I: before 1919; Part II: between the wars, 1919-42. This study is approached in terms of the audience, performer, publisher, and composer.

430 *SUCOFF, Herbert. A Catalog and Evaluation of Stefan Wolpe's Music. M.A., Queens College of the City University of New York, 1969. 40 pp. B13 12, p. 26.

431 *THOMPSON, Geary Scott. The Transcription of Paul Creston's Rhythmicon for Guitar. M.A., Central Washington University, 1972. 28 pp. score (28 pp.); illus.

432 THOMPSON, Sidney Jean. The Piano Works of Norman Dello Joio. M.M., University of Texas at Austin, 1962. B18 UT-1962-17, p. 86.

433 *TRIBLE, Bruce Clarence. The Chamber Music of Henry Cowell. A.M., Indiana University, 1952. 116 pp.

434 *TUCKER, Wayne G. The Development of Original Compositions for the Concert Band during the 1950's. M.M.E., University of Missouri-Kansas City, 1974. 95 pp.

435 *TUREK, James John. Timothy Swan, His Life and His Music. M.Mus.Ed., Hartt College of Music of the University of Hartford, 1970. 112 pp. illus.

436 *UNGRODT, Judith Joan. The Music of Francis Hopkinson. M.A., Eastman School of Music of the University of Rochester, 1962. 101 pp. illus.

437 VANTILBURG, David E. Louis Moreau Gottschalk: United States Ethnic and Patriotic Music. Master's thesis, Bowling Green State University, 1981. A2 2000, p. 142.

438 *VINQUIST, Mary. The Psalm-Settings of Charles Ives. M.M., Indiana University, 1965. 102 pp. illus.

439 *VOORHEES, Larry Donald. A Study of Selected Vocal-Choral Works of Samuel Barber. M.A., Eastern Illinois University, 1965. 105 pp.

440 WAGNER, John W. James Hewitt: His Life and Works. Master's thesis, Indiana University, 1969. B13, p. 23.

441 *WALGREN, Carol L. Nelson. A Study of the Solo Piano Works of Paul Creston. M.A., Eastern Illinois University, 1967. 98 pp.

442 *WALKER, Marvin Ray. Band and/or Wind Compositions of Francis Johnson. M.M.Ed., Memphis State University, 1974. 133 pp.

443 WARD, Tom Robert. The Parthias for Wind Instruments of D. M. Michael. Master's thesis, University of Pittsburgh, 1966. B13, p. 20.

444 WEAVER, Robert E. The Piano Works of Charles T. Griffes. M.M., University of Texas at Austin, 1956. B18 UT-1956-32, p. 80.

445 *WEAVER, Susannah J. E. Music of the Early American Moravians as Reflected in the Compositions of George Godfrey Mueller, Minister and Musician. M.A., Syracuse University, 1952. 103 pp. illus.

    Bound in are the notes to an "Early American Moravian Music Festival and Seminar," Bethlehem, Pennsylvania, June 26 to July 2, 1950. 8 pp.

446 *WEBB, Lucile Hammill. A Study of the G Major Symphony for Organ by Leo Sowerby. Master's thesis, Eastman School of Music of the University of Rochester, 1945.

447 *WELLEFORD, Paul Bailey. The Sacred Choral Works of Jean Berger, 1941-1963. M.C.M., Southwestern Baptist Theological Seminary, 1965. 2 vols. in 1. 85 pp. illus. B18 SBS-1965-5, p. 44.
Volume 2 is an index, or list of the sacred choral works analyzed.

448 WENDT, Rudolph. A Study of Charles Ives' Second Pianoforte Sonata, *Concord, Mass., 1840-1860*. M.Mus., Eastman School of Music of the University of Rochester, 1946. 77 pp.

449 *WHISLER, John A. The Songs of John Philip Sousa. M.M., Memphis State University, 1975. 184 pp. B9 34, p. 5.

450 *WILSON, Janice Y. Black Serious Composers. M.A., Eastern Michigan University, 1971. 96 pp.
Includes lists of recordings, pp. 73-76, and works, pp. 81-96.

451 WOEPPEL, Louise B. W. Howard Hanson: A Song of the Middle West Pioneers in American Music. M.A., Creighton University, 1941. 230 pp. L1 259, p. 33.

452 *WRIGHT, Josephine Rosa Beatrice. A Study of Two Operas by Hugo Weisgall. M.A., University of Missouri-Columbia, 1967. 135 pp. illus.

453 WYNN, Virginia S. Charles Griffes: His Life, Songs, and Piano Works. Master's thesis, Central Missouri State College, 1965. F1 1700, p. 75.

454 *YOUNG, John Walter. A Study of Contemporary, Unpublished Compositions for Band. A.M., Washington University, 1959. 116 pp.
American composers include Thomas Beversdorf, Will Gay Bottje, Charles Cushing, Anthony Donato, Jonathan Elkus, Norman Heim, George F. McKay, Kemble Stout, and Robert Wykes.

455 *YUNGTON, Alvin H. Riegger and Bartok: A Comparative Study. M.A., Wayne State University, 1970. 86 pp.

PERFORMANCE. INDIVIDUALS

456 BANZETT, Donna Lee. An Analysis of Organ Recitals of the Conventions of the American Guild of Organists. S.M.M., Union Theological Seminary, 1953. B8 806, p. 57.

457 *BELLISTON, Bona. The Life and Accomplishments of Simeon Bellison. M.A., Brigham Young University, 1956. 113 pp. plates.
Bellison (1881-1953) was a Russian-American clarinetist.

458 *BLANKENSHIP, Gay Grace. The DeMoss Family Musicians: Lyric Bards of Oregon. M.A., University of Oregon, 1966. 112 pp. A1 (5/1) 13-01044, p. 12.

459 BLITCH, Lila Marie. Sidney Lanier: Artist, Critic, and Human Being. M.A., English, University of Maryland, 1935. 122 pp. B9 37, p. 5.
Lanier was flutist of the Peabody Symphony Orchestra, Baltimore, in 1873.

460 *BOGLE, Gary W. A Comparative Study of Two Choral Conductors B. R. Henson and Lloyd Pfautsch. M.Mus., North Texas State University, 1972. 245 pp.

461 *COMPTON, Annie Rosella. John J. McClellan, Tabernacle Organist. M.A., Brigham Young University, 1951. 73 pp. B8 1499, p. 105.

462 *CORAY, John Louis. Emma Lucy Gates (Bowen), Soprano — Her Accomplishments in Opera and Concert. M.A., Brigham Young University, 1956. 113 pp.

463 *ERVINE, Beverley Ann. Francis Hopkinson Smith and His Grand Harmonica. M.A., Ohio State University, 1975. 94 pp.

464 *FREY, Eugene Victor. Jullien in America. M.M., University of Cincinnati, 1956. 141 pp.

465 *GRIFFITH, Margaret Kathryn Blackman. Analysis of the Vocational Activities of Blind Musicians in the United States as Shown by a Nation-Wide Survey. M.A., Syracuse University, 1939. 100 pp.

466   GRIFFITHS, Philip Ray. A History of the Emerson Minstrels on the San
      Francisco Stage, 1870-1889. M.A., Stanford University, 1954. 142 pp. D2
      (8) 1496, p. 145; D3 98, p. 12.

467   INGALLS, David M. Francis Scala: Leader of the Marine Band from 1855 to
      1871. M.A., Catholic University of America, 1957. 138 pp. B9 19, p. 3.

468   *JOHNSON, Dale A. The Life and Contributions of Evan Stephens. M.A.,
      Brigham Young University, 1952. 129 pp. photos.
      Performer, composer, and music educator.

469   JONES, Maxine Carrie. Resource Materials on Mahalia Jackson: A Chronicle
      of Her Life, an Annotated Bibliography and an Analytical Discography.
      M.A., Morgan State University, 1980. 136 pp.

470   LAQUE, Rosemarie S. Maria Callas: The Controversial Career of a Prima
      Donna. M.A., Catholic University of America, 1979. 50 pp.

471   LOGAN, Margaret Ann. The Musical Life of Theodore Thomas and His Young
      People's Concerts. M.M., Catholic University of America, 1973. 96 pp.
      Discusses Thomas' conducting of symphony concerts in New York (1861-68 and
      1880-90), Chicago (1891-1905), and other places in the U.S. One chapter is devoted
      to his directorship of the Cincinnati College of Music (1878-80).

472   *MINOR, Andrew C. Piano Concerts in New York City, 1849-1865. Master's
      thesis, University of Michigan, 1947.

473   POTTHAST, Anne Colette. Austin Conradi, Piano Artist and Teacher. M.M.,
      Catholic University of America, 1975. 91 pp. B9 25, p. 4.
      Conradi (1890-1965) taught at Catholic University of America. Included are a
      number of recital programs.

474   *WOLBERT, Nancy. Richard Buhlig, a Concert Pianist: His Career and Influence
      in the Twentieth Century. M.A., California State University at Long Beach,
      1978. 142 pp. A1 (17/3) 1312805, pp. 216-17; A2 3212, p. 139.

PERFORMANCE. ORCHESTRAS AND BANDS

475   ADAMS, David. Community Bands in Kandiyohi County, Minnesota. Master's thesis, University of Minnesota, 1970. B13, p. 32.

476   ADKISON, Dan E. Establishment and Growth of the Wind Band at Central Methodist College. Master's thesis, Central Missouri State University, 1977. F1 1351, p. 73.

477   ANDERSON, Leslie A. Sun Devil Pride: A History of the Sun Devil Marching Band. Master's thesis, Arizona State University, 1979.

478   *BARBER, Sue E. Music and Politics: The Philadelphia Orchestra in the People's Republic of China. Master's thesis, University of Michigan, 1977.

479   *BARTNER, Arthur Charles. The Evolution and Development of the University and College Marching Band. Master's thesis, University of Michigan, 1963.

480   BELT, Byron Harold. The Chicago Symphony Orchestra and Its Repertoire. M.M., Northwestern University, 1952. B15 46, p. 6.

481   *BILLINGS, Melvin D. A Survey of Marching Bands in the State of Utah with Emphasis on Types of Materials in Use. M.S., University of Utah, 1957. 71 pp.

482   *BIRKHEAD, Carole Caudill. The History of the Orchestra in Louisville. M.A., University of Louisville, 1977. 183 pp. A1 (15/4) 13-10304, p. 230.
    The study begins with the St. Cecilia Society Orchestra in 1822.

483   BISHOP, John J., Jr. The History of Bands in Union City, Tennessee. M.M.E., Florida State University, 1954. B12, p. 83.

484   BOURLAND, Ellen Y. The History of the Dallas Symphony, 1900-1980. M.S., History, Southern Methodist University, 1981. 92 pp. A2 2955, p. 143.

485   *BROWN, Deane Wakley. Growth and Development of Utah Professional Symphonic Orchestras Prior to 1940. M.A., Brigham Young University, 1959. 171 pp.

486 BUNDY, Orrin Richard, Jr. A Concise History of the Penn State Blue Band to 1982. Master's thesis, Pennsylvania State University, 1982.

487 CALDWELL, Kenneth V. The History of the Band in the United States. M.A., Sam Houston State University, 1963. B18 SHS-1963-4, p. 33.

488 *COOK, Martha Tingey. Pioneer Bands and Orchestras of Salt Lake City. M.A., Brigham Young University, 1960. 84 pp. illus.

489 COVINGTON, Verna Y. The Growth of Texas School Orchestras since 1946-47. M.M., University of Texas at Austin, 1956. B18 UT-1956-6, p. 78; F1 1076, p. 51.

490 DABNEY, Ray F. The History of the Band at Sam Houston State Teachers College. M.A., Sam Houston State University, 1963. B18 SHS-1963-5, p. 33; L7 (79), p. 82.

491 DEL MONACO, John. A History of the Bands of the University of Southern California, 1880-1952. M.M., University of Southern California, 1952. B12, p. 75.

492 DOUGHT, Clinton J., Jr. Growth of the High School Band and Orchestra in Dade County, Florida. M.Ed., University of Miami, 1953. B12, p. 82.

493 DOUGLAS, Sharrard H. A History of the San Antonio Symphony Orchestra. M.A., Incarnate Word College, 1971. L7 (78), p. 320.

494 EAGLE, Charles T., Jr. A Survey of the Organization and Administration of College and University Bands in the United States. M.M., University of Texas at Austin, 1956. B18 UT-1956-10, p. 78; F1 1080, p. 51.

495 *EBY, Margarette F. The Detroit Symphony Orchestra during the Time of Gabrilovitch: An Oral History. M.A., Wayne State University, 1962. 134 pp. illus.

496 FELTS, Jack H. Some Aspects of the Military Wind Band during the Civil War. M.M., Baylor University, 1968. B18 BU-1968-2, p. 4.

497   FORQUE, Charles E. Growth and Development of Texas High School Bands. M.A., Sam Houston State University, 1970. B18 SHS-1970-4, p. 35; L7 (79), p. 82.

498   *FOX, Charles Clayton. A Survey of Important Historical Data of One Hundred and Eight Symphony Orchestras in the United States. Master's thesis, DePaul University, 1950. 133 pp.

499   FREDRICK, Robert. A Study of the Cherry Hill New Jersey Wind Symphony as a Possible Model for Community Bands. Master's thesis, Glassboro State College, 1973. F1 1271, p. 65.

500   *GOLDBERG, Norman Albert. A History of the Band in the United States since 1860. Master's thesis, University of Illinois at Urbana-Champaign, 1942. 88 pp.

501   *GOOD, Jonathan E. John S. Duss and the American Band Movement, 1800-1930. M.M., Ohio State University, 1973. 120 pp.

502   *HAFNER, James T. A History of the Mason City (Iowa) Public High School Concert Band (1931-1971). M.A., Northeast Missouri State University, 1973. 124 pp. A1 (12/4) 13-06256, p. 439; F1 1274, p. 65.
        Includes a tape recording of nineteen compositions performed by the band.

503   *HARRIS, Dana Douglas. The Organization and Unit History of the 399th Army Band. M.A., Northeast Missouri State University, 1977. 282 pp. illus. A1 (16/2) 13-10910, p. 111.
        Activated at Fort Leonard Wood, Missouri.

504   HARRIS, Frederick A. A Survey of the Organization and Administration of College Bands in New England. Ed.M., Boston University, 1950. B12, p. 104.

505   HARTER, Ruth Ellen. Development of the Junior Orchestra in the Medina City Schools. M.Ed., Ohio State University, 1955. B12, p. 131.

506   HOLLIMAN, Marcia Pelton. The Development of the San Antonio Symphony, 1919-1966. M.A., Trinity University, 1966. L7 (80), p. 420.

507 HOWENSTEIN, Marshall C. The Organization and Function of the Community Orchestra in Indiana. M.A., Jordan College of Music of Butler University, 1955. B12, p. 95.

508 JETER, Norman Lafayette. A Descriptive and Evaluative Analysis of Northwestern University's First High School Band Day. M.M., Northwestern University, 1956. B12, p. 91.

509 JOHNSON, Clarance. Displacement of Black Band Directors in Mississippi Following School Desegregation, 1967-1972. Master's thesis, Jackson State College, 1975. F1 1071, p. 59.

510 *JOHNSON, James Winfred. The Status and Administration of Student Dance Bands in Colleges and Universities in the United States. M.Mus., North Texas State Teachers College, 1947. 69 pp.

511 *JOINER, Thomas Witherington. A History and Analysis of the Repertoire of the Louisville Orchestra: Seasons 1937-38 through 1977-78. M.C.M., Southern Baptist Theological Seminary, 1978. 175 pp.

512 LAMBRECHT, Clarence Julius. A Survey of Texas High School Dance Bands. M.M., University of Texas at Austin [no date cited]. B12, p. 145.

513 *LANEER, Larry. Marshall's Band of Topeka: A Study of the Golden Age of Bands in Kansas. M.A., Musicology, University of Kansas, 1978. 156 pp. illus.

Discusses the founding of John Bromell Marshall's Band in 1884; the "second generation" of the band, 1910-32, under the leadership of D. G. Kline, 1910-16, and J. B. Marshall, Jr., 1916-32; and the "third generation" of the band, 1933-78. Included are illustrations of concert programs, four compositions related to Marshall's Band, various business papers, and rosters of the band.

514 *LINDSKOOG, Wesley Milton. An Analysis of the Style of the Stan Kenton Orchestra. Master's thesis, Eastman School of Music of the University of Rochester, 1948.

515 LUND, Anton Monroe. The Iowa Band Law, Major George W. Landers and the Iowa Bandmasters Association: A History. Master's thesis, University of Northern Iowa, 1961. F1 1357, p. 61.

516 *LYONS, Nick Louis. A Brief Historical Sketch and Present Status of the United States College and University Orchestras. Master's thesis, DePaul University, 1950. 136 pp.

517 McCUEN, Joseph Molina. A History of Bands in the United States Navy. M.M., University of Maryland, 1967. 128 pp. B9 58, p. 7; B13, p. 32.

518 McFARLAND, Anne A. The Atlanta Symphony Orchestra: The Sopkin Years. Master's thesis, University of Georgia, 1976. A2 2798, p. 115.

519 *McGUIRE, Ann Calhoun. The Central Kentucky Youth Symphony Orchestra: 1947-1969. Master's thesis, University of Michigan, 1969.

520 *McKEWEN, Robert William. The Development of Union Military Bands in the Civil War. M.A., San Diego State College, 1966. 112 pp. illus.

521 MANNING, Carroll. The Orchestra in the Public Schools of the United States: Its Growth and Development. M.A., University of Southern California, 1951. B12, p. 77.

522 MARQUIS, Robert Lincoln, Jr. The Development of the Symphony Orchestra in Texas. M.A., University of Texas at Austin, 1934. B18 UT-1934-2, p. 67.

523 MARTIN, Glenn M. An Investigation into the Development of the Band in the United States and Its Emergence into Public Education. Master's thesis, University of Mississippi, 1977. F1 1410, p. 75.

524 MARTIN, Mary Karen. An Evaluation of Buffalo's First Orchestra, 1887-1899. M.A., Catholic University of America, 1964. 135 pp. illus.; plates.

    Also discusses a number of musical activities in Buffalo prior to the formation of the orchestra as well as "guests of the Buffalo Orchestra," including L. M. Gottschalk. Included is a selection of early concert programs.

525 *MATTSON, Lynne Marie. A History of the Detroit Symphony Orchestra. Master's thesis, University of Michigan, 1968.

526 MONTGOMERY, John Marvin. A Survey of School Orchestras in Oklahoma. M.M., University of Texas at Austin [no date cited]. B12, p. 145.

527   MORGAN, Richard Sanborn. Critical Reaction to Serge Koussevitzky's Programming of Contemporary Music with the Boston Symphony Orchestra, 1924-1929. M.A., North Texas State University, 1982. 101 pp. A1 (21/2) 1319421, p. 182.

528   *MUNN, John H. A History of Bands at Eastern Michigan University: 1894 through 1964. M.A., Eastern Michigan University, 1979. F1 1048, p. 67.
      Discusses the following conductors: Cornelius A. Woodcox, John F. Barnhill, Duane Chester Ryan, William D. Fitch, and Mitchell M. Osadchuk.

529   NAGEL, Richard J. The Growth and Development of Bands in the United States. Master's thesis, Colorado College, 1958. F1 1036, p. 49.

530   *NASH, Dennison James. The Construction of the Repertoire of a Symphony Orchestra: A Study in Social Interaction. Master's thesis, Sociology and Anthropology, Washington University, 1950. 114 pp. illus.

531   OLSON, Dean R. A Survey of Selected Community Symphony Orchestras of the Middle West. Master's thesis, Mankato State College, 1964. F1 1489, p. 67.

532   *PAPINCHAK, Andrew Ernest. The History of the Johnstown Symphony Orchestra. M.Ed., Indiana University of Pennsylvania, 1969. 214 pp.

533   *PARKS, Rosemary. The Preparation for, the Repertoire, and the Follow-up of Symphony Orchestra Concerts for Students in Eighteen Cities of the United States from 1959-1964. M.M.Ed., University of Missouri-Kansas City, 1965. 133 pp.

534   PETERSON, Milo. A Survey of Summer Band Programs in Twelve Kansas Communities. M.S., Kansas State Teachers College, 1954. B12, p. 97.

535   PHILLIPS, Wendell B. The Status of School Orchestras and Bands in the Counties of Nassau and Suffolk, Long Island, New York. M.M.Ed., Boston University, 1950. B12, p. 106.

536   RAILSBACK, Tom. Military Bands and Music in the Frontier. Master's thesis, Fort Hays State University, 1979. A2 3171, p. 137.

537 *REMINGTON, Marjorie W. History of the Oakland Symphony Orchestra. M.A., California State University at Hayward, 1973. 100 pp. K2 174, p. 21.

538 *RESNICK, Felix. The History, Development, and Future of the Symphony Orchestra in the United States. M.A., Wayne State University, 1947. 103 pp.

539 *SCHNEIDER, Betty M. Comparative Survey of the Programs of the Boston, Chicago, and New York Symphony Orchestras of the Past Twenty-Five Years. M.A., Music, University of Kansas, 1950.

540 *SEDORE, Robert N. An Analysis of the Increase and Decrease in Performance Frequency of Orchestra Repertoire in America. M.M., University of Kansas, 1950. K8, p. 91.

541 *SHAPP, Elizabeth Irene. A Survey of the Critiques of the First Concert of One Hundred and Fourteen Symphony Orchestras in the United States. Master's thesis, DePaul University, 1951. 201 pp.

542 SHAW, Caroline Kallquist. A Survey of Educational Activities Related to Symphony Orchestra Concerts for School Children and Young People in the United States. M.A., American University, 1970. 94 pp.

543 *SLAUGHTER, Jay L. The Marching Band. M.S., University of Utah, 1950. 83 pp. illus.

544 *SLOAN, David Walter. A Study of the Administration and Organization of Extra-Curricular Orchestras in the State of Texas. M.M.E., Midwestern University, 1964. 72 pp.

545 STOCK, Patricia Gail. Richard Franko Goldman and the Goldman Band. Mus.M., University of Oregon, 1982. 152 pp. A1 (21/2) 1319779, p. 183.

546 STONEBURNER, Bryan C. The Phoenix Symphony Orchestra, 1947-1978: Leadership, Criticism and Selective Commentary. M.A., Arizona State University, 1981. 272 pp. A2 3067, p. 148.

547 TERWILLIGER, Gloria H. "The President's Own": The United States Marine Band, 1798-1964, Chronologically Arranged and Annotated. M.S. in L.S., Catholic University of America, 1967. 115 pp. B9 33, p. 5; G4, p. 447.

548 THOMPSON, Charles Elmer. A Survey and Analysis of the Activities of Ten Small College Bands of Ohio and Their Relation to the Music Education Program. M.A., Ohio State University, 1950. B12, p. 130.

549 TOUTANT, William Paul. An Analysis of Symphonic Programming Techniques of the Leading Orchestras at the Turn of the Twentieth Century, Drawn from Selected Programs of the Boston and Chicago Symphony Orchestras, 1881-1908. M.A., George Washington University, 1972. 88 pp.

550 *TRACY, Mildred Lyman. The Development of the San Diego Symphony Orchestra. M.A., San Diego State College, 1962. 159 pp. illus.

551 *WATKINS, Clifford. A Comparative Study of Band Training Programs in the United States Military. M.M.Ed., Southern Illinois University, 1966. 154 pp.

552 *WILCOX, Eileen Wilhoit. Adult Educational Activities of Major American Symphony Orchestras. M.A., Brigham Young University, 1974. 93 pp.

553 *WILLIAMS, Larry R. A History of the High School Orchestra Movement in Kansas. M.M.Ed., University of Kansas, 1968.

554 WOODRUFF, Jean. A History of the Atlanta Community Orchestra (1958-1978) as Founded and Sponsored by the Atlanta Music Club, Inc. Master's thesis, Georgia State University, 1979. A2 3211, p. 139.

555 *WOOTEN, William Chapman. A Study of the Development of High School Bands in Utah. M.A., Brigham Young University, 1950. B12, p. 147.

556 *YATES, Beverly L. A Survey of Children's Concerts of the Thirty Major Symphony Orchestras of the United States. M.M.E., Illinois Wesleyan University, 1956. 84 pp. F1 1215, p. 57.

557 YOUNG, Pamela Fensch. History of the Houston Symphony Orchestra, 1913-1966. M.A., University of Texas at Austin, 1970. L7 (81), p. 439.

558 ZACHMAN, Robert F. Development of the Junior College Honor Band in California from 1961-1963. Master's thesis, Los Angeles State College, 1963. F1 1489, p. 65.

PERFORMANCE. CHOIRS, CHORUSES, AND CHAMBER ENSEMBLES

559 *CLIFFORD, Arthur Charles. Youth Choirs in the Episcopal Churches of America. M.M.E., Illinois Wesleyan University, 1952. 68 pp.

560 COPLEY, Olive Genette. A Comparison of the Choir Programs of Four Methodist Churches in Dallas, Texas. M.R.E., Southern Methodist University, 1954. B8 1440, p. 101.

561 DAUN, Glenn Shields. The Placement of the Choir in Protestant Church in America. S.M.M., Union Theological Seminary, 1949. B8 888, p. 63.

562 *DONALDSON, Alexander. The Status of the Wind Instrument Ensemble in the American School. M.E., Wayne State University, 1950. 61 pp. illus.

563 DORNDORF, Anton Hubert. Historical Analysis of the German-American Singing Societies in California with an Evaluation. M.A., University of the Pacific, 1955. 300 pp. B7 182, p. 25; I2 182, p. 25; K7 411, p. 37.

564 *DORTCH, Clarence William. The Development of an A Cappella Choir at the Southern Missionary College, Collegedale, Tennessee, 1946. M.Mus., North Texas State University, 1946. 74 pp. illus.

565 *GAYLE, (Mrs.) Joe. Youth Choirs and Their Place in Southern Baptist Churches. M.S.M., Southwestern Baptist Theological Seminary, 1947. 89 pp. B18 SBS-1947-1, p. 42; J3 1491, p. 88.

566 HAMMER, Mari Sweeney. History of Louisville's Chamber Music Society. M.A., University of Louisville, 1981. 209 pp. A1 (20/1) 1317032, p. 81; A2 2543, p. 120.

The Chamber Music Society was established in 1938. The author discusses the programs and ensembles associated with the Society. The research is based on Society records and reviews in the *Courier-Journal* and the *Louisville Times.*

567 HOBBS, Odell. A Study of Selected Outstanding Negro College Choirs in the United States of America. M.M., Catholic University of America, 1966. 61 pp.

The college choirs are Fisk University, Howard University, Morehouse College, Morris Brown College, Saint Augustine's College, Saint Paul's College, Tuskegee Institute, Virginia State College, and Virginia Union University. Included is a selection of concert programs.

568 HOUSTON, Clark A. An Investigation of the Development of Community Singing Activities in the United States of America. M.A., Catholic University of America, 1958. 51 pp.

569 KEITH, Gwendolyn Edwards. The Status of Negro Church Youth Choirs in the State of Ohio. M.A., Ohio State University, 1950. B8 1325, p. 91; I3, p. 34.

570 LEWIS, George Daniel. Factors Common to Protestant Church Choirs in Helena, Montana, and Their Relationship to Public School Music. M.M.Ed., Montana State University, 1952. B8 555, p. 41.

571 *McTYRE, Maurine Robles. The Growth and Development of Youth Choirs among Southern Baptists. M.S.M., Southern Baptist Theological Seminary, 1951. 173 pp. B8 430, p. 26; J3 1434, p. 85.

572 MOODY, William. A Study of Choral Activities in Indianapolis Industry and Business. M.M., Jordan College of Music of Butler University, 1953. B12, p. 96.

573 MURPHY, Catherine Amt. The Boy Choir of the Cathedral of St. John the Divine, New York. S.M.M., Union Theological Seminary, 1950. B8 1096, p. 76.

574 RUNKLE, Aleta M. A History of the Choirs in Lamoni, Iowa, of the Reorganized Church of Jesus Christ of the Latter-Day Saints. M.A., University of Iowa, 1952. B8 308, p. 24.

575 SCHEID, Paul. A Study of Boy Choirs: Their Schools and Their Training. M.E., Rutgers University, 1966.

American boy choirs are discussed in Chapter 4, pp. 99-106, including those choirs of the Cathedral Church of St. John the Divine (Episcopal), N.Y.C.; St. Thomas Church (Episcopal), N.Y.C.; and the Columbus, Ohio Boy Choir (secular). Included is a selection of programs.

576 *SCHMOYER, Helen Cecelia. Contribution of the Westminster Choir Movement to American Choral Music. M.M., North Texas State University, 1942. 81 pp. B18 NTSU-1942-11, p. 11.

577 SCHOEPKO, Alfred A. The History of the Chicago Singverein, 1910-1960. M.M., Northwestern University, 1961. B2, p. 151.

578 SCHRAEDER, Marilyn Joyce. The History of the Harlan Boys Choir. M.A., Indiana University, 1976. 117 pp. illus. B17 (10/1) 1753, p. 100.

Harlan City, Kentucky.

579 *SEITZ, Barbara Joan. The History and Significance of the Concert Series Evenings on the Roof, 1938-1954. M.M., Indiana University, 1971. 114 pp.

Evenings on the Roof was a series of monthly chamber music concerts held in Los Angeles in the studio roof apartment of concert pianist Frances Mullen and her husband Peter Yates. Emphasis was on the performance of contemporary music.

580 *SONOMURA, Robert Y. Falsetto Singing in Hawaii and Its Use by Tenors in High School Choral Groups. M.A., Brigham Young University, 1973. 69 pp.

581 *SORENSEN, Merlin Ray. The Ogden Tabernacle Choir: Its History and Contributions to the Cultural History of Utah. M.A., Brigham Young University, 1961. 212 pp. illus.; plates. B8 1509, p. 105.

582 STAIGER, John Norman. The Non-Jewish Choir Director in the American Reform Jewish Temple. M.A., Ohio State University, 1958. B8 1336, p. 92.

583 *THOMPSON, M. Burnette. The Significance of the St. Olaf Lutheran Choir in American Choral Music. M.A., Eastman School of Music of the University of Rochester, 1938. B8 733, p. 52.

584 VOIGHT, Ruth Marie. A Survey of Choral Activities in the Colleges and Universities of the United States. M.M.E., Texas Christian University, 1952. B12, p. 142.

585 WALLS, Brian Scott. Chamber Music in Los Angeles, 1922-1954: A History of Concert Series, Ensembles and Repertoire. M.A., California State University at Long Beach, 1980. 234 pp. A1 (19/1) 1315169, p. 76.

586 WEBSTER, Imogene Rose. A Study of Youth Choirs in the Baptist Churches of Texas. M.M., University of Texas, 1951. B8 1494, p. 104; B18 UT-1951-22, p. 73.

587 WOODS, Genevieve. The Sacred Harp Singers: A Study of the Persistence of a Rural Social Institution. M.A., Southern Methodist University, 1936. 118 pp. H1, p. 237; I2, p. 122.

588 WRIGHT, Mary Louise. The History and Use of the Choral Festival with Special Reference to the Dickinson Choral Festival at Union Theological Seminary, 1935. M.S.M., Union Theological Seminary, 1935. B8 1266, p. 87.

PERFORMANCE. ASSOCIATIONS

589 BLACKWELDER, Harold Gene. The Fort Worth Civic Opera Association from 1946 to 1953. M.F.A., Texas Christian University, 1965. L7 (79), p. 454.

590 *BRITTAIN, James W. A History of the Long Beach Civic Light Opera Association, 1950-1969. M.A., California State University at Long Beach, 1970. 201 pp. plates.

591 FINUCAN, Doreen. The Metropolitan Opera Guild, Inc. M.M., Catholic University of America, 1970. 153 pp.

592 MARTIN, Harold Winthrop. A History of the American Guild of Organists in Boston, Massachusetts (1905-1954). S.M.M., Union Theological Seminary, 1954. B8 1077, p. 75.

593 *ROOT, Deane Leslie. The Performance Guilds of Edgard Varèse. Master's thesis, University of Illinois at Urbana-Champaign, 1971. 108 pp. B13, p. 74.

594 ROSE, Charles. The American Federation of Musicians and Its Effect on Black Musicians in St. Louis in the Twentieth Century. Master's thesis, Southern Illinois University at Edwardsville, 1978. F1 1229, p. 71.

595 *SUBLETTE, Richard Horace. A History of the American Society of Composers, Authors, and Publishers' Relationship with the Broadcasters. M.A., Radio and Television, University of Illinois at Urbana-Champaign, 1962. 94 pp.

596 WRIGHT, Kittye Sneed. Performing Rights Societies in the United States: Their Status and Influence. M.M., Catholic University of America, 1966. 51 pp. B13, p. 31.

SECULAR MUSIC. INSTRUMENTAL

597 BALTZER, Kenneth R. American Instrumental Music of the Revolutionary War Period. Master's thesis, University of Minnesota, 1969. B13, p. 32.

598 BARR, Marilyn. The Contemporary Organ Series of the H. W. Gray Company, Inc., with Emphasis on American Compositions. S.M.M., Union Theological Seminary, 1954. B8 808, p. 58.

599 *BAUER, Margaret Spearly. Salon Piano Music in America as Compared to the Piano Works of Louis Moreau Gottschalk during the Years 1853-1869. M.A., Indiana University of Pennsylvania, 1975. 76 pp.

600 BREAUX, Zelia N. The Development of Instrumental Music in Negro Secondary Schools and Colleges. M.M., Northwestern University, 1939. B15 91, p. 7.

601 *CHAPMAN, Roger E. The American String Quartet, 1924-1949. M.A., University of California at Los Angeles, 1950. 102 pp.

602 *COMBS, Fred Michael. Guide to Percussion Adjudication Procedures. M.A., University of Missouri, 1968. 145 pp.

603 COMSTOCK, Leila Logan. The Development and Present Status of Instrumental Music in the Big Horn Area of the State of Wyoming. M.Mus.Ed., University of Colorado, 1942. 140 pp.

604 *CONRON, Eunice McCormick. Twentieth Century American Keyboard Sonatas. M.A., Brown University, 1963.

605 *DANNEMILLER, Joanne Dilley. The Development of the Importance of the Piano in America. Master's thesis, Kent State University, 1959. 84 pp.

606 *DEMMING, Lanson Frederick. History of the Organ Recital in the United States of America. Master's thesis, University of Illinois at Urbana-Champaign, 1943. 101 pp.

607 DEMUS, Mary Helen. Trends in the United States, 1920-30, as Reflected in Piano Music. M.A., West Texas State University, 1968. B18 WTS-1968-4, p. 99.

608 *EDGE, Rebecca Jane. The Solo Piano Sonata in the United States since 1945: A Survey. M.Mus., North Texas State University, 1971. 64 pp. illus. B18 NTSU-1971-7, p. 29.

Includes a discussion of the piano sonata in the United States prior to 1945. Chapter 3 consists of brief analyses of eight piano sonatas written in 1945-70: Samuel Barber, Sonata, op. 26; John Cage, *Sonatas and Interludes;* Elliott Carter, Piano Sonata; Paul Creston, Sonata, op. 9; Norman Dello Joio, Piano Sonata No. 3; Alan Hovhaness, *Poseidon Sonata;* Peter Mennin, Sonata for Piano; and Persichetti, Piano Sonata No. 9.

609 EGAN, Rita Cecile. A Comprehensive Survey of the Piano Sonata in the United States. M.A., Catholic University of America, 1949. 133 pp.

610 HUNTER, David S. A History of the Development of String Music Activities at Wisconsin State University, Platteville. Master's thesis, Wisconsin State University at Platteville, 1970. F1 1457, p. 70.

611 *JONES, Brent M. The Nocturne in Piano Literature from John Field to Samuel Barber. M.A., Brigham Young University, 1971. 112 pp. B13, p. 72.

612 *JOSEPH, Ralph W. The Changing Demands of Performance on the Trombone, Beethoven to the Present. Master's thesis, Kent State University, 1972. 34 pp.

American music is used for most of the examples of modern requirements.

613 *KNOX, Carol Ruth. American One-Movement and Associated Symphonies. M.A., Brown University, 1964.

614 LOCKE, James Eric. Early American Piano Theme and Variations, 1790-1830: A Survey of Music and Musicians. M.A., California State University at Fullerton, 1980. 104 pp. A1 (19/1) 1315260, p. 76.

Includes biographies of composers and analyses of music.

615 McDANIEL, Walter H. A History of the Competition-Festival Movement in Instrumental Music in Middle Tennessee. Master's thesis, University of Tennessee at Knoxville, 1967. F1 1676, p. 74.

616 McNERNEY FAMERA, Karen. Mutes, Flutters, and Trills: A Guide to Composers for the Horn. M.M., Yale University, 1967. 200 pp. illus. B17 (9/3) 4398, p. 295.

Illustrations from works of Gunther Schuller are included.

617 MATHAY, Angela P. Piano Music by Selected American Composers as Evaluated in Musical Criticism. Master's thesis, Jersey City State College, 1971. F1 1521, p. 71.

618 MEREDITH, Maudell Dukeminier. Organ Music in America since 1900. M.M., Baylor University, 1956. B8 1416, p. 99; B18 BU-1956-2, p. 2.

619 *PAUGH, Sharon L. American Piano Music in Print. Master's thesis, Kent State University, 1971. 189 pp. G3, p. 52; G4, p. 58.

620 PEACH, Lynda Coffman. The Use of Folk Music in Twentieth Century Piano Compositions by Composers of the United States of America. M.M., Baylor University, 1972. B18 BU-1972-5, p. 5.

621 *RAGER, Brenda Marie. The Oboe in Early American Music, 1600-1861. M.Mus., North Texas State University, 1970. 60 pp. B18 NTSU-1970-17, p. 29.

622 RICHARDS, John K. The Brass Sextet: A Study of Its Instruments, History, Literature and Position in Instrumental Music Education. M.Mus., University of Southern California, 1947. B3 380, p. 175.

623 RICHARDSON, Larry Samuel. A Study of the Applicability of Makah Indian Music as Material for Concert Band Composition. 46 pp. M.Ed., Central Washington State College, 1961. I1 6463, p. 276.

624 SHEPHERD, Norma Irene. Early American Clavier Music and Its Influence on the Work of Lowell Mason (The Background of Early Music Education in the United States). M.A., University of Maryland, 1951. 120 pp. illus. F1 906, p. 48.

Emphasis is on the works of Reinagle, Moller, Carr, and Pelissier. Includes a "Bibliography of Early American Clavier Music" which lists over 500 works.

625 *SHIREY, Betty. String Quartets by American Born Composers. M.M., University of Cincinnati, 1949. 74 pp.

626 SLOAN, Frances. A Historical Survey of Violin Literature in America from the Colonial Period to 1880 (Composer's Birthdate). M.A., University of North Carolina, 1950. 167 pp. B6 S634, p. 27; K5, p. 201.

627 *SMITH, Nancy Page. The American String Quartet, 1850-1918. M.A., University of North Carolina at Chapel Hill, 1949. 143 pp. K5, p. 201.

628 THEODORE, Peter C. A Survey of Published Sonatas and Sonatinas for Flute by American Composers since 1920. M.A., Catholic University of America, 1967. 87 pp.

One work from each of 25 composers is discussed.

629 *TRAWICK, Fawn Grey. The Organ Chorale Prelude and the American Composer. M.Mus., Florida State University, 1947. 139 pp. B8 164, p. 14.

630 TYSKA, Theodore Charles. Technical Problems in Contemporary American Violin Sonatas. M.A., American University, 1961. 61 pp.

Composers discussed appear in this order: Burrill Phillips, Aaron Copland, Roy Harris, Walter Piston, Ben Weber, Harold Shapero, Henry Cowell, Robert Ward, David Diamond, and Ross Lee Finney.

631 *VAN CITTERS, Mary Lavina. Some Approaches to Violin Technique in the Twentieth Century. M.S., New Mexico State University, 1971. 76 pp. illus.

632 *WILSON, Dora Jean. Selected Piano Compositions of Contemporary Black Composers in America. A.M., Washington University, 1970. 63 pp. B10, p. 33; B13, p. 33.

The composers include in the order of discussion: John E. Price, Ulysses Kay, Howard Swanson, George Walker, Arthur Cunningham, and Hale Smith.

633 *WILSON, Norman Gerald. Salon Piano Literature Published in the United States, 1850-1875. M.M., University of Illinois at Urbana-Champaign, 1971. 112 pp. illus. B13, p. 73.

634 WISEMAN, Steven Gayle. Contemporary American Piano Music for the Beginning Student: A Study of Selected Composers and Materials. M.A., Northeast Missouri State University, 1981. 107 pp. A1 (20/1) 1317356, p. 82.

Musicians discussed include Karp, Finney, Persichetti, Starer, Riegger, Wuorinen, and Helm.

635 *WOLTER, Richard Arthur. A Description and Analysis of Selected Music Written for the Concert Band Performable by American High School Bands. A.M., Washington University, 1959. 130 pp.

Composers discussed include: Samuel Barber, Robert Russell Bennett, Henry Cowell, Paul Creston, Frank Erickson, Howard Hanson, Roy Harris, Gerald Kechley, Dai-Keong Lee, William Schuman, and Clifton Williams.

636 ZIRNER, Ludwig Ernst. Stylistic Developments in Music since the End of the Romantic Period and Their Reflection in American Piano Music of 1910 to 1925. M.Mus., University of Illinois at Urbana-Champaign, 1948. 115 pp. B6 Z81, p. 31.

SECULAR MUSIC. VOCAL

637 *ADAMS, James Kenneth. Six Concepts of Choral Singing in the United States. M.M., Mississippi College, 1977. 45 pp.

638 AKIN, Katherine O. Song and Prose of the Cattle Trails. M.A., English, University of Texas, 1948. B18 UT-1948-1, p. 69; H1, p. 226; I2, p. 196.

639 ALLGOOD, Mary Alice Neely. Modulatory Devices in Selected Contemporary American Choral Music. M.M., Southern Methodist University, 1962. B18 SMU-1962-3, p. 40.

640 ANDRUS, Lynn S. Southwestern Song. M.A., Education, Adams State College, 1965. I2, p. 320.

641 ANGELL, Ruth Speer. Background of Some Texas Cowboy Songs. M.A., English, Columbia University, 1938. 94 pp. H1, p. 226; I2, p. 131.

642 ANTHONY, A. Eugene. Campaign Songs as a Factor in American Politics. M.A., University of the Pacific, 1951. 153 pp. B7 17, p. 5.

643 *BISHOP, Frances Blackburn. Some Problems of Contemporary American Art Song. M.A., University of Missouri-Columbia, 1958. 89 pp. illus.

644 *BUDWORTH, Frederick Norman. The American Fuging Tune: Its Origins, History, and Educational Implications. M.A., University of California at Los Angeles, 1959. 225 pp. I2, p. 277.

645 *BURTS, Richard C. *The Village Harmony,* an Early American Tunebook. M.A., University of North Carolina at Chapel Hill, 1972. 129 pp. J1.

646 *CAMPBELL, Richard R. Oratorio in America. Master's thesis, Kent State University, 1962. 69 pp.

647 CHIDAMIAN, Claude. The Programmatic Use of English and American Literature in Symphonic, Operatic, and Larger Choral Forms: An Abbreviated List. Master's thesis, English, University of Southern California, 1944. H1, p. 365.

Discusses George Washington Cable, Joel Chandler Harris, DuBose Heyward, and Sidney Lanier.

648 CHISHOLM, Mary L. Stephen Collins Foster and His Folk-Songs. M.A., English, Western Kentucky State College, 1936. 66 pp. I2, p. 114.

649 COOPER, Carl D. The American Popular Song in the Nineteenth Century as Represented by Daniel D. Emmett, George F. Root, and Henry C. Work. M.M., Baylor University, 1972. B18 BU-1972-1, p. 5.

650 CORZINE, Gwenyth Storrar. Musical Treatment of the Poetry in Songs Representing the Developing American Art Song before 1900. M.M., University of Lowell, 1977. 97 pp. A1 (16/1) 13-10562, p. 46.

651 *CROOK, Charles Ernest. Some Factors Affecting the Study and Performance of Contemporary American Songs. M.A., Ohio State University, 1955. 71 pp.

652 DAVIDSON, Caroline Richards. An Eighteenth-Century Music Collection [of Francis Hopkinson, 1737-1791]. M.A., University of Pennsylvania, 1968. 102 pp. B6 D253, p. 12; B13, p. 20.

653 *DELVIN, Robert Carlton. The Lansing Music Book. M.A., Eastern Michigan University, 1972. 51 pp. illus.

This manuscript, compiled during the years 1798-1830, is named after the Lansing family who owned it. Included are 39 pieces of hymns, art songs and arias, patriotic songs, dance tunes, and keyboard pieces. Also discussed are Francis Hopkinson and Moravian hymnody.

654 DEVINE, George John. American Songsters, 1806-1815. M.A., English, Brown University, 1940. B7 176, p. 24; I2, p. 149.

See also nos. 669 and 685.

655 DUNLAVY, Katerine. The Bases of the Early American Anthem. M.A., DePauw University, 1935. B8 261, p. 21.

656   EGAN, Marilyn Michalka. American Folk Songs in Combinatorial Counterpoint for Treble Voices. M.M., Duquesne University, 1978. 134 pp. A1 (17/3) 1312858, pp. 215-16.

657   EVANS, Marguerite. Slavery's Lament Leavens America's Song. M.M., Westminster Choir College, 1943. 164 pp. I2, p. 172.

658   *GOLDENBERG, June Lazare. Urban Folk Song as Exemplified by a Selection of New York City Songs of the Nineteenth Century. M.A., Queens College of the City University of New York, 1976. 225 pp. A2 2751, p. 113.

659   GONGOL, Suzanne M. An Analysis of the Lyrics of Protest Music Published between 1962 to 1967 in Terms of Protest Ideas Expressed. Master's thesis, Glassboro State College, 1969. F1 1509, p. 70.

660   *HALL, Lindley Lawrence. A Study of the Musical Settings of Poems by Emily Dickinson and Robert Frost. M.A., Ohio State University, 1964. 146 pp.

661   HARDIE, Thomas C. An Analysis of American Choral Folk Music Currently Available in Domestic Publication. M.M., North Texas State University, 1949. B18 NTSU-1949-9, p. 16; I2, p. 207.

662   *HARMS, Paul A. Nineteenth-Century American Art-Song: An Annotated Guide and Analysis of Selected Compositions. M.A., California State University at Fullerton, 1973. 152 pp.

663   HAWKINS, Ulista A. Themes in Civil War Songs. Master's thesis, English, George Peabody College, 1929. H1, p. 231.

664   HEAPS, Porter W. Songs of the Civil War. Master's thesis, History, Northwestern University, 1932. H1, p. 232.

665   JENKINS, Kathleen D. Popular Song Models of Tin Pan Alley, 1890-1899: A Theoretical and Stylistic Interpretation. Master's thesis, University of Texas, 1979. A2 3134, p. 136.

666   *KAUFMAN, Harold Christian. The American Folk Song on the Concert Repertoire. M.A., Ohio State University, 1953. 103 pp.

667 KLEIN, Frances Ann. A Survey of Commemorative and Patriotic Songs Inspired by the American Revolution Written and Sung at That Time. M.A., Catholic University of America, 1955. 77 pp.

Approximately 60 songs are discussed. Texts and some music are provided.

668 *LEMBO, Frank Ralph. American War Songs. M.M., Cincinnati Conservatory of Music, 1947. 164 pp. B14 91, p. 28; I2, p. 192.

669 LEWIS, Arthur Ansel. American Songsters, 1800-1805. M.A., English, Brown University, 1937. 306 pp. B7 454, p. 58; I2, p. 126.

See also nos. **654** and **685**.

670 *L'ROY, DiAnn. Songs of the American Temperance Movement. Master's thesis, University of Michigan, 1967. B13, p. 32.

671 *LUPO, Gloria Nell. Expressiveness in Musical Settings of Poems by Robert Frost. M.A., University of North Carolina at Chapel Hill, 1963. 72 pp.

Includes songs by John Duke and Randall Thompson.

672 MASTROIANNI, Lena. Notre Dame Academy, Waterbury, Connecticut: A Survey of Choral Literature Scored for Female Voices, 1936-1969. M.M., Catholic University of America, 1969. 64 pp.

673 *MILLER, Harold Amadeus. Sight-Singing Yesterday and Today (Particularly from 1700-1900 in England and the U.S.). Master's thesis, Eastman School of Music of the University of Rochester, 1941.

674 MITCHELL, Rosanne. Contributions of Charles Ives to Contemporary American Song Literature. M.A., Texas Woman's University, 1971. B18 TWU-1971-5, p. 63.

675 *MONTAGUE, Glenn Adwin. A Study of American Folk Songs for A Cappella Choir. M.A., Brigham Young University, 1951. 166 pp. B12, p. 147; I2, p. 225.

676 MORAN, Mary Anita. A Survey of the Development of the Art Song in the United States. M.A., Catholic University of America, 1949. 89 pp.

Actually only chapter 4 deals with American art song, the other chapters emphasizing the European tradition. The following composers are discussed in this order: Mrs. H. H. A. Beach, John Alden Carpenter, Charles W. Cadman, Richard Hagemann, Bainbridge Crist, Charles T. Griffes, Marion Bauer, and A. Walter Kramer.

677 NELSON, Wanda. The American Art Song since 1900. M.M., Baylor University, 1952. B18 BU-1952-3, p. 2.

678 NUNN, Varina Richard. A Survey of American Poetry Set to Music. M.M., Northwestern University, 1945. B15 583, p. 22.

679 *PAUL, Roschelle Zella. Song Tradition of the University of California at Berkeley. M.A., University of California at Berkeley, 1945. 233 pp. I2, p. 183.

680 PRENTISS, Barbara G. Labels, Styles, and Voices, Part I: A Source Book of Solo Vocal Practices in Secular American Music. Master's thesis, Wesleyan University, 1980. A2 3655, p. 163.

681 SLOCOMB, Alice Louise. Twentieth Century American Choral Styles. M.M., Northwestern University, 1942. B15 755, p. 27.

682 SPRUNGER, Orlo Omer. The North American Saengers Union. M.A., Ohio State University, 1951. 76 pp.

Includes a history of singing societies in Germany and German immigration, the beginnings of German singing societies in America, and the founding, growth, and present status of the North American Saengers Union and its member societies.

683 *STACKHOUSE, Margaret Elise. A Study of the American Composer's Stylistic Use of the Folk-Song "Black Is the Color of My True Love's Hair." M.A., Eastman School of Music of the University of Rochester, 1956. 130 pp. illus. B14 152, p. 33; I2, p. 265.

684 *STEESE, Ruth Zimmerman. Choral Music in the American Colleges. M.M., Eastman School of Music of the University of Rochester, 1933. 31 pp.

685 THORPE, Alice Louise. American Songsters of the Eighteenth Century. M.A., English, Brown University, 1935. 365 pp. B7 784, p. 97; I2, p. 112.

The subject is continued in the Arthur Ansel Lewis thesis, no. 669, and the George John Devine thesis, no. 654.

SECULAR MUSIC. OPERA

686 *BALDINGER, Beatrice Joy. Contemporary Chamber Opera. M.A., Tulane University, 1955. 171 pp. illus.

687 *BELSOM, John A. Reception of Major Operatic Premieres in New Orleans during the Nineteenth Century. M.A., History, Louisiana State University, 1972. 206 pp. H3 2865, p. 183.

This study is divided into the following sections: Opera in New Orleans, an Overview; The Théâtre d'Orléans in Its Formative Period, 1819-36; Rivalry with the St. Charles, 1836-42; The Golden Age of the Théâtre d'Orléans, 1842-61; and Postwar Recovery and the French Opera, 1871-99.

688 BENOWITZ, Zelda. A Study of Opera Staging at the Metropolitan under the Management of Rudolph Bing. M.A., University of Michigan, 1954. D2 (8) 1572, p. 148.

689 *BRICKER, Bernita June. The American Theme in American Opera, 1900-1950. M.A., University of Missouri-Columbia, 1951. 200 pp.

690 *BRIGGS, Harold E. The North American Indian as Depicted in Musical Compositions, Culminating with American "Indianist" Operas of the Early Twentieth Century, 1900-1930. M.M., Indiana University, 1976. 273 pp.

691 *BYRD, William Clifton. Recent Trends of Opera in the United States. M.M., University of Cincinnati, 1953. 46 pp.

692 CAIRNS, Holly A. The Performer's Investigation of Magda's Role in Menotti's Musical Drama *The Consul.* M.M., Bowling Green State University, 1981. 66 pp. A2 2958, p. 143.

693 CARNEY, Margaret Earls. Growth of the Grass Roots Opera Movement in North Carolina. M.A., Baylor University, 1955. B18 BU-1955-1, p. 2.

694 CRAWFORD, Sylvia Lee. A Survey of American Opera since 1947. M.M., Baylor University, 1967. B18 BU-1967-2, p. 4.

695 DAHLBERG, Susan J. The Effect of Contemporary Programming on Opera Company Box-Offices. M.A., Arts Administration, American University, 1981. 117 pp. A1 (20/2) 1317509, p. 234.

The opera companies surveyed include the Opera Company of Boston, New York City Opera, the Cincinnati Opera, the Greater Miami Opera Association, the Houston Grand Opera, the Dallas Civic Opera, Lyric Opera of Chicago, the Minnesota Opera, Lyric Opera of Kansas City, Santa Fe Opera Company, San Francisco Opera, and the Seattle Opera.

696 EDGE, Turner W. A Dramatic Analysis of Six American Opera Libretti. M.A., Cornell University, 1957. D2 (11) 2320, p. 148.

697 GLASS, James William. American Opera at the Metropolitan, 1910-1920. M.M., University of Texas at Austin, 1971. B18 UT-1971-17, p. 96.

698 *GORDON, Diane Kestin. Folklore in Published and Unpublished American Opera of the Twentieth Century. M.A., University of California at Los Angeles, 1955. 370 pp. B14 83, p. 28; I2, p. 252.

699 *HODGE, John Edward. The Collapse of the Chicago Civic Opera Company. M.A., History, University of Illinois at Urbana-Champaign, 1960. 85 pp.

700 *JACKSON, Richard Hammel. The Operas of Gertrude Stein and Virgil Thomson: A Binomial Study. M.A., Tulane University, 1962. 144 pp. plates. B6 J14, p. 19.

701 *KAPLAN, Lloyd Saul. A Study of Twentieth Century American Chamber Opera. M.A., Brown University, 1962.

702 KNAFEL, Stephen Robert. A Joan Sutherland Chronicle, Emphasizing Her San Francisco Opera Engagements. M.A., California State University at Long Beach, 1977. 111 pp. A1 (15/4) 13-10184, p. 231.

703 KNOX, Robert Erskine, Jr. *The Lady of the Lake:* A Reconstructed Piano-Vocal Score with Commentary on the Historical Background. M.Mus., North Texas State University, 1979. 143 pp. A1 (17/4) 1313119, p. 278.

Includes a history of the American premieres.

704 KOBART, Ruth. "The Ballad of Baby Doe": A Manifestation of Opera in Post-World War II in America. Master's thesis, Hunter College of the City University of New York, 1967. B13, p. 26.

705 MILLER, Lucile. Trends in Opera since 1925. M.A., University of Pennsylvania, 1950. 126 pp. illus.

Includes an overview of "Opera in the United States."

706 NASH, Ellen B. Gertrude Stein: Opera Librettist. M.A., Columbia University, 1965. 90 pp. H2 5465, p. 202.

707 *NORWOOD, Donald Jerry. A Historical Study of Opera in New Orleans, 1919-1960. M.A., Louisiana State University, 1962. 223 pp.

708 *OAKES, Mildred C. Light Opera in America. M.Mus., Syracuse University, 1934. 31 pp. illus.

709 OLSON, Marjorie Douglass. Ballad Opera in the American Colonies. M.A., University of Washington, 1951. 177 pp. I2, p. 226.

710 *PEACHY, Burt Haines. Standards of Production at the Metropolitan Opera House during the Tenure of Rudolf Bing, 1950-1966. M.A., California State University at Long Beach, 1968. 254 pp.

711 PILCHER, Diane L. A Singer's Guide to Auditioning for American Opera Companies. Master's thesis, California State University at Fullerton, 1978. A2 3483, p. 147.

712 *RICHARD, Lenis Joseph. The Development of Opera in New Orleans from the Civil War to the Burning of the French Opera House in 1919. M.M., Louisiana State University, 1959. 280 pp.

713 *SCHLEIS, Thomas Henry. Opera in Milwaukee, 1850-1900. M.M., University of Wisconsin at Madison, 1974. 83 pp.

714 SQUARES, Roy. The Washington Opera, Inc., 1956-1977. M.A., American University, 1977. 109 pp. A1 (16/2) 13-10920, p. 112; B9 30, p. 4.

The artistic programming of the Washington Opera from 1956 until 1977 is examined. Includes a list of operas produced at the Kennedy Center, 1971-77; operas produced at Wolf Trap Farm Park, Vienna, Va., 1971-78; and operas produced by the Opera Society of Washington, 1956-77.

715 WEISENTHAL, Gary Jack. An Anatomy of Regional Opera: A Study of American Opera, Its Development, Practice, and Place in the Community. M.A., University of Louisville, 1980. 133 pp. A1 (19/2) 13-15482, p. 178.
Includes a discussion of the Kentucky Opera Association.

SECULAR MUSIC. MUSICAL COMEDY, MINSTREL SHOWS, AND VAUDEVILLE

716 *BOULDIN, Brent. Ten Productions of Non-Dramatic Literature in the Broadway and Off-Broadway Theatre in 1974. Master's thesis, Speech, Louisiana State University, 1976.

717 CHAMBERS, V. Blaine. The Choreography of the Musical *Cabaret*. Master's thesis, Madison College, 1972. F1 1276, p. 63.

718 COYNE, Mary Eileen. Main Trends in Musical Comedy 1900-1950. M.A., Speech and Drama, Catholic University of America, 1951. 120 pp. D2 (5) 633, p. 169.
This study is divided into three principal parts: "History of Musical Comedy," "Main Trends in Musical Comedy Libretto, 1900-1950," and "Through the Years with the Elements of Musical Comedy."

719 *DAUM, Glen Allen. Some Problems in Commercial Arranging: Five Arrangements and a Discussion of Techniques. M.M., Southern Illinois University, 1964. 26 pp.
Discusses the music of Richard Rodgers.

720 DAVIS, Elaine. Major Trends in Contemporary American Musical Comedy. M.A., Stanford University, 1949. D2 (3) 216, p. 151.

721 EGAN, Frank. Minstrelsy in San Francisco, 1848-1870. M.A., California State University at Sacramento, 1971. D3 62, p. 9.

722 *EINACH, Charles D. Restatement of the Play Script in Musical Theater Terms Exemplified by Oscar Hammerstein II. M.A., Drama, Syracuse University, 1953. 84 pp. D2 (7) 1352, p. 159.

723 ELLIOTT, Eugene Clinton. History of Variety Vaudeville in Seattle from the Beginning to 1914. M.A., University of Washington, 1941. D3 1355, p. 151.

724   GOLDMAN, Harry M. *Pins and Needles:* An Oral History. M.A., Speech and Drama, Catholic University of America, 1976. 122 pp.

Consists of interviews with the writer, director, and original set designer, actors, and actresses.

725   GUNNISON, John S. An Investigation of the Origins and Growth of Negro Minstrelsy in the United States. M.A., University of Denver, 1949. D2 (3) 80, p. 146.

726   *HARDEE, Lewis J., Jr. The Musical Theater of Douglas Moore. M.A., University of North Carolina at Chapel Hill, 1970. 231 pp.

727   HARRISON, Grant. The Broadway Revue, 1907-1940. M.M., Howard University, 1973. 127 pp.

Discusses stage music forms before the development of the revue in the 20th century, such as American ballad opera and variants, minstrelsy, the extravaganza, "Evangeline" by Edward E. Rice and the burlesque, satires on city life, and operetta. The Ziegfeld Follies (1907-31) are discussed as well as a number of small revues after Ziegfeld. Included are lists of all of the songs in the Ziegfeld Follies and songs in the first editions of the other revues treated in the study.

728   HAWES, William K., Jr. The Development of the Style of the Ziegfeld Follies. M.A., University of Michigan, 1956. D2 (10) 2071, p. 144.

729   HENNEY, Deloris. A Study of the Development of the American Musical Comedy. M.A., University of Nebraska, 1959. D2 (13) 2828, p. 124.

730   HENRY, Mari Lyn. The Origin, Development, and Significance of Dramatic Entertainment in American Vaudeville, 1893-1925. M.A., Catholic University of America, 1968. 93 pp. D1 17443, p. 358.

Discusses the development of drama in vaudeville. Includes an appendix consisting of a partial list of dramatic works performed in vaudeville during the period studied.

731   HOTTENROTH, A. Elaine. A Study of the Adaptation of Plays into Modern American Musical Comedies. M.A., Bowling Green State University, 1959. D2 (13) 2829, p. 124.

OLD DAN TUCKER. SOLO & CHORUS.

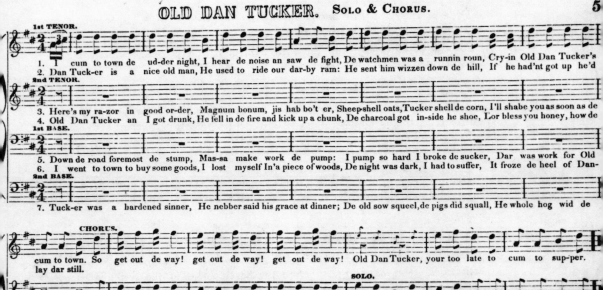

An early example of a minstrel tune arranged for four voices. "Old Dan Tucker."
Words by Daniel Decatur Emmett.
From *The Ethiopian Glee Book* (Boston: Elias Howe, 1848).

732 HUTCHINSON, Robert B. A Review of Musical Stage Productions in Secondary Schools with Special Emphasis on the Opera Laboratory at Tucson High School, Tucson, Arizona. M.M.E., University of Arizona, 1956. B12, p. 71.

733 *JACOBS, Mark Dennis. The Emergence of American Musical Comedy. M.A., University of California at Los Angeles, 1975. 318 pp.

734 JENSEN, Jack A. The Contributions of Kurt Weill to the American Theatre. M.A., University of Michigan, 1950. D2 (4) 454, p. 151.

735 JONES, Jan Lynn. The History and Development of Casa Mañana Musicals, 1958-1980. M.S., Theater, North Texas State University, 1981. 237 pp. A1 (20/1) 1316717, p. 114.

This study discusses Casa Mañana Musicals, Inc., Fort Worth, Texas from its establishment in 1958, and traces various influences dating back to the Casa Mañana production by Billy Rose in 1936.

736 KEZER, Claude D. Development of American Musical Comedy. M.A., University of Oklahoma, 1967. D1 18095, p. 379.

737 KIELTY, Patricia M. A Study of the Structure of the Musical Plays Written by Richard Rodgers and Oscar Hammerstein II. M.A., Speech and Drama, Catholic University of America, 1951. 74 pp. D2 (5) 728, p. 171.

738 KING, William E. A Design Study of the Musical Drama "The King and I" by Richard Rodgers and Oscar Hammerstein II. M.A., Florida State University, 1961. D2 (15) 2449, p. 171.

739 KVAPIL, Otto Arthur. An Investigation of the Ten Largest Gross Income Musical Comedies Performed in New York City between 1941 and 1950 and Their Outlay for Advertising Expenditures. M.A., Speech and Drama, Catholic University of America, 1963. 82 pp. D2 (10) 2073, p. 144; K3, p. 65.

The works are discussed in this order: *Lady in the Dark, By Jupiter, Oklahoma, Bloomer Girl, Carousel, Annie Get Your Gun, Finian's Rainbow, Where's Charley?, Kiss Me, Kate,* and *South Pacific.*

740 LOFGREN, Norman R. The Development and Performance of Musical Theater in the American Schools. M.M., Baylor University, 1970. B18 BU-1970-4, p. 5.

741   LUSCOMBE, Robert H. A Study of the Techniques Used in Adapting the Elements of Character and Diction from the Play "Kismet" and the Play "Pygmalion" to the Musical "My Fair Lady." M.A., Wayne State University, 1967. D1 18396, p. 389.

742   *MATHES, James Farrell. A Survey of Leonard Bernstein's Contribution to American Musical Theater. M.A., University of Cincinnati, 1968. 117 pp. illus.

743   *MOOREHOUSE, Vera. Benjamin Franklin Keith, Vaudeville Magnate: The First Fifty Years, 1846-1896. M.A., Eastern Michigan University, 1975. 145 pp. illus.

744   NELSON, Edwin L. A History of Road Shows in Seattle from the Beginning to 1914. M.A., University of Washington, 1947. D3 1354, p. 151.

745   PHILLIPS, Jean Ann. The American Musical in the 1960's. M.M., Baylor University, 1972. B18 BU-1972-6, p. 6.

746   ROESNER, Francis B. Development of a Style of Acting in American Musical Comedy. Master's thesis, Speech, Kansas State University, 1970. K9 510750, p. 181.

747   *SCARPATO, Robert Hagen. Understanding the Musical Revue. M.A., Drama, Syracuse University, 1962. 79 pp. illus.

748   *SHERMAN, Dianne Lorraine. Vaudeville and the Performance Experience. M.A., Syracuse University, 1972. 60 pp.

749   *SHUMWAY, Peter Carleton. A Discussion of Show Boat as an Innovation in the American Musical Theater and a Related Set Design for the Smith College Theater. M.A., Smith College, 1968. 53 pp. illus.

750   *STEIN, Karen S. Vaudeville in New York City, 1900 to 1910. Master's thesis, Speech, Louisiana State University, 1973.

751 STEWARD, Ronald Maurice. The American Musical Theatre from 1943 to 1963: A Consideration of the Music, the Dance, and the Libretto as Integrated Elements of the Musical Play since the Writing of *Oklahoma!* M.M., Howard University, 1964. 75 pp.

The author's approach to this subject is historical, not analytical. Most of the more important productions of the period are discussed.

752 STOWE, William McFerrin, Jr. Vaudeville at the Majestic Theater of Dallas, 1905-1910. M.A., Southern Methodist University, 1972. L7 (79), p. 208.

753 TAMPLIN, Robert Stockton, Jr. Musical Comedy on Broadway from 1943-1949 with Changes Occurring during This Period. M.A., University of Michigan, 1949. D2 (3) 141, p. 148.

754 TOMASELLI, Daniel John. The Historical Development of Musical Comedy in America. M.M., Catholic University of America, 1965. 67 pp. illus. K3, p. 110.

The five principal sections in this study are: "Trends Affecting the Growth of Musical Comedy to 1880," "Influences Exerted on the Americal Lyric Theater, 1880-1900," "Branches of the American Musical Theater, 1900-1927," "Musical Comedy as an Integrated Artistic Creation, 1927-1943," and "American Musical Play, 1943 to Present."

755 WEISSMAN, Gerald. The Musicalization of *Pygmalion* into *My Fair Lady*. M.A., Stanford University, 1957. D2 (11) 2326, p. 148.

756 WELSH, John D. Play into Musical: A Comparative Study of Sidney Howard's "They Knew What They Wanted" and Frank Loesser's "The Most Happy Fella." M.A., Tulane University, 1961. D2 (15) 2453, p. 171.

757 WILDON, Lorna Marie. A Survey of Contemporary American Musical Arena Theatres. M.A., Michigan State University, 1957. D2 (11) 2325, p. 148.

758 WILLIAMS, Jene Nonnemacher. Rodgers and Hammerstein: Their Concept of Musical Theatre. M.A., University of North Carolina, 1967. D1 17947, p. 375.

759 ZENOR, Mina L. Choreographic Problems Involved with the Production of "Show Boat." M.A., Bowling Green State University, 1961. D2 (15) 2458, p. 171.

SECULAR MUSIC. JAZZ, BLUES, ROCK, AND POP

760 ANTONICH, Mark E. The Style and Analysis of the Music of Charlie Christian, Based upon an Examination of His Improvised Solos and Various Components of His Playing. Master's thesis, Duquesne University, 1982. A2 2946, p. 143.

761 BALL, Carolyn Denise. Bob Dylan: Contemporary Minstrel. M.A., English, University of Maryland, 1967.

762 *BASTIN, Wilton James Bruce. The Emergence of the Blues Tradition in the Southeastern States. M.A., Folklore, University of North Carolina at Chapel Hill, 1973. 120 pp. B5 (22), p. 512.

763 *BAUER, Raymond Miles. Jazz Piano Style (1937-50). M.M., Eastman School of Music of the University of Rochester, 1950. 105 pp.

Contains an original version of *Coquette* by Gus Kahn, Carmen Lombardo, and Johnny Green, an improvised version thereof by Teddy Wilson, and an original creation by Nat Cole.

764 BAUMAN, Dick. A Dissection of the History and Musical Product of Stan Kenton, Jazz Education in the Public School Program, and the Third Stream. M.A., Education, Northwest Missouri State University, 1970.

765 BENNINGTON, Billy D. A Brief History of Jazz. M.S., East Texas State University, 1950. B18 ETS-1950-2, p. 6.

766 *BIRD, Robert Atkinson. Methods and Categories of Jazz Analysis: A Critical Review of Five Approaches to Jazz History and Musical Analysis. M.A., University of Wisconsin at Madison, 1976. 150 pp.

767 BLACK, Timuel K. The Hope of a Song: Towards an Interpretation of the Meaning of Blues and Spirituals. Master's thesis, University of California at Berkeley, 1980. A2 3118, p. 139.

768 *BRINKMAN, Gary. Certain Harmonic Structures of Stravinsky, Ravel, and Milhaud Compared with Selected Jazz Composers, 1940 to the Present. M.M., Southern Illinois University, 1975. 46 pp. illus.

769 *CHMEL, Robert D. A Concise History of Jazz Percussion. Master's thesis, Kent State University, 1974. 58 pp.

Includes an analysis and transcription of drum solos of Max Roach and Buddy Rich, and a discography.

770 CHRISTNER, Deborah Dawson. The Romantic Ideal of the Artist in the Music Industry. M.A., California State University at Fullerton, 1982. 157 pp. A1 (21/1) 13-19307, p. 8.

The primary focus is on rock music and American culture.

771 *CLARK, Robert Douglas. Tradition and Style in the Blues: An Ethno-Musicological Approach. M.A., Brown University, 1976.

Clark restates some of his material in "Pitch Structures in Vocal Blues Melody," *Southern Folklore Quarterly* 42/1 (1978): 17-30.

772 COIN, Gregory McAfee. Developmental Parallels in the Evolution of Musical Styles: Romanticism, Jazz, Rock 'n' Roll, and American Musical Theatre. M.A., University of Louisville, 1974. 87 pp. A1 (12/3) 13-05804, p. 281.

773 *DEMPSEY, Harry J. A Study in Composition for Large Jazz Ensemble. Master's thesis, Kent State University, 1977. 125 pp. illus.

As a practical demonstration, an original three-part composition *No Parking* has been written and appears as part of this study.

774 EVANS, David. The Blues of Tommy Johnson: A Study of Tradition. M.A., Folklore and Mythology, University of California at Los Angeles, 1967. 212 pp. B5 (12), p. 440.

This is a biography of Tommy Johnson, and his musical repertory. Included is a brief history of blues. Most of the musical material derives from commercial phonograph recordings issued since 1920 and from field recordings which the writer made since 1964. Also discussed are musicians and musical life of Drew, Jackson, and Tylertown, Mississippi. Included is an appendix of texts and music.

775 *FAHEY, John Aloysius. A Textual and Musicological Analysis of the Repertoire of Charley Patton. M.A., University of California at Los Angeles, 1966. 176 pp. B5 (12), p. 138.

Charley Patton sang blues-songs, blues-ballads, religious songs, and songs of Tin Pan Alley. Analyzed are tunes and tune families, and texts. Included are forty musical transcriptions, texts, and a discography.

776 *FANTA, Karen Lee. The Blues of Charlie Parker. M.A., Ohio State University, 1964. 69 pp. I3, p. 34.

777 FELDMAN, Mitchell Evan. Impressions of Newport: A Content Analysis of the Coverage of an American Jazz Festival in Six Publications between 1954 and 1978. M.A., University of Georgia, 1980.

The publications are *Time, New York Times, Billboard, Village Voice, Down Beat,* and *New Yorker.*

778 *GENOVA, Vincent. Melodic and Harmonic Irregularities Found in the Improvisations of Art Tatum. M.A., University of Pittsburgh, 1978.

779 GENTRY, Hollis. A Brief History and Musical Analysis of Fusion Jazz. Master's thesis, University of California at La Jolla, 1981. A2 2884, p. 137.

780 *GILES, John Edwin. American Popular Music in the Early 1970's: A Statistical Study of Billboard Charts and Music Listening Habits. M.M., University of Illinois at Urbana-Champaign, 1975. 153 pp.

781 GRANETZ, Ruth Pearl. The Symbolic Significance of the Elvis Presley Phenomenon to Teen-Age Females: A Study in Hero Worship through the Media of Popular Singers and Songs. M.A., Human Development, University of Chicago, 1958. 48 pp. I2, p. 274.

782 GRAY, James M. An Analysis of Melodic Devices in Selected Improvisations of Charlie Parker. M.F.A., Ohio University, 1966.

783 *HANLON, Gloria. A Comparison of Jazz Influences on Selected American and French Composers from 1917 to 1930. M.M., Southern Illinois University, 1971. 45 pp. B13, p. 74.

784 *HANSEN, Barret Eugene. Negro Popular Music, 1945-1953. M.A., University of California at Los Angeles, 1967. 169 pp. B5 (12), p. 440; B13, p. 74; B17 (10/4) 14242, p. 754.

The author's premise for this study is that "there exists in America a genre of popular music created chiefly by Negroes especially for Negro audiences." Discusses Negro popular music before 1945 and instrumental and vocal styles heard on best-selling Negro popular music records, 1945-53. Included is a discography.

785 HARALAMBOS, Michael. Soul Music and Blues: Their Meaning and Relevance in Northern United States Black Ghettos. Master's thesis, University of Minnesota, 1969. I4 0821, p. 71.

786 HARLOFF, Steven. Bob Dylan and the Culture of the 1960s. Master's thesis, Bowling Green State University, 1976. A2 2448, p. 101.

787 HATHERICK, G. The Blues of Chicago's West Side: Towards a History. M.A., University of Sussex, 1976. M2 (26/1) 174, p. 4.

788 *HILBORN, William Dean. A Discriminative Study on the Influence of Jazz on Serious Composers. M.A., University of Missouri-Columbia, 1962. 86 pp. illus.

789 HISCHKE, Jon. The Origins and Development of Kansas City Jazz. Master's thesis, University of Nebraska, 1978. A2 3432, p. 146.

790 HOWARD, Laura Pratt. Ragtime. M.M., Eastman School of Music of the University of Rochester, 1942.

791 IACOBONI, Ricci E. Cleveland Rocks: An Industry Side Pattern for Achieving Commercial Success in Popular Music in Cleveland. Master's thesis, Bowling Green State University, 1980. A2 3581, p. 160.

792 JENSEN, Robert. A History of American Jazz Music Illustrated with Stone Lithography. M.F.A., Ohio University, 1952. B2 (2), p. 169.

793 KIDD, Wayne. The Evolution of Jazz. Master's thesis, Northern Illinois University at DeKalb, 1979. A2 3136, p. 136.

794 *KLEIN, Stephen Tavel. The Improvisational Style of Charlie Parker. M.A., University of Rochester, 1973. 62 pp.
     Includes a discography.

795 LADD, Charles T. Distribution of Jukebox Music Styles in Syracuse and Onondaga County, N.Y. Master's thesis, Syracuse University, 1979. A2 3140, p. 136.

796 LITZINGER, Herman Anthony. Jazz: Its Value and Implications in the Secondary Instrumental Program. M.M., Catholic University of America, 1965. 62 pp.

797 *LONG, Ralph Gerald. Materials of Jazz Improvisation. M.A., Eastman School of Music of the University of Rochester, 1957. 66 pp. illus.

798 *LORNELL, Christopher. A Study of the Sociological Reasons Why Blacks Sing Blues: An Examination of the Secular Black Music Found in Two North Carolina Communities. M.A., Folklore, University of North Carolina at Chapel Hill, 1976. 68 pp. B5 (22), p. 512; L11, p. 85.
Durham, Durham County; Cedar Grove, Orange County.

799 *MEDCALF, Lawrence D. "But I'll Know My Song Well before I Start Singin'": The Rhetoric of Bob Dylan. M.A., Speech, California State University at Hayward, 1976. 145 pp. K2 245, p. 31.

800 MERRIAM, Alan Parkhurst. Instruments and Instrumental Usages in the History of Jazz. M.M., Northwestern University, 1948. B15 528, p. 20.

801 MESSNER, Walter. The Philosophical and Theological Trends of Popular and Folk-Rock Music in the United States, 1960-1972. Master's thesis, University of Wisconsin at Oshkosh, 1971. F1 1525, p. 72.

802 *MEYER, Karen Elaine. The Common Tradition of Stephen C. Foster and the Beatles. M.A., University of Oregon, 1976. 138 pp. illus.

803 OSBORN, P. A. The Piano Music of Ferdinand "Jelly Roll" Morton. Master's thesis, University of Alberta, 1982. A2 3039, p. 147.

804 *OWENS, Thomas. Improvisation Techniques of the Modern Jazz Quartet. M.A., University of California at Los Angeles, 1965. 2 vols.: 105, 106, pp. B6 097, p. 24; B13, p. 75.
Volume 2 consists of seven complete pieces and three fragments transcribed from recordings of the Modern Jazz Quartet.

805 *PACKARD, Donald Wheeler. The Blues, 1912-1927. M.A., Eastman School of Music of the University of Rochester, 1947. 100 pp. illus. I2, p. 193.

806 *PARKINSON, William M. Innovations in the Jazz Trumpet Styles of Louis Armstrong, Dizzy Gillespie, and Miles Davis. Master's thesis, Kent State University, 1975. 40 pp.

807 RADANO, Ronald M. A Cultural and Musical Analysis of Avant-Garde Jazz. M.A., University of Michigan, 1981. 255 pp.

808 RUDINA, Rima. Hot Jazz and the Violin. M.Mus., Eastman School of Music of the University of Rochester, 1944. 83 pp.

809 SCHONING, Fred P. The Theme of Infidelity of the Negro Blues and Songs. M.A., University of Omaha, 1966. I2, p. 328.

810 SIMCOE, George. Critical-Historical Analysis of Rock Music as a Medium of Communication. Master's thesis, Murray State University, 1970. L14, p. 353.
Discusses Nashville's music industry.

811 SIMON, Tom. An Analytical Inquiry into Thelonious Monk's "Ruby, My Dear." M.A., University of Michigan, 1978.

812 *STALVEY, Kenneth Dorrance. Interrelationships in Jazz and Contemporary Music: An Essay. M.M., University of Cincinnati, 1955. 33 pp.

813 *STANLEY, John W. An Analysis and Comparison of Four Texts on Arranging and Composing for Jazz Orchestra. M.A., Sam Houston State Teachers College, 1964.

814 STEBBINS, Robert Alan. The Minneapolis Jazz Community: The Conflict between Musical and Commercial Values. M.A., Sociology, University of Minnesota, 1962. 87 pp. B7 751, p. 93; I2, p. 302.
Fifteen commercial and fifteen jazz musicians were interviewed.

815 STEIN, Richard. The Jazz Trumpet: Development of Styles and an Analysis of Selected Solos from 1924 to 1961. Master's thesis, University of Miami at Coral Gables, 1978. A2 3517, p. 149.

816 TANNER, Paul W. A Technical Analysis of the Development of Jazz. M.A., University of California at Los Angeles, 1962.

817 *TAYLOR, Curtis Benjamin. The Transcription and Stylistic Comparative Analysis of Two Recordings of Duke Ellington's *Black and Tan Fantasy*. M.A., Cornell University, 1974. 115 pp. B9 32, p. 5; B17 (10/4) 14392, p. 759.

818 THOMPSON, Gordon Ross. "Georgia on My Mind": The History of an American Popular Song. M.A., University of Illinois at Urbana-Champaign, 1978. 166 pp. B5 (23), p. 324.

819 THOMPSON, Merle. Ohio Composers of Popular Music. M.M., Northwestern University, 1942. B7 783, p. 97; B15 834, p. 29.

820 TOWLER, Carmen. African Oral Tradition and Black American Jazz Structures in Langston Hughes' *Montage of a Dream Deferred*. Master's thesis, California State University at Carson, 1978. A2 3521, p. 149.

821 VOLONTS, John George. Rock Music and Youth Identity. M.A., American Studies, University of Maryland, 1973. 97 pp.

822 VON HAUPT, Lois. Jazz: An Historical and Analytical Study. M.A., New York University, 1945.

823 WALKER, Vanessa G. Hubert Laws-Observations of His Life, Philosophy, and Jazz Improvisational Techniques. Master's thesis, Bowling Green State University, 1980. A2 3713, p. 166.

824 *WOODSON, Craig DeVere. Solo Jazz Drumming: An Analytic Study of the Improvisation Techniques of Anthony Williams. M.A., University of California at Los Angeles, 1973. 2 vols.

Volume 1: background and analysis of musical variables; Volume 2: transcriptions. Includes a phonotape and discography.

SACRED MUSIC. GENERAL

825 ASK, Bertha C. Church Music in America from 1620 to 1800. S.M.M., Union Theological Seminary, 1930. B8 800, p. 57.

826 *BAKER, Arthur Ray. A Conducting Handbook for Church Musicians. M.S.M., Southern Baptist Theological Seminary, 1956. 74 pp.

827 *BAKER, John Wesley. A Study of the Factors, and Influences Involved in the Administration of Music in the Rural Church. M.C.M., Southwestern Baptist Theological Seminary, 1960. 130 pp.

828 BARBOZA, Joseph, Jr. Liturgical Trends in the Music of the Protestant Churches in America. M.A., Boston University, 1954. B8 375, p. 29.

829 BOYD, Jack H. Religious Music in New England, 1620-1800: A Vernacular Tradition. Master's thesis, Baylor University, 1978. A2 3394, p. 144.

830 BREITMAYER, Douglas Reece. Seventy-Five Years of Sacred Music in Cleveland, Ohio, 1800-1875. S.M.M., Union Theological Seminary, 1951. B8 836, p. 59.

831 *CHAN, Jse Him. The Development of American Protestant Church Music in the Nineteenth Century from 1800-1865. M.M., Southern Illinois University, 1978. 74 pp. illus.

832 *CHASTEEN, Jo Beth. Contemporary American Gospel Music and Its Potential Use in Music Therapy. M.Mus., Florida State University, 1975. 107 pp.

833 DENNISTON, Robert James. The Development of Sacred Music at Chautauqua. S.M.M., Union Theological Seminary, 1956. B8 894, p. 63.

834 DORAN, Carol Ann. The Influence of Raynor Taylor and Benjamin Carr on the Church Music in Philadelphia at the Beginning of the Nineteenth Century. M.A., Eastman School of Music of the University of Rochester, 1970. B17 (10/4) 9966, p. 582.

835 EVANS, James Willis. A Consideration of the State of Music in the Rural Church of the United States. M.S.M., Union Theological Seminary, 1941. B8 905, p. 64.

836   FERLAN, David J. Plenary, Provincial, and Synodal Legislation concerning Liturgical Music in the United States as Causative and Resultant of the Enactments of the Third Plenary Council of Baltimore. Master's thesis, Catholic University of America, 1955. B9 47, p. 6.

837   *FREITAG, Marvin August. Spanish Religious Music in the Southwest, a Survey of the Music during the Colonization of the Southwestern United States. M.A., University of Missouri-Columbia, 1951. 153 pp. B8 548, p. 40.

838   GOTTSHALL, Miles Bowman. The Contributions of Ohio Wesleyan University to Sacred Music. S.M.M., Union Theological Seminary, 1951. B8 937, p. 66.

839   GRADY, Edythe Rachel. Sacred Music of the Negro in the U.S.A. S.M.M., Union Theological Seminary, 1950. B8 939, p. 66.

840   HALFPENNY, Rowland Barnes. Music in Our American Churches: A Criticism of Prevalent Practices. M.M., New England Conservatory of Music, 1934. B8 459, p. 34.

841   HARVEY, Alonzo A. A Survey of the Church Music Program in Non-Liturgical Churches in Greenville County, South Carolina. M.M.Ed., Furman University, 1955. B8 1389, p. 97.

842   LADABOUCHE, Paul Arthur. The Contribution of Our Southern Pioneers to American Church Music. M.A., Boston University, 1938. B8 413, p. 31.

843   LAWRENCE, Arthur Kelton, Jr. The Problem of Music in the Negro Church. M.A., Ohio State University, 1947. B8 1326, p. 91; I3, p. 34.

844   McKISSICK, Marvin Leo. A Study of the Function of Music in the Major Religious Revivals in America since 1875. M.M., University of Southern California, 1957. 168 pp. B8 69, p. 7; B14 102, p. 29.

845   McRAE, William Duncan, Jr. A General Survey of the Various Educational Forces Tending toward Better Sacred Music in the Protestant Churches of America. S.M.M., Union Theological Seminary, 1947. B8 1068, p. 74.

846 OLIVER, Ruth Enid. New England Composers and Compilers of Sacred Music of the Eighteenth Century. S.M.M., Union Theological Seminary, 1955. B8 1104, p. 76.

847 PACKER, Mina Belle. A Brief Survey of Sacred Music in Pittsburgh, Pennsylvania, Past and Present. S.M.M., Union Theological Seminary, 1955. B8 1112, p. 77.

848 *RENFRO, Robert Chase. A Historical Survey of Revival Music in America. M.S.M., Southern Baptist Theological Seminary, 1950. 95 pp. B8 346, p. 26; J3 1436, p. 85.

849 RYAN, Mary Grace. The Progress of Liturgical Music in the United States since 1903. M.A., Catholic University of America, 1941.

850 SISTARE, Lee Chamness. Music for the Church Year Following the Suggested Plans as Outlined by the Federal Council of the Churches of Christ in America. M.S.M., Union Theological Seminary, 1937. B8 1182, p. 81.

851 WILSON, Larry Kyle. Music in Fundamentalist Churches: A Survey of Current Attitudes. M.A., California State University at Fullerton, 1980. 95 pp. A1 (18/4) 1314936, p. 305; A2 3720, p. 166.
   Based on interviews with pastors and music directors of seventeen churches.

852 *WOLFE, A. Edward. A Correlation of Musical Activity and Numerical Church Growth in Selected Southern California Churches. M.A., California State University at Fullerton, 1978. 142 pp.

SACRED MUSIC. VOCAL AND INSTRUMENTAL

853 *ADAMS, Adele. A Survey of Two Hundred English and American Sacred Anthems for Use by Small Church Choirs. M.A., Brown University, 1962.

854 ADAMS, Nelson Falls. Criteria of Five New York Church Musicians Regarding Selection and Performance of Twentieth-Century Sacred Choral Music. S.M.M., Union Theological Seminary, 1954. B8 787, p. 56.

855 *ATWELL, Shirl J. A Musical Analysis of Fifteen Southern Folk Hymns. M.M., University of Louisville, 1976. 215 pp. A1 (15/3) 13-09712, p. 162; A2 2713, p. 112.

856 *BARRINGTON, James Oris. The Beginnings of Psalmody in the English Speaking American Colonies (1607-1700). M.C.M., Southwestern Baptist Theological Seminary, 1962. 68 pp. B18 SBS-1962-1, p. 44; J3 1458, p. 86.

857 *BOLTON, Jacklin Talmage. Religious Influences on American Secular Cantatas. Master's thesis, University of Michigan, 1964.

858 *BOYER, Horace Clarence. The Gospel Song: A Historical and Analytical Study. M.A., Eastman School of Music of the University of Rochester, 1964. 211 pp.

859 BURNETT, Madeline Land. The Development of American Hymnody, 1620-1900. M.M., Southern California University, 1946. 112 pp. B7 109, p. 17; B8 31, p. 5; I2, p. 186.

860 BYNUM, James Louis. The Gospel Singing Conventions of Rusk County, Texas. M.A., Sociology, Southern Methodist University, 1953. 142 pp. H1, p. 228; I2, p. 238.

861 *CARD, Edith Bryson. The Development of the American Hymn Tune, 1800-1850. M.Mus.Ed., Florida State University, 1957. 46 pp. B8 150, p. 13.

862 CARR, Bruce A. Vital Spark, or The Dying Christian: A Study of the Musical Settings of Pope's Ode as They Appeared in Selected Early American Tunebooks. Master's thesis, State University of New York at Buffalo, 1967. B13, p. 32.

863 *CARRATELLO, John D. An Eclectic Choral Methodology and Its Effect on the Understanding, Interpretation, and Performance of Black Spirituals. M.A., California State University at Fullerton, 1976. 99 pp. illus. A1 (14/2) 13-08016, p. 106.

"A close investigation of the Black spiritual is made in terms of its historical and organic development."

864 *CARSON, Bobby Joe. A Study of *The Social Harp* by John G. McCurry. M.C.M., Southern Baptist Theological Seminary, 1973. 70 pp. illus.

865 COBB, Buell E., Jr. The Sacred Harp: An Overview of a Tradition. Master's thesis, English, Auburn University, 1969. H1, p. 229.

> Published under the title *The Sacred Harp: A Tradition and Its Music* (Athens: University of Georgia, 1978).

866 *COGDELL, Jacqueline Delores. An Analytical Study of the Similarities and Differences in the American Black Spiritual and Gospel Song from the South-East Region of Georgia. M.A., University of California at Los Angeles, 1972. 147 pp. B13, p. 74; B17 (6/1) 954, p. 62.

> The author has published a revised edition of this thesis under the name Jacqueline Cogdell DjeDje, *American Black Spiritual and Gospel Songs from Southeast Georgia: A Comparative Study* (Los Angeles: University of California Center for Afro-American Studies, 1978). 105 pp.

867 COOK, Helen Rawson. The Bay Psalm Book and Its Setting. M.S.M., Union Theological Seminary, 1941. B8 877, p. 62.

868 COURVILLE, Margaret Louise. A Study of the Anthems Used in Divine Worship by the Members of the Choral Conductors Guild of California, Los Angeles Chapter. M.M., Southern California University, 1959. B8 33, p. 5.

869 CRUTCHFIELD, Mary Elizabeth. The White Spiritual. S.M.M., Union Theological Seminary, 1946. B7 158, p. 23; B8 886, p. 62.

870 *DAVIS, Virginia Lucile. The 1651 Revision of the Bay Psalm Book. Master's thesis, Kent State University, 1976. 164 pp.

871 DOWNEY, James C. The Gospel Hymn 1875-1930. M.A., University of Southern Mississippi, 1963. 152 pp. B8 532, p. 39.

872 *ELLIOTT, Alberta Swain. Gospel Hymnody in Eastern North Carolina. M.Mus.Ed., Hartt College of Music of the University of Hartford, 1970. 142 pp. illus.

873 FELTON, Walter Wiest. Twentieth-Century Hymns and Hymn Writers of the New Hymnal for American Youth. M.S.M., Union Theological Seminary, 1941. B8 909, p. 64.

874 *FRENCH, Carol Ann. The Musica Sacra, or Utica and Springfield Collections United, by Thomas Hastings and Solomon Warriner. M.A., Ohio State University, 1960. 116 pp. B6 F873, p. 14; B8 1319, p. 91.

875 GABER, Deborah R. Negro Spirituals and Recent Black Soul Music: A Comparative Study. M.A., Indiana University, 1972.

876 *GEIL, Wilma Jean. Christian Harmony Singing in the Ozarks. M.M., University of Illinois at Urbana-Champaign, 1967. 110 pp. illus. B6 G312, p. 15; B13, p. 32.

877 *GOESSLING, Dolores K. Colonial Hymnology. M.A., Wayne State University, 1940. 118 pp. illus. B8 515, p. 37.

878 GOLD, Charles Edward. A Study of the Gospel Song. M.M., University of Southern California, 1953. 126 pp. B7 260, p. 35; B8 41, p. 5; B14 56, p. 26; I2, p. 239.
"Contains hymns, psalms, and white revival tradition."

879 GRAY, Charles Eugene. A Survey of Early American Hymnals from 1762 to c. 1962: From James Lyon's *Urania* to the Publications of the "Lowell Mason School," Noting Changing Trends and Styles in Texts and Tunes. M.M., Baylor University, 1965. B18 BU-1965-3, p. 3.

880 GRIER, Marion Janet. The Influence of French Psalmody on English, American, and Scottish Psalmody. M.A., University of Pennsylvania, 1952. 103 pp. illus.

881 GRUMAN, Eleanor Weeks. Kentucky Mountain Hymn Tunes. S.M.M., Union Theological Seminary, 1951. B8 950, p. 67.

882 *HALL, Stephen Frederic. The Christian Folk Musical: A Foundational Study. M.C.M., Southern Baptist Theological Seminary, 1973. 99 pp.

883 HALL, William. A Study of Contemporary Literature in Current Use in Divine Worship by the Membership of the Choral Conductors' Guild of Southern California. M.M., University of Southern California, 1958. B8 46, p. 6.

884 *HAMMOND, Paul Garnett. A Study of *The Christian Minstrel* (1846) by Jesse B. Aiken. M.C.M., Southern Baptist Theological Seminary, 1969. 80 pp.

885 HATCHETT, Hilliary Rice. A Study of Current Attitudes toward the Negro Spiritual with a Classification of 500 Spirituals Based on Their Religious Content. M.A., Ohio State University, 1946. B8 1321, p. 91; I3, p. 34.

886 HAYS, Robert Wilson. Hymnology in American Theological Seminaries Together with a Survey of the Study of Sacred Music. M.S.M., Union Theological Seminary, 1940. B8 975, p. 68.

887 *HORN, Dorothy Duerson. Shape Note Hymnals and the Art of Music of Early America. M.M., Eastman School of Music of the University of Rochester, 1942. B8 652, p. 47.

888 HUBBARD, Charles M. Early New England Psalmody and Its Effect on the Works of William Billings. M.A., Boston University, 1949. B8 402, p. 30.

889 INGALLS, Marjorie Stone. A Survey of Anthems Sung in Protestant Churches of Franklin County, Ohio. M.A., Ohio State University, 1955. B8 1322, p. 91.

890 *INSERRA, Lorraine. The Music of Henry Ainsworth's Psalter (Amsterdam, 1612). M.A., Brooklyn College of the City University of New York, 1980.
     The Ainsworth Psalter was used in New England during the 17th century. Published with revisions with the same title as I.S.A.M. Monographs, no. 15 by Inserra and H. Wiley Hitchcock (Institute for Studies in American Music, Brooklyn College of the City University of New York, 1981).

891 JARBOE, Ruth A. A Comparative Study of the Hymn Tunes Common to the Hymnals of the Five Major Protestant Denominations of the United States. Master's thesis, California State University at Sacramento, 1978. A2 3439, p. 146.

892 *JOHNSON, Dorothy Lenore. The Use of Instruments in the Worship Service in New England Churches from Colonial Days to About 1850. M.A., Eastman School of Music of the University of Rochester, 1953. 142 pp. B8 658, p. 48.

893 JOHNSON, Vernon Druckenmiller. A Survey of the Hymnology of the Pennsylvania Germans. S.M.M., Union Theological Seminary, 1949. B8 1012, p. 71.

894 KADEL, Lois. A Survey of American Hymnody during the First Half of the Nineteenth Century. S.M.M., Union Theological Seminary, 1946. B8 1018, p. 71.

895 *KADELBACH, Ada. Das Deutsch-Amerikanische Evangelische Kirchenlied bis 1800. Master's thesis, University of Mainz, Germany, 1967. 96 pp.

This study is available in the University of Kansas Music Library.

896 KANDEL, Carl H. The Use of Brass Choir in the Church Worship Service. Master's thesis, Kent State University, 1969. 247 pp.

Contains annotations of modern compositions as well as traditional music in modern arrangements. Composers and works include: Leroy Anderson, *Suite of Christmas Carols;* Thomas Beversdorf, *Cathedral Music;* William Billings, *Chester;* William Bradbury, *Woodworth;* Richard F. Goldman, *Hymn for Brass Choir;* James Hewitt, *Federal Street;* Oliver Holden, *Coronation;* Andrew Law, *Blendon;* Vaclav Nelhybel, *Chorale;* George W. Warren, *National Hymn;* and Frank Smith, *Three Chorale Settings.*

897 KRAISS, Barbara A. The Contemporary American Popular Church Cantata in Evangelical Renewal since World War II. M.A., California State University at Fullerton, 1982. 177 pp. A1 (20/4) 1318570, p. 376.

Both traditional forms and rock and pop idioms are discussed. Principal composers discussed include John Peterson and Ralph Carmichael.

898 LANEY, Helen Cunningham. Larger Choral Works Heard in New York Churches during the Five-Year Period, 1950-1955. S.M.M., Union Theological Seminary, 1956. B8 1032, p. 72.

899 LAZENBY, Jimmy Ray. The Characteristics of Sacred Harp Music: The Problem of Maintaining the Style of Music in Composition and Arrangements. M.A., Stephen F. Austin State University, 1972. 126 pp. A1 (11/2) 13-04235, p. 130.

"Ten Harp hymn tunes, five fuguing tunes and five non-fuguing anthems were selected and stylistically analyzed."

900 LYMAN, David H. The Anthem in the Early Protestant Church of New England. M.M., University of Southern California, 1948. B8 67, p. 7.

901 McKINLEY, Frank Arnold. The American Gospel Song. M.A., Westminster Choir College, 1946. I2, p. 187.

902 *MALEK, Michael Paul. Trends in Contemporary Hymnody as Reflected in Selected Recent American Protestant Hymnals. M.C.M., Southwestern Baptist Theological Seminary, 1969. 178 pp. illus. B18 SBS-1969-1, p. 45.

903   METCALFE, Howard E. American Hymnology. M.A., University of Maryland, 1935. 135 pp. H1, p. 233; I2, p. 110.

Includes a discussion of Francis Scott Key.

904   MEYER, Henry Edwin. Southern Spirituals for White Singers. M.A., Southwest Texas State Teachers College, 1942. 136 pp. B8 1448, p. 101; B18 SWT-1942-2, p. 42; I2, p. 167.

Discusses religious folk songs, camp meeting songs, and folk hymns. Included are several lists of songs according to ethnic characteristics, melodic characteristics, mode, and meter.

905   *MEYER, Ramon Eugene. Oratorios by American Born Composers in the Eighteenth and Nineteenth Centuries. M.M., University of Cincinnati, 1956. 59 pp.

906   MINARIK, Sharon Lee. The Moody-Sankey Era's Gospel Hymnology Exemplified in *Gospel Hymns* Nos. 1-6. M.C.M., Concordia Teachers College, 1979. 161 pp.

907   OLDS, Dorothy L. The Evolution of Protestant Hymnody in the United States. Master's thesis, University of Oklahoma at Norman, 1979. A2 3160, p. 137.

908   PAYNE, Henry David. Selected Shape-Note Hymns, Anthems, and Fuguing Tunes for Christmas. M.M., Texas Tech University, 1969. B18 TTU-1969-9, p. 60.

909   *PEACH, Everett. The Gospel Song: Its Influence on Christian Hymnody. M.A., Wayne State University, 1960. 113 pp. illus. B8 522, p. 38; I2, p. 287.

910   PECKMAN, John L. German Hymn Writers of the Seventeenth and Eighteenth Centuries and Their Influence on American Hymnology. M.A., Pennsylvania State University, 1915. B8 1382, p. 96.

911   ROLFS, Rodney Dean. The Nineteenth-Century American Tune-Book. M.A., Library Science, University of Chicago, 1967. 63 pp. G2, p. 188; G4, p. 448; I2, p. 333.

912   ROSS, Jean Esther. An Analysis and Criticism of the Modern American Protestant Choir Anthem. M.A., Boston University, 1946. B8 425, p. 32.

913 *RUHL, Jacqueline Gordon. Solo Song Literature for the Christian Year. Master's thesis, Kent State University, 1976. 241 pp.

Includes biographies of contemporary composers and annotations of their works. Numerous composers' works are treated. A typical entry includes the title of the work, composer, publisher, date of publication, source of text, range, and tessitura.

914 SALLEE, James Edward. A Historical Survey of the Gospel Song. M.M., University of Colorado, 1975. 133 pp.

915 SCHMALZ, Robert Frederick. A Survey of German Musical Influence on the American Singing-School Tradition (1865-1890), Gathered through the Examination of Selected Volumes Contained within the Hymnological Collection of the Pittsburgh Theological Seminary, Pittsburgh, Pennsylvania. Master's thesis, University of Pittsburgh, 1966. B13, p. 33.

916 *SCOTT, Sheila Lane McAferty. The Twentieth Century American Mass. M.A., Smith College, 1975. 160 pp.

917 *SHARROCK, Barry Roger. A Survey of the Texts and Music of Representative New Hymns as Found in Selected American Protestant Hymnals. M.C.M., Southern Baptist Theological Seminary, 1975. 84 pp. illus.

918 SHELTON, Edward Eugene. Religion, as Expressed in the Negro Spirituals. M.A., Sociology, University of Pittsburgh, 1951. 77 pp. I2, p. 227.

919 SHOTWELL, Joyce M. The Origin of the Gospel Hymn and Its Development in the Nineteenth Century. Master's thesis, Baylor University, 1976. 72 pp. A2 2829, p. 116.

920 SHUMAKER, John Ressler. A Survey of the Musical Use of the Psalms in the Protestant Churches of Franklin County, Ohio. M.A., Ohio State University, 1950. B8 1331, p. 92.

921 SILTMAN, Bobby Lawrence. The Three-Voice Folk-Hymns of William Walker from *Southern Harmony*. M.M., Hardin-Simmons University, 1963. 127 pp. B18 HSU-1963-2, p. 9; I2, p. 310.

922 SMALL, Katharine Lucille. The Influence of the Gospel Song on the Negro Church. M.A., Ohio State University, 1945. B8 1333, p. 92; I2, p. 184; I3, p. 35.

923 SMITH, Timothy Alan. The Southern Folk-Hymn, 1802-1860: A History and Musical Analysis, with Notes on Performance Practice. M.M., California State University at Fullerton, 1981. 177 pp. A1 (20/1) 1317114, p. 82.

924 SPECHT, Robert John, Jr. The Psalms and Hymns in the Pilgrim and Puritan Churches of New England, 1620-1770. M.A., Western Reserve University, 1962. B6 S741, p. 28; B8 1348, p. 93.

925 STANTON, Royal Waltz. The Quality of Permanence in Protestant Hymn Tunes. M.A., University of California at Los Angeles, 1946. 99 pp. I2, p. 188.

926 STARLING, Earl Alvin. Orders of Service Employing American Negro Spirituals. M.S.M., Union Theological Seminary, 1936. B8 1196, p. 82.

927 STEELE, Algernon Odell. The Concept of Religion Reflected in the Early Negro Spirituals. M.A., Northwestern University, 1930. 189 pp. I2, p. 71; J4 6294, p. 180.

928 STEWART, Rose Belle. A Comparative Study of the Anthem and Organ Repertoire of Representative Franklin County Churches and Some English Speaking Churches in England and on the Continent. M.A., Ohio State University, 1955. B8 1337, p. 92.

929 STIGBERG, David Kenneth. Congregational Psalmody in Eighteenth Century New England: An Analytical Study of the Psalm-Tune Collections of John Tufts and Thomas Walter. Master's thesis, University of Illinois, 1970. B13, pp. 32 and 71.

930 *STRUSS, Janet Sue. River Symbolism in the American Gospel Song. M.A., University of Pittsburgh, 1978.

931 *SUTTON, Joel Brett. The Gospel Hymn, Shaped Notes, and the Black Tradition: Continuity and Change in American Traditional Music. M.A., Folklore, University of North Carolina at Chapel Hill, 1976. 149 pp. B5 (22), p. 513.

932 *THOMAS, Georgia Fletcher. The History of the Shape-Note Hymnal from 1800 to the Present. Master's thesis, Kent State University, 1969. 131 pp. illus.

933 TURNER, Beatrice Seberia. The Effectiveness of Arrangements in Negro Spirituals. M.A., Ohio State University, 1947. B8 1339, p. 92; I3, p. 35.

934 *TYE, James E. Numeral Notation in Early American Tune-Books. M.C.M., Southwestern Baptist Theological Seminary, 1970. 67 pp. illus.

935 *VAN BROCKLIN, Allan John. A Century of Music in American Mass Evangelism. Master's thesis, University of Michigan, 1970.

936 WATKINS, Cole. A Study of Some American Developments in Congregational Church Song. M.A., DePaul University, 1936. B8 262, p. 21.

937 *WEBB, George Eliga. William Caldwell's *Union Harmony* (1837). M.C.M., Southern Baptist Theological Seminary, 1975. 129 pp.

938 *WILHOIT, Melvin R. The Influence of the Great Awakening on the Transition from American Psalmody to Hymnody. M.M., Mankato State University, 1976. 92 pp. illus.

939 WILLIAMS, Michael Donald. A Historical Survey of Shape-Note Music and Practices in Texas. M.Mus., University of Texas at Austin, 1970. B18 UT-1970-33, p. 95; L7 (81), p. 437.

940 WITT, Raymond C. American Oratorio since 1900. M.M., Baylor University, 1970. B18 BU-1970-7, p. 5.

SACRED MUSIC. INDIVIDUALS

941 ANDERSON, Anne Fournier. The Contributions of Ira D. Sankey to American Protestant Hymnody. M.A., Catholic University of America, 1965. 126 pp.

Includes an extensive listing of all hymns for which Sankey composed the music and/or text, pp. 92-126.

942   BLACK, Nell Woods. The Contribution of American Hymn Writers to Literature. M.A., University of Iowa, 1932. B8 286, p. 22.

943   *FOX, Ellen Mousseau. The Music of Billy Sunday's Revivals. M.A., Eastern Michigan University, 1977. 85 pp.

944   GRAY, Arlene Elizabeth. Lowell Mason's Contribution to American Church Music. M.M., Eastman School of Music of the University of Rochester, 1941. B8 638, p. 46.

945   JOHNSON, Glen Kenneth. August Crull: His Contributions to the Missouri Synod. M.S.T., Concordia Seminary, 1961. B8 539, p. 39.

946   KIDDER, David Harwell. The Contribution of John Greenleaf Whittier in the Field of Hymnody. S.M.M., Union Theological Seminary, 1948. B8 1026, p. 71.

947   *KIRBY, Linnie Sue. The Influence of John Calvin and His Circle on Present-Day Hymnody. M.S.M., Southern Baptist Theological Seminary, 1955. 118 pp.

948   MAHER, Mary Annata. Nicola A. Montani (1880-1945), a Pioneer in the Reform of Church Music in America. M.A., Catholic University of America, 1961. 56 pp. photos. K3, p. 71.

    Montani's life and friends are discussed in view of his endeavor as a Catholic church music reformer. Included is a copy of the first page of his composition "Salve Regina," for three-part chorus.

949   *MOTYL, Jeanne Marie. Reverend N. L. Williams: A Contemporary Singer of Spirituals. M.M., Florida State University, 1980. 88 pp. photos.

    Includes transcriptions (unaccompanied melodies) of six songs.

950   OLSON, Oscar Emanuel. A. L. Skoog: Pioneer Musician of the Evangelical Mission Covenant of America. M.M., Northwestern University, 1941. B15 589, p. 22.

951   *SPIGENER, Tommy Ray. The Contributions of Isham E. Reynolds to Church Music in the Southern Baptist Convention between 1915-1945. M.C.M., Southwestern Baptist Theological Seminary, 1962. 87 pp. B18 SBS-1962-8, p. 44; J3 1462, p. 86.

952 *STANTON, Charles Kenny. Henry E. Meyer and American Folk-Hymnody. M.C.M., Southwestern Baptist Theological Seminary, 1975. 99 pp. illus.

The Henry E. Meyer collection of early American tunebooks in the Southwestern Baptist Theological Seminary is inventoried and described.

953 *STEEL, David Warren. Truman S. Wetmore (1774-1861): Connecticut Psalmodist. Master's thesis, University of Michigan, 1976.

954 *STEINER, Stephen Merritt. The Contribution of A. B. Simpson to the Hymnody of the Christian and Missionary Alliance. M.C.M., Southern Baptist Theological Seminary, 1977. 241 pp. A1 (15/3) 13-09861, p. 162.

955 *STEWART, Roger Dean. The Contributions of Edmund S. Lorenz to American Church Music. M.C.M., Southwestern Baptist Theological Seminary, 1967. 158 pp. illus.

956 TESTA, Theresa. Nicola Aloysius Montani, K.C.S.S., Prominent Exponent of the First Half of the Twentieth Century Church Music in America. M.A., Catholic University of America, 1969. 80 pp. illus.; photos.

SACRED MUSIC. DENOMINATIONS
Baptist

957 *BALL, Mary Charlotte. A Study of Southern Baptist Vacation Bible School Music and Its Correlation with Educational Organizations. M.S.M., Southern Baptist Theological Seminary, 1958. 73 pp. B8 324, p. 25.

958 *BARNES, Billy Joe. The Development of the Graded Choir Program in Baptist Churches with a Membership of Seven Hundred or Less. M.M., Mississippi College, 1976. 186 pp. illus.

959 BENSON, David Paul. Church Music in Theory and Practice in Selected Baptist Churches: An Exploratory Study. M.S.M., Southwestern Baptist Theological Seminary, 1961. 91 pp. J3 1459, p. 86.

960 *BOBBITT, Paul Rogers, Jr. A Survey of Music in Southern Baptist Churches of North Carolina. M.S.M., Southern Baptist Theological Seminary, 1953. 183 pp. J3 1452, p. 86.

961 *BRATCHER, Marjorie Ann. The Growth and Development of Church Music in the Southern Baptist Convention. M.S.M., Southern Baptist Theological Seminary, 1948. 125 pp. J3 1432, p. 84.

962 *BROOKS, William Walker. A Study of the Attitudes of Baptist Churches toward the Part-Time Music Ministry of Students from the Southern Baptist Theological Seminary. M.C.M., Southern Baptist Theological Seminary, 1974. 87 pp.

963 *CASEY, L. D. Psalmody and Hymnody of Baptists in the American Colonies. M.C.M., Southwestern Baptist Theological Seminary, 1967. 66 pp. B18 SBS-1967-3, p. 45.

964 *CATES, Jesse Howard. American Baptist Hymnody from 1640 to 1850. M.S.M., Southern Baptist Theological Seminary, 1948. 77 pp. J3 1425, p. 84.

965 COLLIER, Shelby L. The Status of Music in One Hundred Baptist Churches of Texas. M.M., University of Texas at Austin, 1949. B8 1476, p. 103; B12, p. 143; B18 UT-1949-2, p. 70.

966 *HAMPSHER, Harry Frank. American Baptist Hymnody since 1850. M.S.M., Southern Baptist Theological Seminary, 1951. 85 pp. B8 332, p. 25; J3 1426, p. 84.

967 *HARDEN, Timothy Don. A Comparison and Analysis of the Identity and Roles of Southern Baptist Ministers of Music and Combination Ministers. M.C.M., Southern Baptist Theological Seminary [no date cited]. 197 pp.

968 *HORNBUCKLE, William R. The Southern Baptist Church Musician as Conductor. M.C.M., Southern Baptist Theological Seminary, 1965. 41 pp.

969 *HUGGINS, James Leon. The New Baptist Hymnal, 1926. M.C.M., Southwestern Baptist Theological Seminary, 1965. 127 pp. B18 SBS-1965-2, p. 44.

970 *JOHNSON, Winson Ray. A Survey of Music in Southern Baptist Churches of Kentucky. M.S.M., Southern Baptist Theological Seminary, 1951. 61 pp. B8 335, p. 26; J3 1451, p. 85.

971   KEY, Jimmy Richardson. The Use of the Wesley Hymns in Southern Baptist Worship. M.M., University of Texas, 1962. B8 1479, p. 103; B18 UT-1962-13, p. 86.

972   *McCARTY, Rex Byron. A Documentary History of the Music Ministry of Baptist Tabernacle, Louisville, Kentucky, 1891-1976. M.C.M., Southern Baptist Theological Seminary, 1976. illus.

973   *McELRATH, Hugh Thomas. The Improvement of Baptist Worship through Music. M.S.M., Southern Baptist Theological Seminary, 1948. 282 pp.

974   *MILLER, Marian Elaine. Practices of American Baptist Churches in Indiana concerning the Ministry of Music. M.C.M., Southern Baptist Theological Seminary, 1970. 92 pp.

975   MINTER, William John. Church Music in the American Baptist Union of the San Francisco Bay Cities. S.M.M., Union Theological Seminary, 1960. B8 1087, p. 75.

976   PATTERSON, Floyd H., Jr. The Organization and Development of the Statewide Church Music Program among Baptists in Texas. M.M., Baylor University, 1949. B8 1419, p. 99; B18 BU-1949-8, p. 1.

977   *POOLE, Robert Wade. A Survey of Music of Southern Baptist Churches in Louisiana. M.S.M., Southern Baptist Theological Seminary, 1952. 128 pp. B8 345, p. 26; J3 1453, p. 86.

978   *RHODES, Orel Arvid. Considerations Given to Musical Purposes in the Construction of Selected Southern Baptist Auditoriums. M.C.M., Southwestern Baptist Theological Seminary, 1970. 271 pp. illus.

979   *ROBERTS, R. D. John Rippon's Selection of Hymns and Its Contribution to Baptist Hymnody. M.C.M., Southwestern Baptist Theological Seminary, 1972. 147 pp. illus.

980   WALKER, Laddie Leo. The Development of Music among Texas Baptists. M.A., Stephen F. Austin State University, 1955. B18 SFA-1955-1, p. 46.

981 *WALKER, Robert Gary. The Walnut Street Music Reader: A Documentary History of the Music Program of the Walnut Street Baptist Church, Louisville, Kentucky, 1844-1954. M.C.M., Southern Baptist Seminary, 1971. 149 pp. illus.

982 *WALL, Woodrow Wilson. The Development of Baptist Hymnody with Particular Emphasis on the Southern Baptist Convention. M.Mus., North Texas State University, 1955. 68 pp. B8 1436, p. 100; B18 NTSU-1955-19, p. 20.

983 *WESTBERRY, Gilbert Foster. A History of the Music Ministry of the First Baptist Church, Jeffersontown, Kentucky, from 1845 to the Present. M.C.M., Southern Baptist Theological Seminary, 1971. 103 pp.

984 WILLIAMS, James M. A Survey of Worship Music Practices in Southern Baptist Churches. Master's thesis, University of Tennessee at Knoxville, 1969. F1 1569, p. 72.

See also nos. 565, 586, 951, 1138, 1258, 1290, 1311, 1958.

Catholic

985 BALL, Walter Herbert. Music at the Church of Saint Mary the Virgin, New York, since 1930. S.M.M., Union Theological Seminary, 1955. B8 804, p. 57.

986 *BIRD, Mary Faber. Early Catholic Church Music in America. Master's thesis, University of Michigan, 1938. B8 476, p. 35.

987 BRENNAN, Allen John. Music in the Catholic Church in Philadelphia, 1800-1835. M.A., University of Pennsylvania, 1968. 154 pp. B13, p. 24.
Includes discussions of "Hymn Books Used in the Catholic Church" and "Musicians Associated with Catholic Church Music."

988 COLUMBRO, Mary Electa. American Catholic Marian Hymnody, 1880-1965. M.A., Catholic University of America, 1966. 105 pp. illus. B13, p. 26.
Includes a number of facsimiles of hymns which appear in hymnals now out of print or not easily accessible.

989 *FISHER, Helen D. Propagation of the Music of the New Roman Catholic Liturgy in Three Selected Dioceses. M.M.Ed., University of Kansas, 1967.

990   GRABRIAN, Bernadette. The Saint Cecilia Society of Milwaukee: Its Principal Figures and Influence on Catholic Church Music in America. Master's thesis, University of Wisconsin, 1972.

991   GRADONE, Richard Anthony. A Record of Events Employing Music at the National Shrine of the Immaculate Conception in Washington, D.C. from 1914 through 1971. M.A., Catholic University of America, 1972. 860 pp. B9 17, p. 3; B17 (10/4) 17176, p. 890.

992   GRUBBS, Baalis. Modern Use of California Mission Music. M.M., University of Southern California, 1955. B8 45, p. 6; B12, p. 76.

993   HELLMAN, Mary Carol. Survey of Church Music in the Diocese of Covington, Kentucky. M.M., Catholic University of America, 1971. 171 pp. illus.
Includes a "brief description of the background contributing to the historical, educational, and liturgical growth of Covington, Kentucky."

994   HILLMAN, Gloria. A Survey of Church Music in the Diocese of Raleigh, North Carolina. M.M., Catholic University of America, 1970. 76 pp. illus.
Includes a brief history of the Diocese.

995   HOPPS, Gloria Lorraine. Mission Music of California. M.M., Northwestern University, 1949. B8 210, p. 17; B15 342, p. 15; I2, p. 207.

996   KAWICH, Nancy Karol. A Survey of the Music as Used in Liturgical and Para-Liturgical Services in Houses of Study, Convents, and Seminaries in Washington, D.C. and Suburban Maryland. M.M., Catholic University of America, 1972. 42 pp. B9 2, p. 1; B17 (10/4) 17189, p. 891.
Fifty religious houses are studied.

997   KAWICH, Stella Kathryn. Survey of Music Used by Various Parishes in the Washington, D.C. Area for the Celebration of the Liturgy. M.M., Catholic University of America, 1972. 49 pp. B9 3, p. 1; B17 (10/4) 17190, p. 891.
Fifty-four parishes are studied.

998   MILLARD, Daryl John. Music Profile of a Church Community at Keaukaha, Hawaii: Malia Puka O Kalani Catholic Church. M.A., University of Hawaii, 1979. 253 pp. A2 3635, p. 162.

999 NEMMERS, M. Helen. The Catholic Normal School of St. Francis, Wisconsin, and Its Effect upon Catholic Musical Reform in the United States. M.M., Catholic University of America, 1969. 128 pp.

Includes a discussion of the American composers Sister M. Theophane and Michael L. Nemmers and the American organists Caspar P. Koch, Paul Koch, Otto Singenberger, and Charles Balzer.

1000 O'CONNOR, Mary Alice. A Survey of Church Music in the Diocese of Albany, New York. M.M., Catholic University of America, 1969. 79 pp.

This study deals with modern church practice. Topics treated include congregational singing, choirs, folk masses, and organists.

1001 SCHMITT, Robert J. A History of Catholic Church Music and Musicians in Milwaukee. Master's thesis, Marquette University, 1968.

1002 TEICHERT, Adolph. Some Notes on the Music at St. Mary-the-Virgin, New York City, 1870-1906. S.M.M., Union Theological Seminary, 1953. B8 1211, p. 83.

1003 VERRET, Mary Camilla. A Preliminary Survey of Roman Catholic Hymnals Published in the United States of America. M.M., Catholic University of America, 1963. 165 pp.

There are 311 entries. A typical entry includes imprint description, date, number of pages, size of book, location(s), and contents.

See also nos. **41, 331, 948, 956, 1176, 1184, 1195, 1209, 1236, 1301, 1306.**

Church of the Brethren

1004 FISHER, Nevin W. A Historical, Critical, and Comparative Study of the Hymnbooks of the Church of the Brethren. M.M., Northwestern University, 1947. B8 199, p. 16; J2, p. 63.

1005 LITES, Milton. The Function of Music in the Church and Community of the United Brethren in America, 1735-1860. M.C.M., Southwestern Baptist Theological Seminary, 1963. B8 1463, p. 102.

1006 *SANGER, Paul Bowman, Jr. A Study of the Trends in the Use of Music by the Church of the Brethren. Master's thesis, DePaul University, 1948. 126 pp.

See also no. **1297.**

Church of the Nazarene

1007 *MILLER, James Eugene. A Survey of Current Musical Practices in Selected Churches of the Nazarene. M.C.M., Southern Baptist Theological Seminary, 1974. 241 pp. illus.

1008 MOORE, Muriel Payne. History and Practice of Music in the Church of the Nazarene in Texas. M.Mus., University of Texas at Austin, 1966. B13, p. 33; L7 (81), p. 314.

Congregational

1009 STEARNS, Gordon Woodburn. The Ministry of Sacred Music, 1954-1955, in the First Church of Christ, Congregational, West Hartford, Connecticut. S.M.M., Union Theological Seminary, 1956. B8 1197, p. 82.

1010 WILDMAN, Rose Marie. Music in the Riverside Church School (New York). S.M.M., Union Theological Seminary, 1958. B8 1252, p. 86.

Episcopal

1011 GRAEFF, Helen Lorenz. A History of the Hymnal of the Protestant Episcopal Church in the United States of America. S.M.M., Union Theological Seminary, 1949. B8 940, p. 66.

1012 HOOD, Sebron Yates. A History of Music at Trinity Church, New York. S.M.M., Union Theological Seminary, 1955. B8 994, p. 69.

1013 KANTZ, Joseph A. A Study of the Hymnal 1940 of the Protestant Episcopal Church in the United States of America. M.M., University of Southern California, 1952. B8 61, p. 7.

1014 QUADE, Robert Milton. A History of the Washington Cathedral, Its Structure and Its Music. S.M.M., Union Theological Seminary, 1955. B8 1135, p. 78; B9 26, p. 4.

1015 SMITH, David Neal. History of Music, the Church of the Holy Trinity, Brooklyn, New York. S.M.M., Union Theological Seminary, 1955. B8 1184, p. 82.

1016   TRAUTMANN, Jean Elizabeth. A History of Music at Saint Bartholomew's Church, New York. S.M.M., Union Theological Seminary, 1951. B8 1215, p. 84.

1017   VOLLSTEDT, Don August. A History of the Music at Saint Thomas' Church, New York. S.M.M., Union Theological Seminary, 1955. B8 1227, p. 85.

1018   WILHITE, Charles. The Episcopal Organist-Choirmaster (New York). S.M.M., Union Theological Seminary, 1953. B8 1253, p. 86.

   See also nos. **559, 573, 575, 1966.**

   Hebrew

1019   FRANK, Emmet A. The Attitudes toward Music and Ritual in the Evolution from Orthodoxy to Reform in the American Synagogue. M.H.T., Hebrew Union College, 1952. B8 1296, p. 89.

1020   *JACOBS, Henry Switzer. The Influence of Reform Judaism on Jewish Liturgical Music. M.A., Tulane University, 1954. 160 pp. illus.

   See also no. **582.**

   Hutterite Brethren

1021   MARTENS, Larry D. Musical Thought and Practice in the Hutterite Community. M.A., Education, University of Kansas, 1960. 67 pp. F1 1254, p. 57; I2, p. 286.

   The first two chapters are a history and the social organization and practice of the Hutterites. Chapter 3 discusses the hymnology and folksongs of that culture.

1022   *RANKIN, Diana M. Hutterite Music: Sixteenth Century Melodies in a Twentieth Century World. M.M., Mankato State University, 1972. 149 pp. illus.

1023   SCHILLING, Arnold J. The Music of the Hutterites of Tschetter Colony [South Dakota]. Master's thesis, University of South Dakota, 1955.

   Additional master's theses on Hutterite topics are listed in John A. Hostetler's *Hutterite Society* (Baltimore: Johns Hopkins University Press, 1974), pp. 373-92.

Lutheran

1024 ARCHIE, Victor Robert. An Analysis of the Symbolism in the Words and Music of the Hymns Pertaining to the Resurrection of Our Lord as Published in the Common Service Hymnal of the United Lutheran Church in America. M.A., Garrett Theological Seminary, 1956. B8 173, p. 15.

1025 CRESSMAN, Herbert Detweiler. A Handbook to the Hymnal of the Common Service Book of the United Lutheran Church of America. M.S.T., Lutheran Theological Seminary at Philadelphia, 1941. B8 1373, p. 95.

1026 ENGELBRECHT, Luther T. Martin Luther's Hymn Texts, with Special Reference to Their Use in Some Hymnals Commonly Used in England and America. M.S.T., Concordia Seminary, 1954. B8 537, p. 39.

1027 GRANT, Maryanne. Music of the Liturgy of the Lutheran Church of America. S.M.M., Union Theological Seminary, 1955. B8 942, p. 66.

1028 KNAUTZ, Philip Frederick. The Status of Music in the Texas District of the American Lutheran Church Synod. M.M., University of Texas, 1954. B8 1480, p. 103; B18 UT-1954-16, p. 76.

1029 KRAUSE, David. The Philosophy and Development of Contemporary Choral Music Written for the Worship Service in the Lutheran Church, Missouri Synod. M.M., Southern California University, 1963. B8 62, p. 7.

1030 KRING, William G. Criteria for the Evaluation of the Anthem for Use in Divine Worship of the Lutheran Church of the United States. M.M., Southern California University, 1963. B8 63, p. 7.

1031 MILLER, Lester David. The Use of the Liturgy in the United Lutheran Church in America. S.M.M., Union Theological Seminary, 1947. B8 1083, p. 75.

1032 SCHNEIDER, Theodore Jacob. The Choral Service for the Reformed Church in the United States. M.S.T., Lutheran Theological Seminary at Philadelphia, 1934. B8 1379, p. 95.

1033 THOMPSON, Dixie C. A History of the Lutheran Hymnal in America. Master's thesis, Fort Hays State University, 1982. A2 4433, p. 214.

1034 TRAMPE, Ronald Charles. Music Administration in Texas District, Missouri Synod Lutheran Churches. M.M., University of Texas, 1958. B8 1493, p. 104; B18 UT-1958-25, p. 82.

1035 WAGGONER, William L. An Investigation into the Use of Instrumental Music in the Lutheran Church of North America. M.A., Sam Houston State University, 1961. B18 SHS-1961-5, p. 33.

1036 ZIELKE, Dorothy Helen Meyer. A Study of the Liturgical Settings for the Communion Service of the Lutheran Church-Missouri Synod. M.M., University of Texas at Austin, 1966. B13, p. 33; B18 UT-1966-23, p. 90.

See also nos. **583, 1268, 1362.**

Mennonites and Amish

1037 BURKHARD, Samuel Theodore. Music among the Mennonites and Amish of North America. M.S.M., Union Theological Seminary, 1938. B8 849, p. 60.

1038 *BURNS, Deborah A. The Role of Music as a Reinforcement in the Lives of the Mennonites of Rockingham County, Virginia. M.A., East Carolina University, 1974. 118 pp. illus.; photos.

This study focuses on the Mennonite community in and around Harrisonburg, Va. Included are chapters on the historical background of the Mennonite sect, sources of Mennonite hymnody, Mennonite hymnals, and the performance practice of Mennonite music. The principal musician discussed is Joseph Funk. The author includes photographs of Funk's home, built in 1804, as well as various Mennonite churches.

1039 *LEHMAN, Earl Wade. Music in the Swiss Mennonite Churches of Ohio and Indiana. M.A., Ohio State University, 1953. 76 pp. B8 1327, p. 91.

1040 *McKEAN, Gary Franklin. *Ausbund,* an Historical and Analytical Study. M.C.M., Southwestern Baptist Theological Seminary, 1970. 217 pp. illus.

The *Ausbund, Das ist: Etliche schöne Christliche Lieder* (1742) was the principal hymn book for the Mennonites in America.

1041 TOEWS, Abraham Peter. The Roots, Development and Application of American Mennonite Worship. M.S.T., Concordia Seminary, 1958. B8 546, p. 40.

See also no. **1167.**

Methodist

1042 BICKLEY, Thomas F. *David's Harp* (1813), a Methodist Tunebook from Baltimore: An Analysis and Facsimile. M.A., American University, 1983. 220 pp.

Includes a biography of John Cole and a survey of Methodist tunebooks to 1813.

1043 BOYER, Daniel Royce. A Survey of the Music Programs in the Alexandria District Methodist Churches, Virginia Conference. M.A., Catholic University of America, 1963. 60 pp. B9 70 p. 9; K3, p. 19.

1044 *ELLENBERGER, William B. A History of Hymn Tunes Used by the Methodist Church in America. M.M., University of Cincinnati, 1956. 59 pp.

Includes a general history of the Methodist church, the hymnals, sources of hymn tunes in Europe and America, and a list of 69 hymn tunes composed by William Billings that appear in the hymnals discussed. Also discussed is *The Southern Harmony* and Tansur's *Royal Melody Complete*.

1045 HOOKS, Sylvia Marquita Cartwright. The Status of Music in the Methodist Churches of Texas. M.M., University of Texas, 1954. B8 1477, p. 103; B18 UT-1954-13, p. 76.

1046 *LONGSTRETH, Mary Kinney. A History and Chronology of the Methodist Hymnal, Edition 1935. M.A., University of Missouri-Columbia, 1962. 209 pp. illus. B8 549, p. 40.

1047 *ODEN, Mary Anne. The Growth and Development of Methodist Hymnody in the United States. M.S.M., Southern Baptist Theological Seminary, 1948. 114 pp. B8 343, p. 26; J3 1433, p. 85.

Examines the 18th-20th centuries. Included is a table of 57 authors and composers.

1048 *PLYLER, Esther Petre. A Survey of American Methodist Non-Official Hymn and Song Collections. M.A., University of Missouri-Columbia, 1962. 147 pp. illus. B8 550, p. 40.

1049 WESTRA, Dorothy Louise. A Historical Analysis of the New Methodist Hymnal. M.S.M., Union Theological Seminary, 1936. B8 1245, p. 86.

See also no. **560**.

Moravian

1050 *BAHR, Marian Hughes. A Study of the Published Editions of Early American Moravian Sacred Arias for Soprano. Master's thesis, Kent State University, 1969. 98 pp. illus.

1051 BALLENGER, Larry Desmond. The Music of the Moravians. M.A., Fresno State College, 1967. J1.

1052 *BOWMAN, Emily Jane. Music of the Early American Moravians. Master's thesis, University of Michigan, 1963. J1.

1053 HERTEL, Marilyn. The Development of the Moravian Sacred Music. M.A., Bob Jones University, 1968. J1.

1054 KEEN, James Alvin. Some Musical Aspects of the Moravian Church including the Easter Service at Winston-Salem, North Carolina. M.A., University of Iowa, 1935. B8 302, p. 23; I2, p. 109.

1055 *McCORKLE, Donald Macomber. An Introduction to the Musical Culture of the North Carolina Moravians in the Eighteenth Century. A.M., Indiana University, 1953. 112 pp. B6 M131, p. 22; B14 100, p. 29; I2, p. 241; J1.

1056 MECHERLE, Elizabeth Lillian. Morning Services for the Moravian Church of New York City. M.S.M., Union Theological Seminary, 1936. B8 1082, p. 75.

1057 *RAUCH, Ralph Frederick. An Analysis of the Moravian Chorales. M.M., Eastman School of Music of the University of Rochester, 1952. 67 pp. illus.

1058 *SCOTT, Ruth Holmes. Music among the Moravians, Bethlehem, Pa., 1741-1816. M.M., Eastman School of Music of the University of Rochester, 1938. B8 718, p. 51.

1059 TAYLOR, J. C. The Moravian Trombone Choir Tradition in America. Master's thesis, University of Alberta, 1982. A2 3071, p. 148.

1060 WOLFE, Lucy Louise. Moravian Church Music in Wachovia, North Carolina. S.M.M., Union Theological Seminary, 1951. B8 1262, p. 87.

1061 *WOODINGS, Terry G. A Study of the Published Editions of American Moravian Choral Music. Master's thesis, Kent State University, 1967. 70 pp. illus.

See also nos. **37, 72, 223, 233, 291, 297, 394, 400, 445, 653, 1414, 1578, 1595.**

Mormon

1062 BARNES, Mary Musser. An Historical Survey of the Salt Lake Tabernacle Choir of the Church of Jesus Christ of the Latter-Day Saints. M.A., University of Iowa, 1936. B8 285, p. 22.

1063 *CASTLETON, Don Bernard. The Concept of Zion as Reflected in Mormon Song. M.A., Religious Instruction, Brigham Young University, 1967. 164 pp.

1064 DURHAM, Lovell M. The Role and History of Music in the Mormon Church. M.A., University of Iowa, 1942. I2, p. 165.

1065 WEBB, Ina T. Congregational Singing in the Church of Jesus Christ of Latter-Day Saints. M.A., Brigham Young University, 1931. B8 1511, p. 106.

1066 *WEDDLE, Frederick O. Philosophy and Development of Music in the Reorganized Church of Jesus Christ of Latter-Day Saints. M.S., University of Kansas City, 1957. 93 pp. illus.

See also nos. **574, 581, 1310, 1974, 2368.**

Presbyterian

1067 ALVIS, Sarah Elizabeth. A Survey of the Music of the Pacific Coast Presbyterian Churches. M.A., San Francisco Theological Seminary, 1941. B8 3, p. 3.

1068 *HAAS, William Dan. The Metrical Psalmody of the Reformed Presbyterians of North America. M.C.M., Southwestern Baptist Theological Seminary, 1971. 102 pp. illus. B18 SBS-1971-2, p. 45.

1069 HAYDEN, Margaret E. A Survey of the Church Music Sung by Presbyterian Young People of the West Coast. M.A., San Francisco Theological Seminary, 1945. B8 16, p. 4.

1070   HORN, Leroy Bernard. Toward an American Presbyterian Tradition in Worship: Being an Examination of the Concept of Worship in America as Reflected in the Records, Events, and Men from the First Presbytery (1706) to the First Book of Common Prayer of the Presbyterian Church in the United States of America (1906). Th.M., Austin Presbyterian Theological Seminary, 1962. B8 1409, p. 98.

1071   *KADEL, Richard William. The Evolution of Hymnody in the Presbyterian Church in the United States, 1850-1900. M.Mus., Florida State University, 1968. 101 pp. B17 (10/4) 17233, p. 893.

1072   McCLEERY, Carolyn. Some Musical and Historical Aspects of the United Presbyterian Psalter of 1872. M.A., University of Iowa, 1933. B8 305, p. 24.

1073   MORRISON, Rheta H. A Correlated Use of the Graded Hymnals in the Presbyterian Church in the U.S.A. M.A., San Francisco Theological Seminary, 1954. B8 22, p. 4.

1074   PENNER, Marilyn Ruth. A History of the Music Program of the First Presbyterian Church, Arkansas City, Kansas. S.M.M., Union Theological Seminary, 1952. B8 1118, p. 77.

1075   SHORT, Naomi Edith Carrington. The Status of Music in the Presbyterian (U.S.) Churches of Texas. M.M., University of Texas, 1957. B8 1489, p. 104; B18 UT-1957-18, p. 81.

1076   STEPHENS, Norris Lynn. The East Liberty Presbyterian Church of Pittsburgh, Pennsylvania: The Church and Its Music. S.M.M., Union Theological Seminary, 1956. B8 1199, p. 83.

1077   *THOMSON, Nancy Jane. A Historical Survey of Music in the Presbyterian Churches in America. M.S.M., Southern Baptist Theological Seminary, 1948. 150 pp. B8 353, p. 27; J3 1435, p. 85.

1078   WEAGLY, William Richard. The Presbyterian Hymnal (1933) and Hymn Anthems. M.S.M., Union Theological Seminary, 1940. B8 1239, p. 85.

See also no. **1303**.

Shaker

1079 *ISQUITH, Aaron. Mary Hazard's "A Collection of Exercize Songs": Historical Background, Transcription and Analysis of a Shaker Manuscript Hymnal. M.A., Brooklyn College of the City University of New York, 1975. 186 pp.

One hundred twenty-five songs are transcribed. Included is a general overview of Shaker notation. The Hazard hymnal is located in the Shaker Museum Foundation Library in Old Chatham, New York.

1080 PATTERSON, Daniel Watkins. Folk-Song Elements in the Shaker Spiritual. M.A., English, University of North Carolina, 1955. 131 pp. I2, p. 255.

See also Patterson's *The Shaker Spiritual* (Princeton University Press, 1979).

1081 ZIMMERMAN, Karen Voci. Symbol, Structure and Reality: Forms of Worship of the New England Shakers. M.A., Sociology, American University, 1973. 254 pp.

Discusses music and dance as a form of worship among the Shakers.

Other Denominations

1082 BAVER, Marlene Jeannette. The Music of the Cathedral Church of St. Mark, Minneapolis, Minnesota. S.M.M., Union Theological Seminary, 1955. B8 812, p. 58.

1083 *BENTON, Franklin Frederick. Music in the Christian Reformed Church: Its Calvinistic, Systematic Theological Influence and Its Development since 1857. M.M., Mankato State University, 1975. 97 pp.

1084 *BROWN, Glenna Nance. An Investigation of the Musical Practices of Churches of the Wesleyan-Arminian Persuasion. M.A., Ohio State University, 1968. 102 pp.

1085 *HARRELL, Donald Robert. The Contemporary Use of Music in the United Church of Christ. Master's thesis, University of Michigan, 1971.

1086 MOMANY, Sharon. Music in the Harmonic Society, 1805-1847. M.M., Indiana University, 1963. B8 280, p. 22.

1087 PEEK, Richard Maurice. A Brief History of Music at the Church of the Ascension, New York City. S.M.M., Union Theological Seminary, 1952. B8 1115, p. 77.

1088 *SCHMID, Roy Ralph. Music – A Discipline of the Ephrata Community. S.T.M., Temple University, 1959.

1089 SHEPARD, Dane K. An Analysis of Three Hymnals Used by the Churches of Christ. M.A., California State University at Fullerton, 1980. 386 pp. A1 (19/3) 1316049, p. 259.

   The hymnals are *Great Songs of the Church, Number Two* (1937), compiled by E. L. Jorgenson, *Sacred Selections for the Church* (1957), edited by Ellis J. Crum, and *Songs of the Church* (1971), compiled by Alton H. Howard.

1090 SYKES, Richard E. The Development of "American" Unitarian Hymnology: A Content Analysis in American Studies. Master's thesis, University of Minnesota, 1966. B13, p. 33.

1091 TWEED, Myron. A Study of the Hymn in the Worship Services of the United Missionary Church. M.M., University of Southern California, 1958. B8 93, p. 9.

   See also nos. **317, 891, 1160, 1190, 1194, 1214.**

EDUCATION. GENERAL

1092 REISS, Muriel. Development of Music Education in the United States. M.M., New England Conservatory of Music, 1949. B12, p. 108

1093 ROSS, Carolyn W. History of Music Education in the United States since 1900. M.M., Catholic University of America, 1968. 115 pp.

   Discusses education in both elementary and secondary schools, federal legislation affecting music education, and current trends in music education.

1094 SPELL, (Mrs.) Lota. A History of Musical Education in the United States. M.A., University of Texas at Austin, 1919. B18 UT-1919-1, p. 67.

1095 SWINEY, James Marvin. The Effect of Musical Education on Musical Trends in the United States, 1940-1960. M.A., American University, 1962. 95 pp. A1 (1/2) 13-00411, p. 45.

   This study is based on the premise that music teaching, educational technology, and the quality of music consumption has changed during the period examined.

An example of an American illuminated manuscript based on medieval practice brought to the colonies by the Pennsylvania Germans. Shown here is the "Halleluja" from the *Paradisches Wunder-Spiel,* 1751, Ephrata Cloister, Pennsylvania.

1096 WEBB, Harriet I. Societal and Educational Influences on Music Education in the United States in the Twentieth Century. Master's thesis, Eastern Kentucky University, 1981. F1 1070, p. 68.

1097 *WELLES, Sherrie L. The Arts in Education: An Overview of Current Trends and Practices. M.M.E., Southern Illinois University, 1979. 141 pp.

EDUCATION. INDIVIDUALS

1098 *ALBAUGH, David H. Will Earhart: Music Educator. Master's thesis, University of Michigan, 1960.

1099 *BARR, Ann Helen. The Aesthetics of Susanne K. Langer: Implications for Music Education. M.A., University of California at Los Angeles, 1973. 102 pp.

1100 *BARR, Clyde Milton. William Paris Chamber, 1854-1913: His Life and Contribution to Music. M.Ed., Indiana University of Pennsylvania, 1973. 98 pp.

1101 BINGHAM, Joanne L. A Biography of Frances Elliott Clark and Her Place in the Development of the Music Educators National Conference. M.M., Peabody Conservatory of Music, 1956. 40 pp.

1102 *BROWN, Bruce A. Nadia Boulanger: Her Influence on American Music. M.M., Midwestern University, 1974. 177 pp.

1103 BUFFALOE, Bonnie Gail. The Pestalozzianism of Lowell Mason: Its Identification and Importance to the Development of American Music Education during the Nineteenth Century. M.A., University of Denver, 1974. 76 pp.

1104 DOXEY, Mary Bitzer. Lowell Mason, Modern Music Educator. M.M.Ed., University of Mississippi, 1957. B8 529, p. 39.

1105 FLAHERTY, Avellina. Ralph Lyman Baldwin (1872-1943): Musician and Educator. M.A., Catholic University of America, 1960. 85 pp. K3, p. 42.
Although Baldwin was known primarily as an educator, he was also a church organist, choir director, and composer. Included is a list of his compositions, both vocal and instrumental.

1106 *GREER, Leslie Kathleen. Morris Hutchins Ruger: A Biography. M.A., California State University at Long Beach, 1977. 167 pp. illus. A1 (16/1) 13-10668, p. 46.

Music teacher and composer in Southern California from 1930 until his death in 1974.

1107 GRIESMAN, Robert J. Early Developments Leading to Peter Dykema's Contribution to American Music Education. M.M., University of Southern California, 1953. B12, p. 76.

1108 *HAMMER, Eleanor Ray. Louis Woodson Curtis, Music Educator. M.A., University of California at Los Angeles, 1961. 98 pp.

1109 *HELIODORE POKORNY, Mary. Lowell Mason's Contribution to the Field of Music Education in America. Master's thesis, DePaul University, 1952. 54 pp. B2, p. 30.

1110 HOLLANDER, Goldye. The Life and Works of Dr. Lowell Mason, the Father of Public School Music. M.S., Texas A & I University, 1941. B18 TA & I-1941-2, p. 46.

1111 *HUNTER, Michael Rolland. The Application to Music History of a Concept of Continuity Based on the Writings of John Dewey. M.M., Southern Illinois University, 1972. 51 pp.

1112 INGALLS, Janyce Greenleaf. Nathaniel Duren Gould, 1781-1864. M.M., University of Lowell, 1980. 45 pp. A1 (18/4) 1314731, p. 303.

Gould established singing schools in New England and New York, and compiled various collections of music.

1113 JOHNSON, Marjorie S. Noah Francis Ryder (1914-1964): A Study of His Life, Works, and Contributions to Music Education. M.M., Catholic University of America, 1968. 89 pp.

1114 JONES, James Nathan. Alfred Jack Thomas (1884-1962): Musician, Composer, Educator. M.A., Morgan State University, 1978. 45 pp. B9 53, p. 7.

Thomas, first black bandmaster in the U.S. armed services, founded the Aeolian Conservatory of Music in Baltimore. His many accomplishments included a guest conductorship of the Baltimore Symphony Orchestra in 1946.

1115 KELLY, Karen L. Dr. James Neilson: His Contribution to the Fields of Instrumental Music Education and Conducting. Master's thesis, Bowling Green State University, 1982. A2 3011, p. 146.

1116 KING, Carl Darlington. Charles Faulkner Bryan: Tennessee Educator and Musician. M.S., University of Tennessee, 1965. 284 pp.

This biography discusses Bryan's musical life as a vocalist, instrumentalist, conductor, and composer. Includes the music of six of Bryan's compositions and the complete text of a paper entitled "The Appalachian Mountain Dulcimer" delivered by Bryan at a meeting of the Tennessee Folklore Society on November 6, 1954.

1117 *LENDRIM, Frank Torbet. Music for Every Child: The Story of Karl Wilson Gehrkens. Master's thesis, University of Michigan, 1961.

1118 *MARCH, Hunter C. Hollis Dann and the Pennsylvania Public School Music Program 1921-25. Master's thesis, University of Michigan, 1970.

1119 *MARKOVICH, Victor Alan. The Contributions of John W. Wainwright to the Public School Band Movement and Music Education in Ohio. Master's thesis, University of Michigan, 1977.

1120 MELCHER, Rita Mary. Leonard Bernstein: His Impact on the Field of Music Education. M.M., Catholic University of America, 1968. 67 pp.

Includes a list of titles and dates, 18 January 1958 to 26 May 1968, of the New York Philharmonic Young People's Concerts.

1121 *MILLER, Samuel Dixon. W. Otto Miessner and His Contributions to Music in American Schools. Master's thesis, University of Michigan, 1962.

1122 *MILLER, Terry Ellis. Alexander Auld and American Shape-Note Music. M.M., Indiana University, 1971. 116 pp.

1123 MITCHELL, Charlie H. Historical Research on Rosa Lillian Carpenter: A Study of Her Life and Influence on Music Education in Kentucky. M.M.Ed., University of Louisville, 1981. A1 (20/2) 1317540, p. 198.

1124 MOORE, Douglas. The Activities of Lowell Mason in Savannah, Georgia, 1813-1827. M.F.A., University of Georgia, 1967. 46 pp. B6 M821, p. 23.

1125 *MURADIAN, Thaddeus George. Lowell Mason: His Philosophy and Contribution to Music Education. M.A., San Diego State College, 1967. 150 pp.

1126 NOGAMI, Toshiyuki. Meijishoki No Ongakukyoiku Ni Okeru L. W. Mason No Igi (The Significance of the Achievement of L. W. Mason in the Development of Music Education in the Early Meiji Era). M.A., Kunitachi M. College, 1977. B17 (11/1) 1727, p. 102. 252 pp.

1127 *REES, James Lester. Leonard Bernstein's Informative Speaking in the 1965-1966 Young People's Concerts. M.A., Speech, Syracuse University, 1966. 287 pp.

1128 RICHARDS, Marie Juliette. The Role of William Mason in American Music Education. M.A., Catholic University of America, 1959. 58 pp.

1129 *ROBERTS, Benjamin Mark. Anthony C. Lund, Musician, with Special Reference to His Teaching and Choral Directing. M.A., Brigham Young University, 1952. 76 pp. photos.

1130 *ROBISON, Richard W. Albert Miller, His Musical Achievements and Contributions to the Teaching of Music at Brigham Young University. M.A., Brigham Young University, 1957. 38 pp. illus.

1131 SCANLON, Mary Browning. Lowell Mason in Music Education. M.A., Eastman School of Music of the University of Rochester, 1940. 216 pp.

1132 SILANTIEN, John Joseph. William Channing Woodbridge: His Life and Contributions to American Music Education. M.M., Catholic University of America, 1972. 105 pp.

Includes a discussion of Woodbridge's activities in Hartford, Conn., and Boston, Mass.

1133 SUEHS, Hermann C. The Legacy of William Augustus Hodgdon, School Music Teacher. M.M., Catholic University of America, 1971. 86 pp. photos.

Hodgdon (1825-1906) taught in Barnstead, New Hampshire and St. Louis, Missouri.

1134   WATKINS, Gladys Manigault. An Analytical and Comparative Study of Two Nineteenth Century Music Courses by Luther Whiting Mason. M.M., Catholic University of America, 1968. 117 pp. illus.

The *National Music Course* and the *Educational Music Course* were both published in Boston.

1135   YOUNG, Pauline. Significant Contributions by New England Music Educators, 1875-1940. M.M.Ed., Boston University, 1951. B12, p. 107.

EDUCATION. PRIMARY AND SECONDARY

1136   ADAMS, Alice. A Study of the Attitudes of Primary Classroom Teachers toward the Teaching of Music in Schools Staffed by the Sisters of Charity of Nazareth, Kentucky. M.M., Catholic University of America, 1968. 57 pp.

1137   AIELLO, Edgar. Music Education in Catholic Schools of Pittsburgh. M.S., Duquesne University, 1941. B8 1353. p. 94.

1138   ALLEN, Fred M. The Relationship of Objectives of the Church Graded Choir Program of the Southern Baptist Convention and Public School Music Programs for the Junior High School Student. M.C.M., Southwestern Baptist Theological Seminary, 1963. B8 1450, p. 101.

1139   *BAE, Owen Richard. A History of Instrumental Music in the Chico Public Schools, 1946-1966. M.A., California State University at Chico, 1967. 145 pp.

1140   BAKER, Genevieve G. An Evaluation of Music in One-Teacher Rural Schools in Arizona. M.A., University of Arizona, 1952. B12, p. 71.

1141   *BALLMER, Emerson A. Historical Survey of Music in the Secondary Schools of Detroit. M.A., Wayne State University, 1945. 80 pp.

1142   BARTLEY, Ruby Ruth. A Brief Survey of the Historical Background and of the Present Status of Music Education in the Negro Schools of Texas. M.A., Southwest Texas State University, 1950. B12, p. 141; B18 SWT-1950-1, p. 42.

1143   BECKETT, Elizabeth. The Status of Music Education in the Public Junior
        Schools of Massachusetts as of the Year 1954-1955. Ed.M., Boston Univer-
        sity, 1955. B12, p. 102.

1144   BILLUPS, Kenneth Brown. The Inclusion of Negro Music as a Course of Study
        in the School Curriculum, M.M., Northwestern University, 1947. B7 60,
        p. 10.

1145   BINGHAM, Carl W. A Comparison of Certain Phases of Musical Ability of
        Negro and White Public School Pupils. M.A., University of Texas, 1925.
        B7 61, p. 10.

1146   BOYER, Benjamin F. A History of Music Education in the Evansville-
        Vanderburgh School Corporation, Evansville, Indiana, from 1853-1978.
        Master's thesis, Southern Illinois University at Edwardsville, 1981. F1 1021,
        p. 66.

1147   *BOYER, Elizabeth Barry. Integration in the Elementary School Program through
        Vocal Music. M.A., Wayne State University, 1948. 119 pp.

1148   BOYTER, Haskell L. The Status of Public School Music among Negroes in
        the State of Georgia. M.M., Eastman School of Music of the University
        of Rochester, 1944. B7 81, p. 13.

1149   BRENTON, Thelma G. A Survey of Music Education in District 51, Mesa
        County, Colorado. M.A., Western State College of Colorado, 1953.
        B12, p. 81.

1150   BURGESS, Eleanor. History of Children's Music in the Public School. Master's
        thesis, Ball State Teachers College, 1951. F1 847, p. 45.

1151   CALDERWOOD, R. D. Status and Trends of Music Education in the Public
        Secondary Schools of Maine. Ed.M., Boston University, 1949. B12, p. 102.

1152   CAMARA, Joseph Anthony. Survey of Junior High School Music in
        Massachusetts. M.M.E., Boston University, 1956. B12, p. 102.

1153 *CAMPBELL, Jay J. A Study of the Values of Public School Music Competition Festivals in Utah, Idaho, Wyoming, and Colorado. M.S., University
of Utah, 1951. 90 pp.

1154 CARLSON, Roy. A Century of Public School Music in Fresno, California.
Master's thesis, California State University at Fresno, 1981. F1 1026, p. 66.

1155 CARPENTER, James F. A Survey and Evaluation of the Music Programs of
State-Supported Training Schools in Seven Southern States. M.M.E.,
Mississippi Southern College, 1954. B12, p. 114.

1156 CAVALIERI, Louise T. A Survey of Existing Music Programs and Scheduling
Practices in Junior High Schools of Large Cities in the United States. Ed.M.,
Boston University, 1951. B12, p. 102.

1157 CIERPIK, Anne F. History in the Development of Music Education in the
Chicago Public Schools. M.A., DePaul University, 1941. B2, p. 27.

1158 *COOKE, Frederick. Survey of Public Music Education in Cincinnati, Ohio.
M.M.Ed., University of Kansas, 1936.

1159 COSARO, Frank. The Status of Music Education in the Public Schools of
Massachusetts as of the Year 1948-1949. Ed.M., Boston University, 1950.
B12, p. 103.

1160 CROOK, Stewart Johnson. Evaluation of the Music Curricula in Seventh-Day
Adventist Academies and Recommendations for Improvement as Based on
a Survey of Former Students. M.S., University of Tennessee, 1962. B8 1404,
p. 98.

1161 DALLAS, George M., Jr. A Study of Music Education in the Meigs County
Public Schools for the Year 1955-1956. M.A., Ohio State University, 1956.
B12, p. 127.

1162 DAY, Robert L. The Development of Music and Music Education in Ector
County. M.M., Hardin-Simmons University, 1956. B18 HSU-1956-1, p.8.

1163 *DENTON, Floyd Chandler. A Study of School Administrators' Opinions of the Values of Public School Music Competition-Festivals in Utah, Idaho, Wyoming, and Colorado. M.S., University of Utah, 1953. 81 pp.

1164 DOWNING, Alvin Joseph. An Analysis of the Administration of High School Instrumental Programs in the State of Florida. M.M., Catholic University of America, 1961. 77 pp.

1165 DURSO, Ann Marie. The Afro-American's Contribution to American Music: A Summer Music Curriculum for Junior High Students. M.M., Catholic University of America, 1972. 85 pp.
Includes a selective and annotated bibliography of audio-visual materials.

1166 ELLSWORTH, Margaret S. Survey and Evaluation of Elementary Music in the Central Community Schools of Decatur County, 1959-1964. Master's thesis, Drake University, 1965. F1 1625, p. 72.

1167 EWERT, John L. Music Education in Mennonite Academies. M.S., Kansas State Teachers College, 1951. B12, p. 97.

1168 FABRIZIO, Mark. Contemporary Trends of American Music in the Secondary School. M.E., Wayne State University, 1956. B12, p. 113.

1169 GHRIST, James Creighton. Instrumental Music Education in the Liberty Union Local School District, Delaware County, Ohio. M.A., Ohio State University, 1956. B12, p. 127.

1170 GIBBS, Mary Inez. A History of Texas, Portrayed in Music, Chronologically Arranged for Use in the Fourth Grade. M.A., Texas Woman's University, 1967. B18 TWU-1967-2, p. 62; L7 (80), p. 319.

1171 GILLETTE, Elizabeth A. Music in Rural High Schools in Maine and New Hampshire. M.M.Ed., Boston University, 1950. B12, p. 104.

1172 GOODE, Anna Johnson. Survey of Music Education in the County Schools of North Carolina. M.A., Boston University, 1954. B12, p. 104.

1173 GREAR, Effie Carter. A Survey of the Progress and Development of Instrumental Music in Selected Negro Public Schools of Florida. M.A., Ohio State University, 1955. B12, p. 127; I3, p. 34.

1174 HEINLEN, Glenn Frederick. A Survey and Evaluation of Instrumental Music Education in the Public Schools of Columbus, Ohio. M.A., Ohio State University, 1951. B12, p. 127.

1175 HENLEY, Glenice. A Historical Survey of Music Appreciation in the Public Schools of the United States. M.A., University of Arizona, 1951. B12, p. 71.

1176 HILL, Mary K. The Status of the Music Specialist in the Catholic Elementary School at Evansville, Indiana. M.A., Catholic University of America, 1969. 66 pp.

1177 HINE, Robert J. A Survey of Summer Music Programs in the Public Schools of Indiana, 1953. M.M., Jordan College of Music of Butler University, 1954. B12, p. 95.

1178 HIXON, Paula Marcheta. The Status of Junior High School Choral Music in the State of Texas. M.M., University of Texas at Austin, 1949. B12, p. 144.

1179 HUGHES, Ola Irene. The Development of Music in the Amarillo Schools, 1889-1942. M.A., Texas Tech University, 1942. B18 TTU-1942-1, p. 58.

1180 JONES, Jamesetta Liddel. The Status of Public School Music in the Negro Elementary Schools of Brunswick County, Virginia. M.M., Chicago Musical College of Roosevelt University, 1956. B12, p. 87.

1181 *KARPOWICH, Michael Paul. The Development of Instrumental Music in the Shasta County Rural Elementary Schools. M.A., California State University at Chico, 1956. 128 pp. illus.

1182 *KEAGLE, Roger M. The Growth and Development of Instrumental Music in the Public Schools of America. M.M., University of Michigan, 1950. B12, p. 50.

1183 KINNEY, Sally J. A History of Public School Instrumental Music in the United States. Master's thesis, Wisconsin State University at Platteville, 1969. F1 1530, p. 70.

1184 LAETSCH, Florence Gardner. A Survey of Catholic Elementary School Music in Texas. M.M., University of Texas at Austin, 1952. B8 1481, p. 104; B12, p. 145; B18 UT-1952-12, p. 73.

1185 LAMBACH, Mona. A Survey of the Early History of the Development of Music Education in the Denver Public Schools, Considering Origins, Functions, and Philosophies of Eminent Music Educators. Master's thesis, Adams State College, 1967. F1 1673, p. 74.

1186 LANE, James William. A Survey of Music Education in the Small Secondary Schools of Illinois. M.A., University of California at Los Angeles, 1950. B12, p. 73.

1187 LASSEN, Martin Gerhardt. A Survey of the Music Programs of the Local Schools of Three Ohio Counties. M.A., Ohio State University, 1955. B12, p. 128.

1188 LEE, James Potter. A Survey of the Music Education Program in the Public Schools of Licking County, Ohio. M.A., Ohio State University, 1951. B12, p. 128.

1189 LENNON, Madison Cuyler. A Survey of Instrumental Music Education in Selected Negro Public Schools of North Carolina. M.A., Ohio State University, 1950. B12, p. 128.

1190 LESTER, Vera Fay. A Critical Survey of Music Instruction in Seventh-Day Adventist Academies of North America. M.M.E., Boston University, 1950. B8 414, p. 31; B12, p. 105.

1191 LIEBERMAN, Milton. Development of Music in the Hartford, Connecticut Public Schools to Their Consolidation in 1934. M.Mus., Hartt College of Music of the University of Hartford, 1951. 41 pp. illus. B12, p. 81.

1192 McCARTY, Diane. The History of Public School Music in Baldwin City, Kansas. M.Mus.Ed., University of Kansas, 1981. F1 1045, p. 67.

1193 McCOWEN, Edward Reginald. The History and Development of Public School Music in Scioto County, State of Ohio. M.M., Northwestern University, 1942. B15 502, p. 19.

1194 *McELWAIN, Juanita. Music in the Curricula of Seventh-Day Adventist Schools of Florida. M.Mus.Ed., Florida State University, 1959. 43 pp. B8 157, p. 13.

1195 McGOVERN, Mary Immaculate. A Survey of Piano Instruction in the Secondary Schools of the Archdiocese of Newark, New Jersey. M.M., Catholic University of America, 1966. 86 pp.

1196 MACHLES, Leonard. A Survey of Music Education in the County Public Schools of Huron County, Ohio. M.A., Ohio State University, 1953. B12, p. 128.

1197 McKOWN, Catherine. Elementary School Music Education in the United States from 1800-1900. M.M., Northwestern University, 1951. B12, p. 91; B15 513, p. 20.

1198 McNATT, Mary R. The Objectives of Public School Music Teaching as Presented in *Music Educators Journal* during the 1965 to 1975 Period. Master's thesis, East Texas State University, 1975. F1 1081, p. 59.

1199 MARR, Marion Emily. A Study of the Traditional Folk Festivals in Iowa — Their Contribution in the School Music Program. M.M., University of Southern California, 1953. 239 pp. I2, p. 241.

1200 *MEACHAM, Elmer D. Changing Philosophies of Music Education in American Public Schools, 1837-1948. M.Mus., Syracuse University, 1948. 108 pp.

1201 *MILLER, Howard Franklin. The History and Present Trends of Inter-School Music Competition in the High Schools of Oregon. M.A., University of Oregon, 1953. 115 pp. B12, p. 133.

1202 *MOORE, Katrina Lee. The History of the Development of Public School Music in Taylor County, Texas. M.S., North Texas State University, 1943. 128 pp. B18 NTSU-1943-6, p. 12.

1203 MORRIS, Robert Othello. The Folk Music of California for the Period 1769 to 1860 Available for Use in the Secondary Social Studies. M.M., University of Southern California, 1948. 163 pp. B14 118, p. 31; I2, p. 201.

1204 *OKAZAKI, Yoshiko. Music Appreciation in Senior High School: The Basic Ideals and a Guide for Teaching Music of Africa, America, and Japan. M.A., University of Michigan, 1976. 127 pp.

1205 O'NEAL, Gloria. Significant Trends, Past and Present, in Junior High School Music Education. M.M., University of Southern California, 1949. B12, p. 78.

1206 OURSLER, Robert Dale. A History of Public School Music in Kansas. M.M., Northwestern University, 1954. B12, p. 92; B15 598, p. 22.

1207 *PARKER, Robert Warren. A History of Music Education in Mount Shasta Schools, 1916-1970. M.A., California State University at Chico, 1970. 158 pp.

1208 *PETRY, Delano Lee. A History of the String Class and Orchestra in the Public Schools of the United States. Master's thesis, University of Michigan, 1955. B12, p. 111.

1209 POLITCO, Jeromine. An Analysis of Music Appreciation in the Catholic Grade Schools of Detroit. M.M., Notre Dame University, 1956. B8 283, p. 22.

1210 PRESCOTT, Marjorie. The Present Status and Trends of Music Education in the Public Elementary Schools of Massachusetts. Ed.M., Boston University, 1952. B12, p. 106.

1211 *PUTNAM, Maxine Schunnep. The Extent to Which the Folk-Song Appears in the Music Study of Elementary Schools. M.A., Florida State University, 1931. 126 pp.

1212 RANDLE, Mary Jo. The Development of the High School Choral Festival in Texas. M.A., Prairie View A & M College, 1965. L7 (79), p. 76.

1213 RAYBURN, Charles Meade. A Survey of the Instrumental Music Program in the Ironton Public Schools for the School Year 1950-1951. M.A., Ohio State University, 1951. B12, p. 129.

1214 READ, John William. A National Survey of Music in Seventh-Day Adventist Secondary Schools. M.M., University of Texas at Austin, 1958. B18 UT-1958-17, p. 81.

1215 REECE, Avalon B. Instrumental Music and Its Contributions to the Negro High Schools and Communities of Oklahoma. M.M., University of Southern California, 1954. B12, p. 78.

1216 ROBBINS, James Edward. An Analysis of the Postgraduate Musical Activities of the Graduates of Pierre High School from the Years 1941 through 1950. M.M., University of South Dakota, 1955. B12, p. 138.

1217 ROBINSON, William Nathaniel. A Music Education Program for Blout County, Tennessee, with Emphasis on Church Music. S.M.M., Union Theological Seminary, 1955. B8 1147, p. 79.

1218 ROYCE, Letha M. Survey of Music Education in Florida Secondary Schools. M.M.E., Florida State University, 1949. B12, p. 84.

1219 SARIBALAS, George Michael. A Study of Music Education in the Fairfield County Public Schools for the Year 1955-1956. M.A., Ohio State University, 1956. B12, p. 129.

1220 *SHACKELFORD, Lucy Evelyn. Arkansas Ozark Folk Songs Presented for Elementary Grades Utilizing the Teaching Procedures of the Kodaly Method of Music Instruction. M.M.Ed., Memphis State University, 1976. 243 pp.

1221 SHINABERY, Elmer Ray. The Study of Instrumental Music Participation by the Graduates of the Public High Schools of Lima, Ohio, 1943-1954. M.A., Ohio State University, 1955. B12, p. 129.

1222 *SLAUGHTER, Nancy Williams. American Folk Music Suitable for Use in the Junior and Senior High School. M.Mus., West Virginia University, 1953. 78 pp.

1223 *SMILEY, Alton Whitney. A Century of American Folk Song Arranged for High School Chorus. Master's thesis, University of Michigan, 1962.

1224 *SMITH, Leonard Adrian. A Discussion of Contests and Festivals in the Public Schools of America. M.S., University of Illinois at Urbana-Champaign, 1943. 76 pp.

1225 SODERBERG, Karl L. A Study of the Band and Music Patron Clubs in the Junior High Schools of Tampa, Florida. M.M.E., Florida State University, 1956. B12, p. 85.

1226 STOLTENBERG, Margaret Mary. The Status of General Music in the Elementary Schools of Selected Cities in the United States with a Population of Approximately 250,000. M.M., Northwestern University, 1955. B12, p. 93.

1227 STRANLUND, Virginia. Swedish Folk Music and Dancing: Use in the American Classroom. M.M., University of Southern California, 1950. B12, p. 79; B14 157, p. 33.

1228 *SUNDERMAN, Carolyn. Using African and Afro-American Music in the General Music Class. Master's thesis, University of Michigan, 1969.

1229 TABOR, Malcolm L. A Study of Music Teacher Certification in the Northwest and California — Western Divisions of the Music Educators National Conference. M.M., University of Southern California, 1951. B12, p. 79.

1230 TAYLOR, Francis Coolidge. Instrumental Music in Boston Public Schools. M.M.Ed., Boston University, 1956. B12, p. 107.

1231 TESACK, Kathryn Elizabeth. A Study of the Oldest Hawaiian Music Culture and a Plan for Its Utilization in the High School Music Courses in That Territory. M.A., University of Washington, 1932. 92 pp. B14 162, p. 34. Includes 23 songs of the old tradition.

1232 TETRICK, William Everal. A Survey of Music Education in the Schools of Pike County, Ohio. M.A., Ohio State University, 1950. B12, p. 130.

1233 THOMSON, Robert Edwin. An Instrumental and Vocal Survey of Music in the Knox County Public Schools, Ohio. M.A., Ohio State University, 1955. B12, p. 130.

1234 TILLMAN, Paul M. The Contributions of the Music Competition-Festival to the Music Education Program in Missouri. M.M., University of Southern California, 1956. B12, p. 80.

1235 *TYLER, Virginia June. A Discussion of American Music To Be Used as a Teacher's Guide for Junior High School Study. Master's thesis, University of Michigan, 1951.

1236 VELCICH, Mary Imelda. The Instrumental Program in Two Diocesan Elementary School Systems of Ohio. M.A., Catholic University of America, 1960. 39 pp.

1237 VON DER HEIDE, Henry J. A Survey of the Music Competition-Festival in the High Schools of Idaho. M.S., University of Idaho, 1956. B12, p. 86.

1238 *WALDROFF, Kenneth. The Historical Development of High School Music Contests in the United States. M.A., University of Portland, 1956. 82 pp.

1239 WARE, Mary Anne. Forty Years of Music in the Lubbock Public Schools (1900-1940). M.A., Texas Tech University, 1941. B18 TTU-1941-2, p. 58.

1240 WEILER, William Joseph. The Status of Music Education in the Parochial Schools, Dioceses of Fargo. M.M., Northwestern University, 1953. B8 246, p. 19; B15 885, p. 31.

1241 WELCH, Thelma Glover. A Study of the Development of Music Programs in Negro Schools of Alachua County, Florida. Master's thesis, Ohio State University, 1958. I3, p. 35.

1242 *WEST, Virginia Brown. A History of Vocal Music in the Louisville Public Schools from 1900-1950. M.Ed., professional paper, University of Louisville, 1953. 87 pp. illus.

1243 WHITE, James R. A Survey of Instrumental Music Instruction in Public Schools of Second Class Cities of Kansas. M.S., Kansas State Teachers College, 1954. B12, p. 98.

1244 WORTHINGTON, Thomas Howard. A History of the Development of Music Education in Austin, Texas. M.M., University of Texas at Austin, 1954. B12, p. 147; B18 UT-1954-34, p. 77.

1245 WRIGHT, Marilyn Jean. Music of the States in the Public Schools in America. M.M.E., Florida State University, 1955. B12, p. 85.

1246 *YUDKIN, Jacqueline Joy. Music Education in the Los Angeles Public Schools, 1890 to 1911. M.A., University of California at Los Angeles, 1975. 120 pp.

EDUCATION. COLLEGES, UNIVERSITIES, CONSERVATORIES, AND OTHER SCHOOLS OF MUSIC

1247 ACKERMAN, J. N. Varied Concepts of Organ and Church Music Departments in Ohio Colleges and Universities. M.A., Ohio State University, 1960. B8 1313, p. 90.

1248 ALEXANDER, Jo Helen. The History of Music Instruction at Howard University from the Beginning to 1942. M.M., Catholic University of America, 1973. 115 pp. B9 4, p. 1.
Contains an appendix of "Instructors in Music from 1869 to 1942."

1249 *BASHAM, Rosemary. The Development of Music Curricula in American Colleges and Universities. M.M.Ed., University of Louisville, 1971. 83 pp. illus.

1250 CATHER, George D. The Trend of Research Studies in Music Education at the University of Southern California, 1924-1949. M.M., University of Southern California, 1950. B12, p. 74.

1251 CHANG, Songsri. Music and Art School for Virginia Polytechnic Institute. Master's thesis, Virginia Polytechnic Institute, 1978. F1 1178, p. 69.

1252 *CHILDRESS, Frances. A Survey of Educational and Professional Background of Piano Teachers in the Colleges and Universities of the United States. M.Mus., North Texas State University, 1948. 66 pp.

1253 COTTINGHAM, Gerald Eugene. A Survey of Northeast Missouri State University Baccalaureate Graduates in Music Education, 1960-1972. M.A., Northeast Missouri State University, 1973. 80 pp. A1 (12/4) 13-06252, p. 439.

1254 COWAN, John R., Jr. A History of the School of Music, Montana State University (1895-1952). M.M.E., Montana State University, 1952. B12, p. 115.

1255   CRAWFORD, Loren Brown. The Music in the Church Supported Colleges and Universities of the State of Kansas. M.M., Eastman School of Music of the University of Rochester, 1939. B8 614, p. 45.

1256   *DALKE, Jacob J. A History of Music Education at the University of Kansas from 1936-1947. M.Mus.Ed., University of Kansas, 1980. 78 pp. illus.

1257   DUERKSEN, Walter. A Survey of Instrumental School Music Activities in Colleges and Universities of the United States. M.M., Northwestern University, 1938. B15 197, p. 11.

1258   *DuRANT, Charles B. The Effectiveness of the 1970 Church Music Institute. M.C.M., Southern Baptist Theological Seminary, 1971. 92 pp.

1259   EVANS, Jesse Gillette. A Study of Music Theory Teaching in Ohio Colleges and Universities. M.A., Ohio State University, 1954. B12, p. 127.

1260   FARRIER, Walter. Academic Training in the Field of Church Music in the United States. M.M., University of Southern California, 1963. B8 38, p. 5.

1261   FIELD, George Franklin. Resource Music for Teaching American History. Ed.M., Boston University, 1950. B12, p. 103.

1262   FLEMING, Frances. A Study of Piano Pedagogy Based on Research in the University of Texas Piano Project. M.M., University of Texas at Austin, 1956. B12, p. 144.

1263   GILLILAND, John Henry. The Department of Music of San Diego State College from 1898 to 1972. M.A., San Diego State College, 1972. 101 pp. L13, p. 3.

1264   GREENE, Mary Hermana. An Historical Study of the Octavo School of Musical Art, Albany, New York. M.M., Catholic University of America, 1969. 106 pp. The school was founded in September, 1924. Included are a number of recital programs.

1265   GRETTIE, Donald V. The History and Development of the Hull House School of Music. M.M., Northwestern University, 1960. B2, p. 129.

1266   HAYES, Marie Therese. The History of the Juilliard School from Its Inception to 1973. M.M., Catholic University of America, 1974. 216 pp.

Based, in part, on the tenures of the four directors of the school: Frank Damrosch (1905-37), Ernest Hutcheson (1937-45), William Schuman (1945-62), and Peter Mennin (1962-present). Also discussed are the Juilliard Opera Theater, the American Opera Center, the Juilliard Orchestra, and the Juilliard Dance Division.

1267   HAZLEWOOD, Mark Phillip. A Survey of Northeast Missouri State University Master of Arts Graduates in Music Education, 1965-1976. M.A., Northeastern Missouri State University, 1977. 66 pp. A1 (16/2) 13-10911, p. 90.

1268   HOLVIK, Karl M. Music in the Evangelical Lutheran Church Colleges. M.A., Eastman School of Music of the University of Rochester, 1947. 259 pp.

1269   *KIRCHOFF, Kim Allyson. A History of Music Education at the University of Kansas from 1866-1936. M.M.Ed., University of Kansas, 1976. 133 pp.

1270   *LACKEY, Sue Andra. The History of Music at Eastern Illinois University, 1899-1963. M.A., Eastern Illinois University, 1967. 80 pp.

1271   LaDUE, George William. Music in Twenty Midwestern Colleges and Universities. M.M., Northwestern University, 1949. B15 436, p. 18.

1272   *LAUGHLIN, Lynn Ann. The Development of the Music Therapy Program at the University of Kansas from Its Inception through 1971. M.M.Ed., University of Kansas, 1975. 81 pp. illus.

1273   *LESTER, Paul Frederick. The Development of Music at the University of Illinois and a History of the School of Music. M.S., University of Illinois at Urbana-Champaign, 1943. 134 pp.

1274   *LEWIS, James Robert. Generating Computer Music at New Mexico State University. M.S., New Mexico State University, 1978. 239 pp. illus.

Includes a cassette, 2-track, 60 minutes.

1275   LINDGREN, Frank E. A Content Analysis of Research Studies in Vocal Music Education at the University of Southern California from 1930-1955, with a View of Establishing Areas of Needful Research. M.M., University of Southern California, 1956. B12, p. 77.

1276 McGRATH, Roberta Mary. A History of the Boston Conservatory of Music. M.M., Catholic University of America, 1968. 47 pp. B13, p. 31.

This study is divided into three sections: the early years under its director, Julius Eichberg; the "period of reorganization," 1896-1902; and 1933 to the present.

1277 McHENRY, Donna K. A Study of Class Voice Instruction in Eleven Southern States. M.M.E., Mississippi Southern College, 1955. B12, p. 114.

1278 *MAYBEE, Harper C. The Development of the Music Education Curriculum in the State Colleges of Education in Michigan. Master's thesis, University of Michigan, 1951. B12, p. 110.

1279 MILES, Dorothy Wilson. A History of the School of Music of Baylor University. M.M., Baylor University, 1950. B18 BU-1950-2, p. 2.

1280 *MONEY, Mary Grace. A History of the Louisville Conservatory of Music and Music at the University of Louisville, 1907-1935. M.M.Ed., University of Louisville, 1976. 121 pp. A1 (15/4) 13-09727, p. 231.

1281 MORRIS, Robert Bower. A Survey of the Various Schools, Seminaries, and Conservatories in the United States of America Offering Training in the Field of Sacred Music. S.M.M., Union Theological Seminary, 1947. B8 1091, p. 76.

1282 MORRISON, Donald Eugene. The Sacred Music Degrees (Protestant) in the Colleges, Universities, and Seminaries of the United States (1956-57). S.M.M., Union Theological Seminary, 1957. B8 1092, p. 76.

1283 NELSON, Carl Leonard. The Teaching of Music in the Private Junior Colleges of the United States. M.S., Education, Northwestern University, 1934. B15 570, p. 22.

1284 NIEMIEC, Mary Martinelle. A Study of Programs for Gifted Students in Music and the Program at the Villa Maria Institute of Music, Buffalo, New York. M.M., Catholic University of America, 1967. 74 pp.

1285 *ORLANDO, Vincent A. An Historical Study of the Origin and Development of the College of Music of Cincinnati. M.M., University of Cincinnati, 1946. 280 pp. illus.

1286 PAGE, Patricia Ann. The Westminster Choir College. S.M.M., Union Theological Seminary, 1953. B8 1113, p. 77.

1287 PETREE, Colbert G. A Survey of the History of Music and Music Education at the University of Tennessee. Master's thesis, University of Tennessee at Knoxville, 1965. F1 1669, p. 74.

1288 PRIEST, Jimmie Ray. A History of the West Texas State University Music Department, 1917-1965. M.A., West Texas State University, 1965. B18 WTS-1965-3, p. 98; L7 (81), p. 446.

1289 RENTSCHLER, David M. A History of the School Music of West Chester College from Its Inception to 1967. Master's thesis, West Chester University, 1968. F1 1674, p. 76.

1290 *RHEA, Claude H., Jr. An Investigation of the Musical Offerings for Theological Students in the Southern Baptist Colleges, Universities and Seminaries. M.Mus.Ed., Florida State University, 1954. 51 pp. B12, p. 84.

1291 *SCHAEFER, Donald George. Contributions of the McCune School of Music and Art to Music Education in Utah, 1917-1957. M.A., Brigham Young University, 1962. 123 pp. illus.; plates.

1292 *SOUDER, Marian Jo. The College-Conservatory of Music of Cincinnati, 1955-1962: A History. M.M., University of Cincinnati, 1970. 147 pp.

1293 STEELE, Charlotte L. A Study of Music Offerings in Eight Florida Junior Colleges. M.M.E., Florida State University, 1951. B12, p. 85.

1294 SWINNEY, Winston S. An Evaluation and Critical Analysis of the Music Program in the Thirteen Public Supported White Junior Colleges in Mississippi. M.M.E., Mississippi Southern College, 1952. B12, p. 115.

1295 *TEAGUE, Webster W., Jr. A Study of Church Music Offerings in Church-Related Colleges in Alabama, Florida, and Georgia. M.Mus.Ed., Florida State University, 1956. 73 pp. illus. B12, p. 85.

1296 *THAYER, Barry Lee. Music Vale Seminary and Normal Academy of Music. M.Mus.Ed., Hartt College of Music of the University of Hartford, 1964. 47 pp.

1297 *TROUT, Philip Edwin. A Study of Certain Factors in the Training of Church Musicians by the Six Affiliated Colleges of the Church of the Brethren. M.Mus., Florida State University, 1958. 86 pp. illus.

1298 *TURK-ROGÉ, Janet Louise Coulson. A History of the Fine Arts School at the University of Kansas. M.M., University of Kansas, 1941. 230 pp.

EDUCATION. ASSOCIATIONS

1299 ESKRIDGE, Charles Sanford. History of the Texas Music Educators Association. M.S., Texas Tech University, 1943. B18 TTU-1943-1, p. 58.

1300 HACKNEY, C. R. A History of the Texas Music Educators Association. M.A., Sam Houston State University, 1939. B18 SHS-1939-1, p. 31.

1301 HAID, Maris Stella. The Organization and Influence of the National Catholic Music Educators Association. M.A., Ohio State University, 1947. B8 1320, p. 91.

1302 *HUNTER, Boyd M. A History of the Utah Music Education Association: Origin to 1965. M.A., Brigham Young University, 1968. F1 1664, p. 74. 184 pp. illus.

1303 JOHNSON, Emory M. A Historical Survey of Leadership Training, Music in Christian Education, and University Work as Organized and Promoted by the Board of Christian Education, Presbyterian Church, U.S.A. M.A., San Francisco Theological Seminary, 1954. B8 17, p. 4.

1304 *JOHNSON, Peter R. The Music Education Department of the National Education Association, 1884-1909. Master's thesis, University of Michigan, 1959.

1305 KUBACH, William Raymond. A Survey of Music Education in District Seven of the Ohio Music Education Association. M.A., Ohio State University, 1956. B12, p. 128.

1306 MURPHY, Rose Marie. A Historical Survey of the National Catholic Music Educators Association. M.A., Catholic University of America, 1959. 95 pp.

1307 SHARTLE, Paul. The Development of the Ohio Music Education Association. M.A., Ohio State University, 1952. B2 p. 206; B12, p. 129.

1308 SOWELL, Brady O. A History of the Texas Music Educators Association, 1940-1953. M.A., Sam Houston State University, 1953. B12, p. 141; B18 SHS-1953-5, p. 32; F1 1186, p. 55.

1309 THERIOT, Leon R. A History of the Texas Music Educators Association, 1953-59. M.A., Sam Houston State University, 1959. B18 SHS-1959-5, p. 33.

EDUCATION. SPECIAL STUDIES

1310 *ANDERSON, Grant Lester. Some Educational Aspects of the Music Training Program of the Church of Jesus Christ of Latter-Day Saints, 1935-1969. M.A., Brigham Young University, 1976. 156 pp. B17 (10/1) 1700, p. 97.

Includes a historical description of the music training program.

1311 ANDERSON, Thomas Wynn. A Study of Musical Training in Graded Choirs of Southern Baptist Churches. M.M., University of Texas, 1956. B8 1473, p. 103.

1312 BALARZS, Mary Ellen Hawthorne. A Study of the Singing Schools in Massachusetts and Virginia and Potential Application of the Singing School Process in Contemporary Society. M.M., Virginia Commonwealth University, 1975. 105 pp.

1313 *BANE, Mildred. The American Folk Song in Music Education. M.M., Illinois Wesleyan University, 1945. B7 37 p. 7; I2, p. 181.

1314 BENNETT, Barbara. The History and Development of Class String Methodology in the United States. M.M., Baylor University, 1967. B18 BU-1967-1, p. 4.

1315 *BRIDGES, Rodney Gustav. Curricular Change in Music as It Relates to the Afro-American Idiom. M.M.Ed., Florida State University, 1971. 87 pp. illus.

1316 BRIGGS, Sharon Lee. A Listening Guide Using American Vocal Music. M.M.Ed., University of Louisville, 1980. 178 pp. A1 (19/4) 1316499, p. 330.

1317 BROWN, Judith A. A Survey of Selected Music Reading Methods in Nineteenth Century America. Master's thesis, Hardin-Simmons University, 1978. A2 3396, p. 144.

1318 BRUMLEY, Thomas Edwin. The Virtuoso Age in American Music History and Its Instruction via Television. M.M., University of Texas at Austin, 1971. B18 UT-1971-6, p. 95.

1319 CAREY, Kathryn M. A Study of Class Piano Instruction in Eleven Southern States. M.M.E., Mississippi Southern College, 1953. B12, p. 114.

1320 *COLOMA, Gemma L. Foreign Influences on American Music Education within the Last Ten Years. Master's thesis, University of Michigan, 1969.

1321 CROOK, J. Don. An Investigation of the Historical, Philosophical and Financial Activities of Choral Workshop Programs in the United States. Master's thesis, University of Tennessee at Knoxville, 1963. F1 1429, p. 64.

1322 *DRABKIN, Jane Lee Daugherty. The Use of the Optacon for Facilitating the Reading of Sighted Music Notation by Blind Persons. M.M.Ed., University of Kansas, 1976. 59 pp. illus.

1323 FIRNHABER, Oscar Ernst. A Study and an Evaluation of Boy Choir and Children's Choir Schools of the United States. M.A., University of Iowa, 1949. B12, p. 97.

1324 *GANTT, Alvin V. Jack. The Eighteenth Century Singing School and Its Effect on the Development of American Church Music. M.C.M., Southwestern Baptist Theological Seminary, 1965. 77 pp. illus. B18 SBS-1966-2, p. 45.

1325 GARABEDIAN, Charles. Music Education in the Massachusetts Community. M.M.Ed., Boston University, 1954. B12, p. 103.

1326 GIBBON, Gladys. Education in Corpus Christi, Texas, 1846-1900. M.S., Texas A & I University, 1941. B18 TA & I-1941-1, p. 46.

1327   GILFILLAN, John Alexander. Singing-Schools in America. M.Mus., Eastman School of Music of the University of Rochester, 1939. 144 pp.

1328   GONS, Marie Otken. Survey of American Music Textbooks, 1830-1890. M.E., Rutgers University, 1974. 118 pp. illus. F1 1042, p. 55.

The introductions of forty music books are studied in terms of techniques, style, and materials. The sources of unusual examples of notations including the "fasola" system, shape notes, and numeral notation are given and their use explained. Also discussed are the roles of William Channing Woodbridge and Lowell Mason in disseminating Pestalozzian philosophy in America. The last section of the survey contains a useful anthology of songs from the music textbooks. The songs are grouped according to the following categories: songs to encourage school attendance, patriotic songs, songs that teach subject skills, exercise songs, songs for girls, songs for teachers, songs about death and illness, temperance songs, holiday songs, and potpourri.

1329   GONZALES, Marie Infanta. The Contribution of the Spirituals to Music Education. M.M., Catholic University of America, 1962. 51 pp. K3, p. 47.

Includes a review of previous studies, the origin of the spiritual, and a survey of the literature.

1330   GOODALE, David W. Music and Music Education in the United States Army. M.A., Catholic University of America, 1963. 87 pp. K3, p. 48.

Discusses the history, structure, and mission of music in the U.S. Army.

1331   *GRAY, Nancy Jean. Women in Music Education. M.S., Syracuse University, 1975. 88 pp.

1332   *GREGORY, Thomas B. An Analysis of the Effect of Various Types of Rhythmic Notation in the Errors Made in Music Sight-Reading. Master's thesis, Education, Kent State University, 1967. 134 pp. illus.

Contains a history of sight-reading teaching and testing.

1333   HARTWIG, Charlotte Mae. An Intercultural Approach to Music Education in Underdeveloped Areas. M.M.E., Indiana University, 1967. 73 pp. B17 (1/2) 1201, p. 51.

Southern black music compared to traditional music of the Baganda, a tribe in East Africa.

1334 *HILL, Terry S. A Comprehensive Analysis of Selective Orchestral Music Lists Published in the United States for Educational Purposes between 1962 and 1976. M.A., Brigham Young University, 1977. 66 pp. B17 (11/1) 1662, p. 98.

1335 *HOBBS, John Marion. Development of Singing Schools. Master's thesis, Northeast Missouri State University, 1955. 81 pp.

1336 HURT, William Jackson. The Beginnings of Music Education Broadcasting. M.M., Southern Methodist University, 1948. E1, p. 28.

1337 JONES, Geraldine Wells. The Negro Spiritual and Its Use as an Integral Part of Music Education. M.M.Ed., Hartt College of Music of the University of Hartford, 1953. B8 128, p. 11; B12, p. 81.

1338 *JUDKINS, Edith Margueritte. The American Singing School and Its Terminating Activities in the North. M.A., Tulane University, 1963. 156 pp. illus. B6 J92, p. 19; B8 363, p. 28.

1339 *KAY, Robert Louis. A Comparative Study of Selected American Folk Songs Found in Some Current Graded Music Textbooks as Related to Source Materials. M.A., University of California at Los Angeles, 1972.

1340 *KLINE, Mary Francella. A Study of American Music with the Teaching of American History. M.M., University of Michigan, 1951. B12, p. 112.

1341 *KNOBLOCH, Ann-Lee. A Comparative Study of Six Well-Known Stringed-Methods in Use in the United States. M.Mus.Ed., Florida State University, 1952. 96 pp. illus.

1342 LEWIS, Thelma Marguerite. Twenty-Five Negro Spirituals Arranged for Use in Schools with Explanatory Notes and Illustrations. M.M.Ed., Boston University, 1950. B12, p. 105.

1343 LIGHT, Patricia A. Choir School Conferences in California. M.A., San Francisco Theological Seminary, 1956. B8 18, p. 4.

1344 LOPEZ, Elmo. The History and Development of Music Education in Laredo, Texas. M.M., University of Texas at Austin, 1957. B18 UT-1957-10, p. 80; F1 1030, p. 48.

1345 McGILL, Lynn D. A Study of Shape-Note Music as a Resource and as a System of Teaching Music. Master's thesis, University of Tennessee at Knoxville, 1968. F1 1662, p. 76.

1346 *MIKITA, Andrew. A Critical History of School Music Contests and Festivals in the United States. Master's thesis, University of Illinois at Urbana-Champaign, 1942. 73 pp.

1347 MILLER, Kathryn L. A Comparison of Several Keyboard Instruction Books Used in the New England Colonies. Master's thesis, Baylor University, 1979. A2 3155, p. 137.

1348 *MOON, Kathleen. Sacred Music in Public Education: A Critical Analysis of the Issues. M.A., University of California at Los Angeles, 1977. 126 pp.

1349 MURPHY, Charles Robert. History of the Piano Class in the United States — An Approach to Piano Playing for Class Instruction (Two Parts: Method and Supplement). M.M.Ed., Boston University, 1950. B12, p. 106.

1350 *NEIL, Lantha-Dale. The Influence of European Educators on School Music Education in the United States. M.S., University of Illinois at Urbana-Champaign, 1941. 122 pp. illus.

1351 PEARLMAN, Blanche. The Modern Dance in Education in America. A Study of Its Background, Influences, and Present Trends. M.A., New York University, 1935. C2 498, p. 38.

1352 QUEEN, James L. Fasola Solmization in England and America. M.M., Baylor University, 1971. B18 BU-1971-7, p. 5.

1353 *RALPH, Marie Michel. Songs, Ballads, and Poems of Value in the Teaching of the Revolutionary War and the Civil War. M.A., Education, Teachers College at the University of Cincinnati, 1948. 189 pp. I2, p. 202.

1354 *ROTHERT, Harold Hanson. The Growth and Development of Music Education in an Historic Town: Madison, Indiana (1892-1936). M.M., Indiana University, 1945. 110 pp.

1355 RUBINSTEIN, Lucille. An Historical Study of the Dance in Education in the United States in the First Quarter of the Twentieth Century. M.A., New York University, 1940. C2 563, p. 43.

1356 SACCA, Vincent John. Teaching and Correlating Music with Socialized History of the United States from 1500 to 1900. Ed.M., Boston University, 1952. B12, p. 107.

1357 SANDERSON, Alice Louise. The Status of Music Instruction in Schools for the Blind in the United States. M.S., Education, Northwestern University, 1933. B15 692, p. 25.

1358 SMIRIGA, Mary Esther. The Relationship of John Cage and His Philosophy to Contemporary Objectives in Music Education. M.M., Catholic University of America, 1974. 103 pp.

1359 SMITH, Charles Howard. Academic Training in the Field of Sacred Music in American Educational Institutions: Present Status and Influence in School and the Protestant Church. M.M., Southern California University, 1949. B8 86, p. 8.

1360 SNYDER, Joan M. The Spanish Influence on Music Education in Early America. M.M., Catholic University of America, 1966. 62 pp. K3, p. 104.

1361 *SOIFER, Joseph Harry. The Folk Spirit in Contemporary American Music and Its Use in Music Education. M.Mus.Ed., Hartt College of Music of the University of Hartford, 1951. 305 pp.

1362 SPEAKER, Lucy Lee. The Status of the Music Education Program in the Churches of the Texas-Louisiana Synod of the United Lutheran Church in America. M.M., University of Texas, 1958. B8 1491, p. 104; B18 UT-1958-23, p. 82.

1363 *TACHIBANA, Taeko. A Comparative Study of Elementary School Music Textbooks in the United States of America and in Japan. M.M.Ed., University of Kansas, 1979. 87 pp.

1364 WOLVERTON, Josephine. Eighteenth Century Music Teaching in America. M.M., Northwestern University, 1937. B15 927, p. 32.

1365 WUNDERLICH, Joyce C. A History of the Teaching of Sight Singing in the United States, 1721-1960. Master's thesis, Ithaca College, 1960. F1 1420, p. 64.

THESES 3 *Theory*

THEORETICAL STUDIES

1366 *AUSTIN, John Charles. A Survey of the Influence of Heinrich Schenker on American Music Theory and Its Pedagogy since 1940. M.M., North Texas State University, 1974. 100 pp. A1 (13/2) 13-06953, p. 87.

1367 *CHANCY, James Melvin. Supplement to Twentieth Century Harmony by Vincent Persichetti. M.A., San Diego State University, 1974. 133 pp.

1368 *CORDES, Robert. Existentialism and Phenomenology: Objectivism and Non-purposiveness in the Music of Selected Twentieth Century Composers. M.A., California State University at Fullerton, 1970. 202 pp.

1369 DEVORE, Richard O. Theories of Harmony in the United States to 1900. Master's thesis, University of Iowa, 1982. A2 2974, p. 144.

1370 KOREY, Judith A. A Survey of Contemporary Trends in Music Notation. M.A., Catholic University of America, 1976. 130 pp. illus.

American composers discussed include Elliott Carter, Leon Kirchner, Earle Brown, Kenneth Gaburo, George Crumb, Larry Austin, Lukas Foss, and Robert Moran.

1371 *LIEMOHN, Edwin. The Background and Contributions of American Authors of Music Theory Texts. Master's thesis, Eastman School of Music of the University of Rochester, 1937.

1372 *METZ, Paul Wesley. A Study of Harry Partch: With Particular Emphasis on His Microtonal Tuning System. M.M., University of Cincinnati, 1978. 103 pp. illus.

ANALYSES OF WORKS

1373 ADAMS, Florence Chenoweth. Structural Form and Analysis of Ernest Bloch's *Schelomo.* M.Mus., Eastman School of Music of the University of Rochester, 1955. 59 pp.

1374 *ADAMS, Kenny L. Pandiatonicism in Three Ballets by Aaron Copland. M.Mus., North Texas State University, 1972. 86 pp. illus.
The works discussed are *Appalachian Spring, Billy the Kid,* and *Rodeo.*

1375 ADAMSON, Cynthia Louise. An Analysis of Menotti's *The Unicorn, the Gorgon, and the Manticore* and a Comparison to Vecchi's *L'Amfiparnasso.* M.A., Eastman School of Music of the University of Rochester, 1959. 99 pp.

1376 *AGEE, Barbara Lee. A Stylistic Analysis of the Sonata for Piano by Roy Henry Johnson. M.M., Eastman School of Music of the University of Rochester, 1956. 80 pp. illus.

1377 ALLEN, Debra Kaye. Drama and Characterization in Opera Settings of *A Midsummer Night's Dream* by Britten and Siegmeister. M.M., North Texas State University, 1982. 209 pp. A1 (21/2) 1319387, p. 181.

1378 ALLEN, Sandra G. Salient Formal and Thematic Structures in the Four Violin Sonatas of Charles Ives. Master's thesis, University of Washington, 1966. B13, p. 30.

1379 *ALLISON, Rosalie. The Style of Roy Harris, as Approached through a Study of Piano and Chamber Works. M.A., Eastman School of Music of the University of Rochester, 1947. 87 pp. illus.
Includes a list of the works of Harris, pp. 83-87.

1380 *ALTENBERND, Nicholas. Form and Rhythm in the Music of Elliott Carter (1946-52). M.A., Cornell University, 1971. 106 pp.

1381 *ANDERSEN, Lawrence Bert. An Analysis of Textures in Compositions of Four Contemporary Composers. M.A., Brigham Young University, 1957. 119 pp. The one American composer discussed is Roy Harris.

1382 *ANDERSON, Wayne D. Twentieth Century Choral Settings of the Twenty-Third Psalm: An Analysis. M.A., West Texas State University, 1974. 191 pp. American composers include Jean Berger, Joseph W. Clokey, Katherine K. Davis, Alan Hovhaness, Ardis M. Irvin, Jack Dane Litten, Austin C. Lovelace, George Matterling, Thomas Matthews, Lloyd Pfautsch, and George Wald. Includes scores of the choral settings being analyzed.

1383 ANDREWS, Patricia Lee. Compositional Freedom of Choice in Selected Works by Milton Babbitt, Pierre Boulez, and John Cage. M.M., University of Texas at Austin, 1971. B18 UT-1971-3, p. 95.

1384 BAKKER, Anne J. Elliott Carter: The Maturing of the Metric Modulation Concept. M.M., Virginia Commonwealth University, 1976.

1385 BALDWIN, Marvette R. An Analysis of the Vocal Style of Howard Swanson. M.M., Bowling Green State University, 1977. 33 pp. A2 3384, p. 144; K1 (22) 3212, p. 200.

1386 BALES, Noreen Putnam. The Piano Music of Houston Bright — A Stylistic Analysis. M.A., West Texas State University, 1968. B18 WTS-1968-1, p. 98.

1387 BARNES, Marsha Korth. Aspects of Pitch Structure in Elliott Carter's Sonata for Cello and Piano, 1948. M.M., University of Maryland, 1975. 58 pp. illus.

1388 BARTMANN, John W. A Structural Analysis of Two Works for Trumpet and Piano: *Sonata* by Paul Hindemith, *Sonata* by Kent Kennan. Master's thesis, Northern Illinois University, 1976. F1 1602, p. 71.

1389 *BAUER, Joyce Griffin. An Analysis of the Third Symphony of Roy Harris. Master's thesis, Eastman School of Music of the University of Rochester, 1948.

1390   BAYREUTHER, Florence. Religious Texts Used by Modern American Composers: A Critical Bibliographical Essay. Master's thesis, Library Science, Long Island University, 1971. G3, p. 5.

1391   BELFY, Jeanne M. A Brief Chronology and Analysis of the Basic Style-Trends of the Music of John Cage. Master's thesis, Ball State University, 1978. A2 3387, p. 144.

1392   *BESTOR, Charles Lemon. An Analysis of the "Rhapsody in Blue" by George Gershwin. M.Mus., University of Illinois at Urbana-Champaign, 1952. 183 pp.

1393   *BOELZNER, David Ernest. The Symphonies of Leonard Bernstein: An Analysis of Motivic Character and Form. M.A., University of North Carolina at Chapel Hill, 1977. 205 pp.

1394   *BOMFORD, Ruth Payne. The Interdependence of Music and Poetry as Taught by Sidney Lanier. M.Mus.Ed., Florida State University, 1951. B9 38, p. 5; B12, p. 83.

1395   *BOSTIC, Stephen Julian. The Use of Imitative Technique by Modern American Composers. M.A., Eastman School of Music of the University of Rochester, 1959. 43 pp. illus.

1396   *BRACKENRIDGE, Margaret Elaine. A Stylistic and Structural Analysis of David Stanley Smith's Sonata in A, Opus 51. M.M., North Texas State University, 1944. 57 pp. illus.

1397   *BRIDENTHAL, Deloris. A Stylistic Analysis of the Concerto for Two Pianos and Orchestra by Harl McDonald. M.Mus., North Texas State University, 1945. 36 pp. illus.

1398   BRILLHART, Jerome Bellamy. Comparative Analysis of Two Symphonies by William Schuman as Documentation of a Critical Judgment. M.M., University of Texas at Austin, 1960. B18 UT-1960-3, p. 83.

1399   *BROWNE, Douglas A. Analyses of Three Songs by Charles Ives. M.A., West Texas State University, 1974. 33 pp.

The three songs are "Tom Sails Away," "The Cage," and "The Circus Band."

1400 *BRYANT, Mary Louise. Form in Ten Contemporary American Piano Sonatas. M.A., University of Kentucky, 1953. 91 pp. illus.

1401 *BURCHAK, Jay Wilbur. An Analysis of Leo Sowerby's Sonata for Trumpet and Piano. M.M., Eastman School of Music of the University of Rochester, 1954. 79 pp. illus.

1402 CALDWELL, George O. A Comparison of Selected Material in Stravinsky's "Fire Bird" with Traditional Negro Folk Music. M.A., University of Iowa, 1932. B7 113, p. 17.

1403 *CHADWICK, Muriel Ann. The Variation Technique as Seen in Selected Piano Works of the Twentieth Century. M.M., Southern Illinois University, 1965. 151 pp.
Includes a discussion of Aaron Copland's *Piano Variations,* pp. 39-66.

1404 *CHRISTIE, John P. A Structural Analysis of the "Symphony for Band" by Vincent Persichetti. M.A., Eastern Illinois University, 1971. 41 pp.

1405 *CLOUGH, Gregory Jay. Sonatas and Interludes for Prepared Piano (1946-48) by John Cage: An Analytical Basis for Interpretation. M.M., University of Arkansas at Fayetteville, 1968. 92 pp.

1406 *COKE, Austin Neil. An Analysis of Some of the Purely Instrumental Works of Samuel Barber between the Years 1930 to 1950. M.A., California State University at Long Beach, 1968. 82 pp.

1407 *CONNOR, Patricia Josephine. A Critical Analysis of the Harmonic Idiom of Songs of Claude Debussy and Its Influence on Compositions of Charles Loeffler and John Alden Carpenter. M.M., North Texas State University, 1941. 98 pp. illus. B18 NTSU-1941-5, p. 10.

1408 COREY, Dean Patterson. An Analysis of Five Works of Contemporary American Band Literature. M.M.E., Texas Christian University, 1961. 134 pp. B18 TCU-1961-1, p. 52.

1409 *COX, Sidney Thurber. The Autogenetic Principle in the Melody Writing of Roy Harris. M.A., Cornell University, 1948. 25 pp.

1410   CRABB, James C. An Analysis and Comparison of Fifteen Marches by John Philip Sousa. M.A., Sam Houston State University, 1962. B18 SHS-1962-2, p. 33.

1411   CRAIG, Barbara Peterson. A Stylistic Comparison of Works by Three Texas Choral Composers: Houston Bright, Theron Kirk, and Lloyd Pfautsch. M.A., Sam Houston State University, 1970. B17 SHS-1970-3, p. 35.

1412   *CRAWFORD, Katharine Elizabeth. A Critical Analysis of the Choral Works of Roy Harris. M.S., North Texas State University, 1942. 73 pp. illus. B18 NTSU-1942-3, p. 11.

1413   *CREIGH, Robert Hugh. Stylistic Characteristics of Randall Thompson's Choral Music. M.Ed., Central Washington University, 1970. 37 pp. F1 1442, p. 69.

1414   CRIM, Jack Smith. The String Quintets of John Frederick Peter: An Analysis. M.M., Cincinnati College-Conservatory of Music, 1956. 56 pp. J1.

1415   DAVIDSON, Marilyn M. A Stylistic Analysis of American Piano Sonatas from 1900-1930. M.M., University of Texas at Austin, 1971. B18 UT-1971-13, p. 96.

1416   *DAVIS, Richard Allen. The Vocal Melody of Menotti's *The Consul*. M.M., West Virginia University, 1970. 65 pp.

1417   DeSIMONE, Carol M. An Analysis of *The Medium*. M.A., Eastman School of Music of the University of Rochester, 1963. 71 pp.

1418   *DeTAR, Francis Edward. An Analysis of Billy Jim Layton's String Quartet, Op. 4. M.A., Eastman School of Music of the University of Rochester, 1973. 75 pp. illus.

1419   *DEWEY, James William. An Analysis of "Little Bat" in the Opera *Susannah*. M.Ed., Central Washington University, 1968. 29 pp.
        The composer of the work is Carlisle Floyd.

1420   DOWDY, Juliet Catherine. The Evolution of a Modern Technique Exemplified in the Works of Wallingford Riegger. M.Mus., Eastman School of Music of the University of Rochester, 1938. 99 pp.

1421 DOWNEY, John. An Analysis of the Jazz Influence in Each of the Following Contemporary Works: Sextet for Clarinet, Piano and Strings, by Aaron Copland; La Creation du Monde, by Darius Milhaud; L'Histoire du Soldat, by Igor Stravinsky. Master's thesis, Ithaca College, 1960. F1 1328, p. 61.

1422 DRANE, Sharon Suzanne. An Analysis and Production of *The Music Man.* M.A., Theater, North Texas State University, 1979. A1 (17/4) 1313109, p. 294.

Includes an investigation of the reviews of the original production.

1423 DRIGGETT, Daniel S. An Analysis of Five Songs by Ernst Bacon. Master's thesis, Northern Illinois University at DeKalb, 1964. F1 1452, p. 65.

1424 *EAGLE, Nancy Louise. The Pianoforte Sonatas of Edward A. MacDowell: A Style-Critical Study. M.A., University of North Carolina, 1952. 194 pp. B6 E11, p. 13; B10, p. 17; K5, p. 202.

1425 *ECKERS, Roger Bruce. An Analysis of Paul Creston's Sonata for E♭ Alto Saxophone and Piano. M.A., Eastman School of Music of the University of Rochester, 1966. 87 pp.

1426 *ELLIS, Lydia Kathryn. An Analysis of Barbara Kolb's Solitaire for Piano, Vibraphone and Tape. M.M., West Virginia University, 1978. 93 pp.

1427 EMLEY, Joseph Frederick. Melodic Characteristics of the Songs and Compositions for Violoncello of Samuel Barber. M.Mus., Eastman School of Music of the University of Rochester, 1957. 99 pp.

1428 *ENGLE, Susan Stancil. A Harmonic Analysis and Comparison of Selected Twelve-Tone Compositions of Krenek and Cordero. M.M., Indiana University at Bloomington, 1969. 145 pp.

1429 ETTER, David D. The Choral Style of George Lynn. Master's thesis, University of Missouri-Kansas City, 1979. A2 3108, p. 135.

1430 FASSINO, Frederick Joseph. A Formal and Stylistic Analysis of *Symphony for Band* by Morton Gould. M.A., Sam Houston State University, 1971. B18 SHS-1971-1, p. 35.

1431 *FERTIG, Judith Pinnolis. An Analysis of Selected Works of the American Composer Miriam Gideon (1906-): In Light of Contemporary Jewish Musical Trends. M.M., University of Cincinnati, 1978. 185 pp. discog.; illus. B17 (12/12) 3020, p. 194.

Includes a review of the history of reform synagogue music and an analysis of *The Hound of Heaven.*

1432 *FISKE, Judy Mayberry. An Analysis of the Solo Organ Works of Daniel Pinkham. M.C.M., Southern Baptist Theological Seminary, 1979. 62 pp.

1433 *FLEISHER, Gerald. Concerto for Clarinet and String Orchestra by Aaron Copland: A Stylistic Analysis. M.A., Eastman School of Music of the University of Rochester, 1961. 77 pp. illus.

1434 FLERLAGE, Alice. The Use of Pre-Existent Material in the Works of Peter Maxwell Davies and George Rochberg. Master's thesis, Northern Illinois University, 1979. A2 3111, p. 135.

1435 *FLINN, Wesley C. Analysis of the Published Songs of Charles T. Griffes. M.A., San Diego State College, 1962. 232 pp. illus.

1436 *FLOYD, Annette Rahm. An Analysis of the Published Dance Music of Wallingford Riegger. M.A., Eastman School of Music of the University of Rochester, 1969. 123 pp.

Includes a list of compositions, pp. 117-20, and a discography, p. 123.

1437 *FORBES, Douglas L. Some Serious Compositions of Victor Herbert: A Study in Musical Style. M.A., Eastman School of Music of the University of Rochester, 1957. 130 pp. illus.

1438 FOSTER, Paul Stephen. Aaron Copland as Radical Traditionalist: "Inscape" (1967). M.Mus., Goldsmiths' (London), 1981.

1439 *FRASER, Violet Lennie. The Style of Henry F. Gilbert. M.M., Eastman School of Music of the University of Rochester, 1947. 48 pp. illus.

1440 FULFORD, William Douglas. An Analysis of Sound Masses in *Hyperprism, Octandre* and *Intégrales,* Three Chamber Works by Edgard Varèse. M.A., California State University at Fullerton, 1979. 120 pp. A1 (18/2) 1313487, p. 116; A2 3543, p. 159.

1441 *GAY, George Errol. Stylistic Developments in the Music of Gunther Schuller: 1949-1961. M.A., University of North Carolina at Chapel Hill, 1965. 186 pp.

1442 GOODING, David. A Study of the Quotation Process in the Songs for Voice and Piano of Charles Edward Ives. Master's thesis, Western Reserve University, 1963. B6 G652, p. 15.

1443 *GREEN, Carol Anne. Melodic and Harmonic Analysis of Selected Piano Works by Aaron Copland. M.M., Indiana University, 1970. 101 pp. B13, p. 27.

1444 GREEN, Sheila A. Impressionistic Devices in Selected Piano Works of Ernest Bloch. Master's thesis, Southern Methodist University, 1980. A2 3556, p. 159.

1445 *HAAS, Eugene Joseph. Notational Practice in Twentieth Century Music: Problems and Developments. M.M., Southern Illinois University, 1965. 147 pp.
Includes a discussion of Earle Brown's *Available Forms I* and Lukas Foss's *Echoi for Four Soloists,* pp. 98-107 and pp. 108-12, respectively.

1446 HALDEEN, Alfred L. A Study of Aspects of Motivic Organization in Selected Works of Beethoven, Schubert, and Sessions. M.A., California State University at Hayward, 1973. 206 pp. K2 159, p. 19.

1447 HAMILTON, Christine A. The Elements of Jazz in George Gershwin's Piano Works. Master's thesis, Bowling Green State University, 1980. A2 3563, p. 160.

1448 *HANKS, Sarah Elizabeth. Charles Ives: The Creative Process of the Composer Especially in the Second Pianoforte Sonata, Concord, Mass., 1840-1860. M.A., Smith College, 1963. 132 pp.

1449 HANTZ, Mary Jane. Walter Piston's Use of Contrapuntal Devices in His Concertino for Piano and Orchestra. M.Mus., Eastman School of Music of the University of Rochester, 1943. 43 pp.

1450 *HARBINSON, William Grady. The Harmonic Language in the Symphonies of Aaron Copland. M.M., University of Alabama, 1977. 71 pp. illus.

1451 *HARER, Carolyn Bertha. Charles Ives and a Stylistic Analysis of His Three Piano Sonatas. M.M., North Texas State University, 1955. 83 pp. illus. B18 NTSU-1955-8, p. 19.

1452 HARKINS, Suzanne MacLean. A Study of Constructional Principles in George Crumb's *Makrokosmos, Volume 1*. M.A., American University, 1974. 217 pp.

1453 HARRIS, Nancy L. An Interpretive Analysis of a Selected Aria by G. C. Menotti in the Context of Twentieth-Century Opera Trends and the Italian Opera Tradition. M.M., California State University at Fullerton, 1981. 98 pp. A2 2997, p. 145.

1454 *HARTZELL, Lawrence W. Phrase Structure, Melody and Rhythm: Their Use as Primary Factors of Movement and Unity in Three Selected Works of Roger Sessions. M.M., Theory, University of Kansas, 1966. B13, p. 29.

1455 *HASTY, Patrick Robert. Aaron Copland's Symphonic Use of Brass Instruments. M.Mus., North Texas State University, 1965. 57 pp. B18 NTSU-1965-5, p. 24.

1456 *HAUGAN, Edwin Lyle. An Analysis of Three Major Piano Compositions by Aaron Copland: The Variations, Sonata, and Fantasy. M.A., Tulane University, 1961. 68 pp. illus.

1457 HAYS, Vivian. Ten Contemporary American Violin Sonatas: An Analytical Study. M.M., University of Texas at Austin, 1954. B18 UT-1954-12, p. 76.

1458 HEATON, Roger James. Elliott Carter's Third String Quartet: An Analysis of Pitch and Form. M.Mus., King's College, 1979.

1459 *HEMINGWAY, Marcia Jean. A Stylistic Analysis of Early American Keyboard Duets between 1780 and 1830. M.C.M., Southern Baptist Theological Seminary, 1977. 245 pp.

Actually these are keyboard duets which were popular in America but not written by Americans. Includes music for keyboard duets by Neville Butler Challoner, Johann Baptist Cramer, Martin Pierre Dalvimar, Ferdinand Franzl, John Gildon, Frantisek Koczwara, Ignaz Pleyel, Theodore Smith, and Jan Vanhall.

1460 *HESTEKIN, Kjellrun Kristine. Structural Elements in Karel Husa's *Apotheosis of This Earth* (1970). M.M., University of Wisconsin at Madison, 1976. 144 pp. illus.

1461 *HIGGINBOTHAM, Mary Kay. A Comparison of the Variation Technique Employed by Beethoven and Copland. M.Mus., North Texas State University, 1964. 81 pp. illus.

1462 HODGES, David W. An Analytical Study of the Songs of Charles Ives. Master's thesis, Central Missouri State College, 1967. F1 1661, p. 74.

1463 *HOFF, Ruth Marion. An Analysis of Some Principles of Music Theory Observed in a Selected Group of Contemporary American Art Songs. M.M., Indiana University, 1954. 130 pp.

1464 *HOOVER, Richard Lee. An Analysis with Historical Background of Selected Compositions of American Organ Music. M.A., California State University at Long Beach, 1974. 22 pp. A1 (12/4) 13-06348, p. 440.

The composers and compositions are John K. Paine, Concert Variations on "The Star-Spangled Banner"; Charles Ives, "Variations on 'America'"; Leo Sowerby, "Arioso"; Daniel Pinkham, "When the Morning Stars Sang Together"; and Ronald Sindelar, "Argo."

1465 *HOUSE, Elizabeth Gaines. Elements of the Vocal Style of Roy Harris. Master's thesis, Eastman School of Music of the University of Rochester, 1944.

1466 HU, Janice S. The Structure of Paul Creston's Sonata Op. 9 for Piano. Master's thesis, Central Washington State College, 1976. A2 2768, p. 114.

1467 *HUBER, John Elwyn. An Analysis of Aaron Copland's *Piano Variations.* Master's thesis, University of Michigan, 1967. B10, p. 20; B13, p. 29.

1468 HUFFMAN, June Hood. Eight Contemporary American Piano Sonatas: An Analytical Study. M.M., University of Texas at Austin, 1956. B18 UT-1956-17, p. 79.

1469 *HUTCHINSON, Mary Ann. Unrelated Simultaneity as an Historical Index to the Music of Charles Ives. M.M., Florida State University, 1970. 145 pp. illus. B13, p. 73.

1470 *HUTCHISON, Merilyn Kae. A Stylistic and Pianistic Evaluation of Aaron Copland's *Piano Fantasy*. M.Mus., North Texas State University, 1968. 91 pp. B18 NTSU-1968-13, p. 26.

1471 *IBBERSON, John B. A Study of Form in Selected Piano Sonatas of Five United States Composers. M.M., Indiana University, 1965. 138 pp. illus.

1472 *INGLEFIELD, Howard Gibbs. The Harmonic Style of Ernest Bloch as Approached through a Comparison of His Concerti Grossi. M.A., Eastman School of Music of the University of Rochester, 1960. 92 pp. illus.

1473 *INGRAHAM, James Leslie. An Analytic Investigation of Four Works by Alan Hovhaness with Emphasis on His Mysterious Mountain (Symphony No. 2), Op. 132 (1955). M.A., Ohio State University, 1973. 251 pp.

1474 *JACKSON, Arthur Wesley. A Conductor's Analysis of Selected Works by Giovanni Pierluigi da Palestrina, Orlando di Lasso, William Byrd, Giovanni Gabrieli, Dietrich Buxtehude, and Daniel Pinkham. M.M., Southwestern Baptist Theological Seminary, 1976. 114 pp.

1475 JACKSON, Eileen Stanza. The Use of Negro Folksong in Symphonic Forms. M.A., University of Chicago, 1941. 42 pp. I2, p. 160.

1476 JACKSON, Sam Oliver. Negro Slave Songs as Found in the Symphonic Works of Negro Composers. M.M.E., Virginia Commonwealth University, 1976.

1477 JACOBSON, Roger F. An Analysis of *The Old King* by John Duke. Master's thesis, Northern Illinois University, 1965. F1 1643, p. 73.

1478 *JAYNES, R. Leiland. Producing a Musical on the Secondary Level: An Analysis and Production of Clark Gesner's *You're a Good Man, Charlie Brown*. M.A., Midwestern University, 1972. 178; 104 pp.

1479 *JENKINS, Gwendolyn N. The Choral Style of Randall Thompson. M.M., Eastman School of Music of the University of Rochester, 1955. 92 pp. illus.

1480 *JENSEN, Ginger Anne. The Performance Interpretation of Paul Creston's Six Preludes, Opus 38 for Piano. M.A., Central Washington University, 1971. 47 pp.

1481   JOHNSON, Barry Wayne. A Comparative Analysis of Five American Trumpet Sonatas. M.A., Sam Houston State University, 1966. B18 SHS-1966-1, p. 34.

1482   *JOHNSON, Myrna Evelyn. The Structure of Paul Creston's Narrative No. 2, Op. 79, No. 2 for Piano. M.A., Central Washington University, 1972. 41 pp.

1483   KEATING, Mary Patricia. Adaptation of Liturgical Themes in Organ Compositions by Some Contemporary American Composers. M.A., Catholic University of America, 1973. 132 pp.

    American composers include Richard Dirksen, August Maekelberghe, Joseph J. McGrath, Leo Sowerby, Everett Titcomb, Camil Van Hulse, Russell Woollen, and Alec Wyton. For each composer there are biographical notes, lists of published organ works with liturgical themes, and style analysis and musical adaptation of certain selected compositions.

1484   KELLY, John J. The Musical Style of Alan Hovhaness. Master's thesis, University of Iowa, 1965. B13, p. 74.

1485   *KENNEDY, Helen Louise. Analysis of the Walter Piston Sonata for Violin and Piano. M.A., Eastman School of Music of the University of Rochester, 1956. 110 pp. illus.

1486   *KENNEY, Scott Glen. Purposeful Purposelessness: Musical Style in the Literary Works to John Cage. M.Mus., University of Utah, 1972.

1487   KRUMMER, Randolph F. An Analysis of the Compositional Techniques Employed in the Requiem by Randall Thompson. Master's thesis, University of Wisconsin, 1966. B13, p. 30.

1488   KUCHENMEISTER, Mary Jeanne. Formal and Thematic Relationships in the First String Quartet of Elliott Carter. Master's thesis, University of Arizona, 1967. 110 pp. B6 K95, p. 20; B13, p. 28.

1489   *KUDO, Elmer Takeo. An Investigation of Twelve-Tone Usage in George Rochberg's Symphony No. 2. M.M., Indiana University, 1974. 66 pp.

1490   *LABRECQUE, Candida Piërina Marsella. Compositional Techniques of Alexei Haieff's Saint's Wheel: Piano Variations on a Circle of Fifths. M.A., Central Washington University, 1973. 52 pp.

1491 *LAMBERT, Georgia P. The Symphonies of the Boston Classicists. M.A., University of North Carolina at Chapel Hill, 1976. 172 pp. illus.

Although the author discusses "The Boston Classicists: An American School of Composers," "The Orchestral Production of the Boston Classicists," and "The Historical Significance of the Boston Classicists' Symphonies" in chapters 1-3 respectively, the major portion of this study is an analysis of the symphonies studied in terms of overall structure, unity of the symphonic cycle, tempo, tonality, length, orchestration, and harmonic treatment.

1492 *LANGILLE, Edward D. An Analysis of Three String Quartets of Quincy Porter. M.M., Eastman School of Music of the University of Rochester, 1953. 97 pp. illus.

1493 LARKIN, James V. An Investigation of Contemporary Trends in Wind Band Instrumentation in the United States. M.M.E., Florida State University, 1955. B12, p. 84.

1494 *LARKIN, John E. An Analysis of Samuel Barber's First Symphony. M.M., University of Cincinnati, 1952. 47 pp.

1495 *LAVERTY, Paul H. Samuel Barber: A Formal Analysis of Three Chamber Works. M.M., Eastman School of Music of the University of Rochester, 1955. 84 pp. illus.

1496 LELAND, Mary Elizabeth. A Study of the Style of Ernest Bloch through the Analysis of Three Chamber Works, String Quartet No. II, Suite for Viola and Piano, and Quintet for Piano and Strings. M.M., Baylor University, 1951. B18 BU-1951-2, p. 2.

1497 *LENGYEL, Peter Myron. An Analytical Study of Particular Aspects of William Schuman's George Washington Bridge. M.M., Indiana University, 1973. 53 pp.

1498 *LERNER, Ellen Dale. The Music of Selected Contemporary American Women Composers: A Stylistic Analysis. M.M., University of Massachusetts at Amherst, 1976. 124 pp. A2 2785, p. 114.

1499 *LEUCH, Ruth. An Analysis of the First Symphony in One Movement by Samuel Barber. M.M., Eastman School of Music of the University of Rochester, 1949. 115 pp. illus.

1500 *LIEN, Beatrix. An Analytical Study of Selected Piano Works by Edward MacDowell. Master's thesis, Eastman School of Music of the University of Rochester, 1940.

1501 LIVESAY, Dan B. Bloch Symphony for Trombone and Orchestra: An Analysis of a Major Work Performed in a Graduate Recital, May 25, 1969, California State College at Hayward. M.A., California State University at Hayward, 1970. 21 pp. K2 164, p. 20.

1502 *LIVINGSTON, Carolyn Lambeth. The Songs of Charles T. Griffes: A Style-Critical Study. M.A., University of North Carolina at Chapel Hill, 1947. 99 pp. K5, p. 200.

1503 LOCKLEAR, Rebecca Anne. *The Cherubic Hymn* by Howard Hanson: An Analytical Study for the Choral Director. M.A., Stephen F. Austin State University, 1982. 128 pp. A1 (21/4) 1320422, p. 360.

1504 LOGAN, Adeline Marie. American National Music in the Compositions of Charles Ives. M.A., Washington University, 1943. 77 pp. B14 96, p. 29; I2, p. 174.

1505 LOGAN, Charles G. A Stylistic Analysis of George Gershwin's *An American in Paris*. M.M., Texas Christian University, 1949. B18 TCU-1949-3, p. 49.

1506 LONG, Jo Harolyn. An Analysis of Representative Compositions by Three Black American Composers. M.M., Southern Methodist University, 1972. B18 SMU-1972-3, p. 41.

1507 *LOUCKS, Donald G. Cadences in the Music of Representative Twentieth Century Composers. M.M., Southern Illinois University, 1966. 48 pp. illus. Includes a discussion of Walter Piston's Symphony No. 6, pp. 18-24.

1508 *LUCAS, Virginia Ruth. A Critical Analysis of the Choral Arrangements of Fred Waring as of May, 1946. Master's thesis, Eastman School of Music of the University of Rochester, 1946.

1509 *LYONS, Joseph C. Some Aspects of the Pitch Relations in Milton Babbitt's Song Cycle *Du*. M.A., Queens College of the City University of New York, 1970. 80 pp. illus. B13, p. 26.

1510 *McELROY, William Wiley. Elliott Carter's String Quartet No. 1: A Study of Heterogeneous Rhythmic Elements. M.M., Florida State University, 1973. 43 pp.

1511 *McHORSE, Claud Denison. A Conductor's Study of Selected Works by Jacobus Clemens non Papa, Orlando di Lasso, Michael Praetorius, Johann Pachelbel, Jean Berger, and Norman Dello Joio. M.M., Southwestern Baptist Theological Seminary, 1977. 198 pp.

1512 MacKAY, John W. An Analysis of Musical Time in Selected Works by George Crumb. Master's thesis, McGill University, 1980. A2 3615, p. 162.

1513 McKINNEY, Janeen E. The Three Symphonies of Leonard Bernstein: An Analysis. Master's thesis, Baylor University, 1981. A2 2950, p. 140.

1514 *McMURRAY, Sue Ellen Zank. Motival Structure of *Susannah,* a Music Drama by Carlisle Floyd. M.A., Central Washington University, 1967. 70 pp. illus.

1515 MACOMBER, Jeffrey R. A Performer's Analysis of the Concerto for Trombone and Orchestra by Walter Ross. M.M., Bowling Green State University, 1977. 100 pp. A2 3461, p. 147; K1 (22) 3179, p. 153.

1516 *MADSEN, Jean. A Discussion and Analysis of Some of the Songs of Schütz, Wolf, Duparc, Falla and Barber. Master's thesis, University of Northern Iowa, 1968.

1517 *MAHDER, William Carl. Elliott Carter's String Quartet, No. 1: An Analysis of the Adagio. Master's thesis, University of Michigan, 1973.

1518 MAIR, Brian. The "Poème Electronique" of Edgard Varèse: Analysis and Transcription. Master's thesis, Queens College of the City University of New York, 1967. B13, p. 26.

1519 *MALYC'KYJ, Andrij. A Stylistic Analysis of Solo by Daniel Perlongo. M.M., Indiana University of Pennsylvania, 1972. 65 pp.

1520 *MANFREDINI, Harry. Aaron Copland Piano Variations: An Analysis. M.A., Western Illinois University, 1967. 50 pp.

1521 *MATHIS, Kitty Borland. The Relationship between Theory and the Interpretation of Twentieth-Century Music. M.M., University of Alabama, 1977. 144 pp.

Discusses a few American composers including George Crumb.

1522 *MAXWELL, Jerome Chester. An Investigation of the Musical Devices Used by Randall Thompson to Compose Works on the Text of Robert Frost. M.A., Ohio State University, 1966. 69 pp.

"Frostiana," seven country songs. Words by Robert Frost, music by Randall Thompson.

1523 *MAYS, Kenneth Robert. The Use of Hymn Tunes in the Works of Charles Ives. M.M., Indiana University, 1961. 130 pp. illus.

1524 *MEEK, Charles Richard. The Crucible by Robert Ward: An Analysis. M.A., Eastman School of Music of the University of Rochester, 1970. 204 pp.

1525 *MENTZER, John George. Jean Sibelius and Howard Hanson: A Study of Compositional Techniques Indigenous to the Nordic Temperament as Evidenced in Each Composer's First Symphony. M.A., University of Utah, 1961. 29 pp. illus.

1526 MESSER, Celinda H. The Contemporary Idiom in the Piano Teaching Pieces of Vincent Persichetti, Norman Dello Joio, and Paul Creston. Master's thesis, Baylor University, 1977. F1 1415, p. 75.

1527 MICHEL, Sarah Belle Skinner. The Relationship of the Poetry to the Melodic Line in Aaron Copland's *Twelve Poems of Emily Dickinson.* M.M., University of Texas at Austin, 1966. B13, p. 30; B18 UT-1966-14, p. 90.

1528 *MILLER, Donald C. A Theoretical Study of the Short Choral Works of Leo Sowerby. Master's thesis, Kent State University, 1958. 84 pp.

1529 *MITCHELL, Johnlyn G. An Analysis of Samuel Barber's Sonata for Piano, Opus 26. M.A., West Texas State University, 1974. 79 pp.

1530 MONTAGUE, Stephen Rowley. The Simple and Complex in Selected Works of Charles Ives. M.Mus., Florida State University, 1967. 111 pp. B13, p. 73.

1531 MOOMAW, Charles Jay. A PL/1 Program for the Harmonic Analysis of Music by the Theories of Paul Hindemith and Howard Hanson. M.M., University of Cincinnati, 1973. 436 pp. A1 (12/1) 13-05230, p. 48.

1532 *MOORE, Gary Winston. A Conductor's Analysis of Psalm Settings by J. S. Bach, W. A. Mozart, Anton Bruckner and Leonard Bernstein. M.C.M., Southwestern Baptist Theological Seminary, 1970. 183 pp. illus. B18 SBS-1970-2, p. 45.

1533 MORSE, Susan K. The Influence of Syrinx, Density 21.5 and Sequenza on Twentieth-Century Flute Compositions. Master's thesis, University of Western Ontario, 1981. A2 2954, p. 140.

1534 MUELLER, Robert E. Contrapuntal Styles in Contemporary American Music. M.M., Northwestern University, 1948. B15 559, p. 21.

1535 MURRAY, Carol J. Formal Analyses of the First Movements of the Eight Symphonies by Walter Piston. M.A., Indiana State University, 1977. F1 1216, p. 71. 77 pp.

1536 *MUSKRAT, James Bruce. A Conductor's Analysis of Look toward the Sea by Alan Hovhaness and Skelton Poems by Jean Berger. M.M., Southwestern Baptist Theological Seminary, 1976. 140 pp.

1537 *NASH, Nancy Lee. Syllogistic Form as a Heuristic Principle in Musical Analysis—Based on the Music of Charles Griffes. M.M., Florida State University, 1972. 286 pp.

1538 NICHOLL, Matthew James. Harry Partch: "And on the Seventh Day Petals Fell on Petaluma." M.M., North Texas State University, 1982. 114 pp. A1 (21/2) 1319424, p. 182.

1539 *O'BRIEN, James Patrick. The Theme and Variations as Used by Four Important Piano Composers in Four Periods of Music History. M.Ed., Central Washington University, 1966. 71 pp.
Discusses Norman Dello Joio's Sonata No. 3.

1540 *OLEWILER, William S. An Analysis of Consonance and Dissonance in Norman Dello Joio's To Saint Cecilia. M.A., Indiana University of Pennsylvania, 1974. 70 pp.

1541 *OSTRANDER, Arthur Eugene. An Analysis of Five Works of Carl Ruggles. M.M., Indiana University, 1969. 101 pp. B13, p. 27.

1542 PAGE, Adele. The Style of Ernest Bloch as Approached through a Study of Piano and Chamber Works. Master's thesis, Eastman School of Music of the University of Rochester, 1940.

1543 PALMER, Lyelle Lee. Some Techniques of Composition Employed by Charles Edward Ives in 114 Songs. M.M., Southern Methodist University, 1963. B18 SMU-1963-4, p. 40.

1544 *PARKER, Mark Mason. Classification of Pitch Material in Three Compositions by Howard Hanson. M.A., Eastman School of Music of the University of Rochester, 1976. 256 pp. illus.
The three compositions are Symphony No. 4, Mosaics, and Symphony No. 6.

1545 PARKS, O. G. A Critical Analysis of the Works of Leo Sowerby. M.M., North Texas State University, 1941. B18 NTSU-1941-14, p. 11.

1546 PEASE, Rhenda Ronfeldt. An Analytical Study of Twentieth-Century Cadential Techniques. M.M., Western Michigan University, 1978. 432 pp. A1 (18/2) 1312606, p. 117.
Includes a discussion of Charles Ives.

1547 *PELLMAN, Samuel Frank. Sentinel: An Overview of Current Practices Regarding the Performance of Electronic Music. M.A., Cornell University, 1978. 2 vols. 173 pp.

1548 PEMBROOK, Randall G. The Nocturne: An Overview Based on a Comparison of Four Examples: Field, Chopin, Fauré, and Barber. Master's thesis, Southern Illinois University at Edwardsville, 1981. A2 2963, p. 140.

1549 *PERRIN, Phil D. Forsaken of Man by Leo F. Sowerby: A Stylistic Analysis. M.C.M., Southwestern Baptist Theological Seminary, 1964. B18 SBS-1964-4, p. 44.

1550 *PETERSON, Ronald Dale. A Brief History and Description of Electronic Music Including an Analysis of Davidovsky's Synchronisms No. 1, 2, and 3. M.M., University of Cincinnati, 1972. 75 pp. illus.

1551 PICKARD, Dorothy Selden. The String Quartets of Robert Frank Kurka: A Style-Critical Study. Master's thesis, University of Maryland, 1967. B13, p. 29.

1552 *PIRRET, Bruce Alan. General Style Characteristics of Music of Aaron Copland. M.A., Central Washington University, 1975. 30 pp.

1553 PISCIOTTA, Louis V. Texture in the Choral Works of Selected Contemporary American Composers. Master's thesis, Indiana University, 1967. B13, p. 27.

1554 POOLER, Marie. Part 1: Analyses of Choral Settings of the "Te Deum" by the Contemporary Composers Benjamin Britten, Leo Sowerby, Halsey Stevens, and Vincent Persichetti. M.A., California State University at Fullerton, 1971. 90 pp. A1 (9/3) 13-02780, p. 154.

1555 *POSTMA, Frank. An Analysis of Six Sonatas for 'Cello and Continuo by Raynor Taylor, as Arranged by Dr. Leroy J. Robertson with Reference to Certain Baroque and Classical Influences Found in Them. M.A., University of Utah, 1964. illus.

1556 *PRATZ, Kathryn Hester Darnielle. Paul Creston's *Narrative No. 1,* Op. 79, No. 1 for Piano: A Rhythmic Analysis. M.A., Central Washington University, 1975. 39 pp.

1557 *PRINGLE, Margaret Ann. An Analysis of the Organ and Harpsichord Music of Vincent Persichetti. M.A., Eastman School of Music of the University of Rochester, 1968. 241 pp.

1558 *PYKE, L. Allen. George Gershwin: A Study of His Style. Master's thesis, University of Michigan, 1946.

1559 *QUACKENBUSH, Margaret Diane. Form and Texture in the Works for Mixed Chamber Ensemble by Charles Ives. M.A., University of Oregon, 1976. 125 pp. illus. B17 (10/2) 3179, p. 195.
Nineteen pieces are analyzed.

1560 RALEY, Randall. American Elements in the Music of Aaron Copland. M.M., University of Texas at Austin, 1950. B18 UT-1950-16, p. 71.

1561   REEDER, Jack Sanborn. Walter Piston: An Analytical Study. M.A., American University, 1959. 161 pp.

Includes a discussion of Piston's life, analysis of representative works, his published musicological contributions, and his role as both composer and teacher. There is also an excellent bibliography comprised mostly of original source material.

1562   *REESE, MonaLyn. The Incorporation of Jazz Elements in Selected Works of Gunther Schuller. M.M., Theory, University of Kansas, 1977. 115 pp.

1563   RENSHLER, Diane B. An Analysis of Tensional Factors Relating to the Performance of Leonard Bernstein's Sonata for Clarinet and Piano. Master's thesis, Bowling Green State University, 1982. A2 3052, p. 148.

1564   *RENZELMAN, Gary Eugene. A Stylistic Analysis and Comparison of the A Cappella Choral Music for Mixed Voices by Three Contemporary American Composers: Aaron Copland, William Schuman, Randall Thompson. M.A., University of California at Los Angeles, 1960. 132 pp.

1565   *REXWINKEL, Alma Ruth. A Theoretical Study of Copland's Piano Fantasy. M.M., Eastman School of Music of the University of Rochester, 1959. 65 pp. illus.

1566   *RHOADS, Mary. Leonard Bernstein's "West Side Story": A Critical Analysis. Master's thesis, University of Michigan, 1964.

1567   RHODES, James C. Towards an Analytical Method: Musical Prosody in Selected Songs of Elie Siegmeister. Master's thesis, University of North Carolina at Greensboro, 1979. A2 3176, p. 138.

1568   RINGENWALD, Richard Donald. The Music of Esther Williamson Ballou: An Analytical Study. M.A., American University, 1960. 20 pp. B9 27, p. 4.

Ballou (1915-73) taught at American University and composed over 100 works.

1569   *ROBERTSON, David Hiram. An Analysis of Aaron Copland's Third Symphony. M.A., Eastman School of Music of the University of Rochester, 1965. 184 pp. illus.

1570   *ROBSON, Margaret. An Analysis and Comparison of the 20th Century Piano Fugues by Barber, Hindemith, Hovhaness, Kabalevsky, and Shostakovich. M.A., Wayne State University, 1974. 289 pp. illus.

1571 *RODGERS, James Bruce. Elements of the Choral Style of Howard Hanson. M.M., Eastman School of Music of the University of Rochester, 1947. 115 pp. illus.

1572 ROGERS, Harold Emery. An Analysis of Six American Operas. M.A., University of Denver, 1962. 140 pp.

Discusses *The Medium* (Menotti); *The Mother of Us All* (Thomson); *Down in the Valley* (Weill); *The Tender Land* (Copland); *Susanna* (Floyd); and *Vanessa* (Barber).

1573 ROMEO, James Joseph. Vocal Parts in the Music of George Crumb. M.M., Michigan State University, 1978. 74 pp. A1 (17/2) 1312558, p. 150.

Analyzed are *Madrigals* Books I-IV and *The Ancient Voices of Children*.

1574 ROSENBLUM, Denise L. Selected Rags of Scott Joplin, James Scott, and Joseph Lamb, 1900-1920: A Theoretical Comparison. Master's thesis, College of St. Rose, 1980. F1 1233, p. 72.

1575 ROSS, Sylvia Lucy. An Analysis of Ernest Bloch's Treatment of Psalm 22, Psalm 114, and Psalm 137. S.M.M., Union Theological Seminary, 1956. B8 1151, p. 79.

1576 *ROSSOMANDO, Fred Edward. A Conductor's Guide to the Third Symphony of Charles Ives. M.M., Indiana University, 1971. 63 pp. illus. B17 (6/1) 739, p. 49.

Discusses the work's evolution.

1577 *ROUSE, Christopher Chapman. Gacela Del Amor Imprevisto: Expansion of Material in the Seventh Symphony of William Schuman. M.F.A., Cornell University, 1977.

1578 SABIN, John T. Analysis of Selected Works of the Moravian Composer Johann Peter. Master's thesis, Illinois State University, 1967. F1 1698, p. 75.

1579 *SACLAUSA, John. The Tonal Setting of Text in Selected Operas of Gian Carlo Menotti. M.M., Eastman School of Music of the University of Rochester, 1957. 101 pp. illus.

1580 SAFANE, Clifford J. A Structural and Tonal Analysis of the Three Piano Sonatas of Roger Sessions. Master's thesis, Boston University, 1976. A2 2823, p. 115.

1581 SATTERFIELD, Jacqueline Creef. Samuel Barber: A Study of His Style and Music for Solo Voice and Piano. M.Mus., University of Houston, 1970. 69 pp. A1 (9/1) 13-02079, p. 33.

The compositions discussed are: "The Daisies," "A Nun Takes the Veil," "Sure on the Shining Night," and "Monks and Raisins."

1582 *SCHALK, Carl Flentge. A Stylistic Analysis of The Christmas Story for Orchestra and Mixed Chorus by Peter Mennin. M.M., Eastman School of Music of the University of Rochester, 1957. 109 pp. B8 715, p. 51.

1583 *SHARP, Mary Elizabeth. A Survey of Musical Quotation from 1940-1975. M.M., University of Louisville, 1979. 91 pp. A1 (18/2) 1314011, p. 117.

Discussed is George Crumb's *Ancient Voices of Children, Vox Balaenae,* and *Makrokosmos* I, II, III, and George Rochberg's *Chamber Symphony, Ricordanza, Sonata Fantasie, Nach Bach, Music for the Magic Theater,* and Symphony No. 3. Charles Ives is also discussed.

1584 SHELNESS, Felicity A. Composition: Piano Quartet. Analysis: String Quartet No. 3 by Elliott Carter. Master's thesis, University of California at Davis, 1978. A2 3509, p. 148.

1585 SHINABERRY, Cathleen. Samuel Barber's Melodies Passagères with Performance Implications. Master's thesis, Bowling Green State University, 1979. A2 3185, p. 138.

1586 SKINNER, William Scott. Harmonic Dimension and Direction in the Fifth String Quartet of George Perle. M.A., Indiana University, 1976. 87 pp. B17 (10/2) 4081, p. 240.

1587 *SLOAN, Julia Margaret. Harmonic Devices in the Compositions of Carl Hugo Grimm, an American Composer. M.M., University of Cincinnati, 1940. 195 pp.

1588 *SLY, Caroline Ware. The Language of Ives's Solo Songs. M.A., Smith College, 1970. 146 pp.

1589 SMITH, Barbara Baranard. John Powell's *Sonate Noble* and His Use of Folk Music. M.M., Eastman School of Music of the University of Rochester, 1943. 65 pp. I2, p. 176.

1590 *SMITH, James Craig, Jr. A Study of the Harmonic Styles of Lowell Mason and Benjamin Franklin White. M.C.M., Southwestern Baptist Theological Seminary, 1959. 72 pp. B18 SBS-1959-3, p. 43; J3 1482, p. 87.

1591 SOLIE, Ruth Ames. Varèse's *Arcana*: An Analysis of Form. Master's thesis, University of Chicago, 1966. B13, p. 29.

1592 SOUTHERN, Eileen Stanza Jackson. The Use of Negro Folksong in Symphonic Form. M.A., University of Chicago, 1941.

1593 SPARROW, Danny R. Alec Wilder's Horn Sonatas: A Stylistic Study. Master's thesis, Georgia State University, 1978. A2 5588, p. 237.

1594 SPECK, Frederick A. An Analysis of *Theme and Variations* by Verne Reynolds (1926-). M.M., Bowling Green State University, 1982. 25 pp. A2 3065, p. 148.

1595 *SPIER, Ronald Michael. The Compositional Style of Johann Friedrich Peter as Influenced by Franz Xaver Richter. M.A., San Diego State University, 1976. 108 pp.

1596 *STANEK, Ethel Lou. Analysis of the Sonata for Cello and Piano by Burrill Phillips. M.M., Eastman School of Music of the University of Rochester, 1953. 187 pp. illus.

1597 STANLEY, Hildegard Jo. The Major Choral Works of Randall Thompson with Particular Emphasis on and Analyses of *The Testament of Freedom*. M.C.M., Southwestern Baptist Theological Seminary, 1962. 76 pp. B18 SBS-1962-9, p. 44; J3 1468, p. 87.

1598 STEPHENSON, Robert. Stylistic Changes in the Works of Aaron Copland. M.M., University of Texas at Austin, 1956. B18 UT-1956-30, p. 79.

1599 *STOGSDILL, Thomas M. A Conductor's Analysis of Selected Works by Thomas Tallis, Johannes Eccard, Samuel Scheidt, Johann Hermann Schein, Johann Pachelbel, Halsey Stevens. M.M., Southwestern Baptist Theological Seminary, 1977. 199 pp.

1600 *SUNDELL, Steven Lynn. Charles Ives' Use of Simultaneity to Conflict and Blur Tonality: The Projection of Multiple Layers of Music in *Putnam's Camp* and Related Sources. M.M., University of Wisconsin at Madison, 1973. 61 pp.

1601 SVAREN, John Cornell. Choral Styles of Samuel Barber. Master's thesis, Moorhead State University, 1976. A2 2837, p. 116; F1 1095, p. 60.

1602 *TAYLOR, Jewel Annabelle. Technical Practices of Negro Composers in Choral Works for A Cappella Choir. M.A., Eastman School of Music of the University of Rochester, 1960. 85 pp. illus.

Composers discussed include R. Nathaniel Dett, William Dawson, Henry Clay Work, and Undine S. Moore.

1603 THOMPSON, Jacqueline K. William Levi Dawson (b. 1898) and an Analysis of His *Negro Folk Symphony* (1932; rev. 1952). Master's thesis, University of Missouri-Kansas City, 1979. A2 3200, p. 138.

1604 THOMPSON, Loren Dean. Comparative Aspects of Variation Technique as Applied to the Keyboard in Selected Works of Scheidt-Mozart-Brahms-Copland. M.A., California State University at Fullerton, 1970. 96 pp. A1 (9/2) 13-02462, p. 81.

1605 TIGAI, Joan E. Kent Kennan's Sonata for Trumpet and Piano: An Analytical Study. M.M., Bowling Green State University, 1971. 42 pp. K1 (16) 1956, p. 73.

1606 *TIROFF, Philip Knight. An Analytical Critique of the Use of Twelve Equal Tones as Utilized in *Sonata-Fantasia* by George Rochberg. M.Mus., North Texas State University, 1968. 61 pp.

1607 *TOMPKINS, Jimmy. Menotti's Use of Dramatic Impact in *The Medium*. M.Mus., North Texas State University, 1968. 172 pp. illus.

1608 *TOWNSEND, Robert C. Technics Used by Charles Martin Loeffler in Music for Four Stringed Instruments. Master's thesis, Eastman School of Music of the University of Rochester, 1948.

1609 TROTTIER, Muriel. A Study of Sound and Timbre in the Music of Edgard Varèse. Master's thesis, Bridgewater State College, 1981. A2 2998, p. 142.

1610 *TULL, Fisher Aubry, Jr. An Analysis of the Works for Solo Trumpet by Alan Hovhaness. M.Mus., North Texas State University, 1957. 70 pp. illus. B18 NTSU-1957-17, p. 21.

1611 UNRAU, Mary Anne. Contemporary and Traditional Influences in the Elliott Carter Piano Concerto. Mus.M., University of Western Ontario, 1973. A2 3706, p. 165.

Also cited in *Canadian Theses* (1972-75), 2 vols. (Ottawa: National Library of Canada, 1980), 1:328.

1612 VAN FOSSAN, Kathryn R. Style in the Songs of Charles T. Griffes. Master's thesis, Illinois State University, 1979. A2 3205, p. 139.

1613 *VARS, Dianne. Rhythmic Structure in Elliott Carter's String Quartet No. 1. M.M., Indiana University, 1973. 129 pp.

1614 WARD, Charles Wilson. The Use of Hymn Tunes as an Expression of 'Substance' and 'Manner' in the Music of Charles E. Ives, 1874-1954. M.M., University of Texas at Austin, 1969. B18 UT-1969-25, p. 93.

1615 *WATKINS, David Hugh. The Use of Polytonality in Selected Works of Aaron Copland. M.M., Indiana University, 1965. 75 pp. illus.

1616 *WEDGEWOOD, Richard Barton. Melodic Construction and Phrase Structure in the Music of Carl Ruggles. M.M., University of Arkansas at Fayetteville, 1967. 45 pp. illus. B13, p. 29.

1617 WIEBUSCH, Janice M. The Piano Concerto since 1950. Master's thesis, University of Nebraska, 1969. 151 pp. B10, p. 51; B16, p. 64.

Includes an analysis of op. 38 of Samuel Barber and the Piano Concerto by Elliott Carter. Over 400 piano concertos composed or published since 1950 are listed.

1618 *WIIG, John. An Analysis of Transcendental Influences in Selected Choral Works of Charles Ives. M.M., Mankato State University, 1972. 107 pp. illus.

1619 *WILCOX, James H. An Analysis of the Third Symphony, Op. 42 by Wallingford Riegger. M.M., Eastman School of Music of the University of Rochester, 1953. 163 pp. illus.

1620 WILEY, Joan Marie. A Comparative Analysis of Charles E. Ives' *First Sonata* and Sonata No. 2. M.A., California State University at Fullerton, 1980. 94 pp. A1 (19/3) 1316054, p. 259.

1621 *WILLIAMS, Jay Thomas. Elements of Form in the Music of Edgard Varèse. M.M., Indiana University, 1966. 121 pp. illus.

1622 WILLIS, Sharon J. A Musical Analysis of the Works of Florence Price. Master's thesis, Georgia State University, 1980. A2 5597, p. 251.

1623 WILSON, Frances P. A Study of Selected Songs by Henry Purcell, Franz Schubert, Giacomo Puccini, Arthur Honegger, and Ned Rorem. Master's thesis, Appalachia State University, 1979. A2 3210, p. 139.

1624 WINDECKER, Anita F. Aaron Copland's *Piano Fantasy* (An Analysis). M.M., University of Texas at Austin, 1963. B18 UT-1963-20, p. 87.

1625 WITUCKI, Alan Philip. Thematic Transformation and Other Considerations in the Six Symphonies of Howard Hanson. M.M., Michigan State University, 1978. 62 pp. A1 (17/2) 1312580, p. 150.

1626 WOICIKOWFSKI, John F. An Analysis of Houston Bright's Choral Music. Master's thesis, Texas Tech University, 1973. F1 1316, p. 67.

1627 *WOLFE, Curtis Scott. Tonality in the String Chamber Works of Walter Piston. M.M., Indiana University, 1963. 70 pp. illus.

1628 *WORTHEN, Ellis Clayton. Musical Techniques Used by Arthur Shepherd in Three Representative Works. Master's thesis, Brigham Young University, 1966. 130 pp. illus.; plates. B13, p. 73.

1629 YEARY, David Maurice. The Second Symphony of Walter Piston: An Analysis. M.M., Texas Christian University, 1968. B18 TCU-1968-9, p. 54.

1630 *YOUNG, John Joseph. The Role of Parameters in *Octandre* by Edgard Varèse. M.M., University of Wisconsin at Madison, 1970. 104 pp. B13, p. 30.

1631 *YOUSLING, Richard S. The Style of George Gershwin's Popular Songs. M.A., Eastman School of Music of the University of Rochester, 1949. 116 pp. illus.
Includes a list of Gershwin's works, p. 109.

1632 *YUEN, Janice Shan-Chen Hu. The Structure of Paul Creston's Sonata, Op. 9 for Piano. M.A., Central Washington University, 1975. 41 pp.

1633 *YUNE, Kuija Lee. A Study of Compositional Processes in John Eaton's Songs for R.P.B. and George Crumb's Songs, Drones, and Refrains of Death. M.M., Indiana University, 1974. 65 pp.

See also nos. **207-455**.

THESES **4** *Ethnomusicology*

FOLK MUSIC. GENERAL

1634 ALLEN, Robert R. Old-Time Music and the Urban Folk Revival. Master's thesis, Western Kentucky University, 1981. A2 2836, p. 135.

1635 *BANGHART, Edward Phillip. The American Folksong: A Study in Its Selection and Performance. Master's thesis, University of Michigan, 1960.

1636 CARRUTH, Mildred L. A Study and Analysis of Six Classifications of American Folk Music. M.Ed., Oberlin College, 1954. 129 pp. B2, p. 163; I2, p. 245.

1637 *COOPER, Jane. Characteristics of American Folk Music. M.M., College-Conservatory of Music, Cincinnati, 1951. 68 pp. B7 145, p. 21; B14 37, p. 24; I1 4312, p. 64; I2, p. 221.

1638 CUTLER, Flory Fenton. Early Interest in Folksong and Folklore in America. M.A., German, University of Illinois, 1915. 71 pp. I2, p. 20.

1639   HAMMOND, Stella Lou. Contribution of the American Indian and Negro to the Folk-Music of America. M.A., Wayne State University, 1936. 97 pp. B7 289, p. 38; B14 61, p. 26; H1, p. 231; I1 1368, p. 136; I2, p. 116.

1640   HERREID, Henry Benjamin. Folk Music in the United States. M.A., University of Wisconsin, 1938. 96 pp. B7 315, p. 41; B14 65, p. 26; I2, p. 133.

1641   JABBOUR, Alan A. A Survey and Analysis of the Collecting, Editing, and Criticism of Folkmusic in England, Scotland, and America. M.A., English, Duke University, 1966. I2, p. 327.

1642   KODISH, Debora Gail. "Good Friends and Bad Enemies": Robert W. Gordon and American Folksong Scholarship. M.A., Folklore, Memorial University of Newfoundland, 1977. 293 pp. B5 (23), p. 457.

1643   MICHAEL, Marian Pendergrass. Child, Sharp, Lomax, and Barry: A Study in Folksong Collecting. M.A., University of Texas, 1960. 197 pp. B18 UT-1960-15, p. 83; I2, p. 287.

1644   NICKEL, Margaret Elizabeth. American Folk-Music. M.M., Northwestern University, 1942. 69 pp. B2, p. 144; B14 125, p. 31; B15 577, p. 22; I2, p. 168.

1645   *RASMUSSEN, Ivan Burdette. A Study of the Folk Music of Europe and America. M.M., Syracuse University, 1933. 57 pp. illus. I2, p. 95.

1646   *SEGALE, Virginia Jean. Development of American Folk Music. M.M., Cincinnati Conservatory of Music, 1947. 100 pp. B14 139, p. 32; I2, p. 195.

1647   TOWNSEND, Arthur Ornes. The American Folk Song and Its Influence on the Work of American Composers. M.A., University of Southern California, 1939. 116 pp. B14 166, p. 34; I2, p. 145.

1648   WHITE, Marie Price. The Status of Rural Music in the United States. M.Ed., University of Texas at Austin, 1951. B12, p. 146.

1649 ADAMS, Charles Siegel. New Hampshire Folklore: A Regional Collection. M.A., Folklore, Indiana University, 1968. 148 pp.

Although most of the study emphasizes folklore, there is a section of songs and ballads sung by Minnie White, pp. 116-39.

1650 ANDERSON, Geneva. A Collection of Ballads and Songs from East Tennessee. M.A., English, University of North Carolina at Chapel Hill, 1932. 317 pp. H1, p. 226; I2, p. 79.

Discusses English and Scottish popular ballads in Eastern Tennessee, other imported ballads and songs, ballads of the dead and dying, love songs, war songs, ballads of wrecks and disasters, songs of orphan children, religious and moralistic songs, and miscellaneous ballads and songs. Although music is not provided, each song text is given with an indication of when and where it was first sung.

1651 AYCOCK, Etholine Grigsby. Americanisms in the Traditional Ballads of the Eastern United States. M.A., English, University of Missouri, 1940. B7 30, p. 6; H1, p. 226.

1652 BARROW, Linda Miller. A Folkloristic Analysis of Representative Eastern North Carolina Religious and Secular Folksongs Sung by Miss Janis Hardison. M.A., Literature, East Carolina University, 1978. 93 pp. L11, p. 98.

1653 BOETTE, Marie D. Selections of Tunes and Variations in the Words of Certain Folk Tunes and Ballads of the Upper Monongahela Valley. M.A., English, Ohio University, 1942. 82 pp. B7 78, p. 13; I2, p. 164.

1654 BONAR, Eleanor Jean. A Collection of Ballads and Popular Songs, Iowa and Appalachian. M.A., English, University of Iowa, 1930. 224 pp. B7 71, p. 12; I2, p. 65.

Discusses 104 songs (music and texts) of home, work songs, temperance songs, songs and ballads of war, children's songs and game songs, and love ballads. The section on songs in Appalachia includes pieces from Kentucky, North Carolina, and Georgia.

1655 BUCKLEY, Bruce Redfern. Ballads and Folksongs in Scioto County, Ohio. M.A., English, Miami University, 1952. 329 pp. H1, p. 228; I2, p. 229.

1656   BUFORD, Mary Elizabeth. Folksongs of Florida and Texas. M.A., English, Southern Methodist University, 1941. 219 pp. B7 107, p. 16; H1, p. 228; I2, p. 157.

Discusses traditional ballads, imported ballads, dance songs, and folk songs. Included is an appendix of tunes.

1657   BUSH, Michael. Murder Ballads in Appalachia. Master's thesis, Marshall University, 1978. A2 3399, p. 144.

1658   CALHOUN, Cecil Warner. Selected Instrumental Folk Music of South Central Kentucky. M.A., University of Iowa, 1941. 88 pp. B7 114, p. 17; I2, p. 157.

Some of the instruments discussed include fiddles, banjos, Spanish guitars and mandolins, accordians, and mouth organs. Each musical selection treated includes background information as well as music. There is a chapter on the social functions related to the music of the area.

1659   CARLISLE, Irene Jones. Fifty Ballads and Songs from Northwest Arkansas. M.A., English, University of Arkansas, 1952. 178 pp. H1, p. 228; I2, p. 230.

Discussed are eleven Child ballads, six British-American songs, three songs of war, six songs of tragedies and disasters, five songs of outlaws, prisoners, and prodigals, four ballads of Indians, three songs on various subjects, nine smiling songs, and three nursery songs. Includes a section on "Notes on the Informants."

1660   CHAMBERLAIN, William Woodrow. Folk Music in the Kentucky Barrens. M.A., English, Stanford University, 1940. 282 pp. B7 125, p. 19; H1, p. 228; I2, p. 148.

1661   *CHANDLER, George W., Jr. The History and Present Status of Folk-Song Scholarship in the South. M.A., English, University of North Carolina at Chapel Hill, 1936. 128 pp. H1, p. 228; I2, p. 115.

1662   CHICKERING, Geraldine J. Some Ballads and Songs from Michigan. M.A., English, Wayne State University, 1934. 178 pp. I2, p. 98; L9 157.1, p. 13.

1663   CHILDS, Alice May. Some Ballads and Folk Songs from the South. M.A., English, University of Missouri, 1929. 208 pp. H1, p. 228; I2, p. 59.

1664   *CHRISTENSEN, June. Folksong in Michigan. Master's thesis, University of Michigan, 1949.

1665   CLEMENTS, Caroline. Old English and Scottish Ballads in the Southern Appalachian Mountains. Master's thesis, English, Columbia University, 1925. H1, p. 229.

1666   *COBB, Lucy M. Traditional Ballads and Songs from Eastern North Carolina. M.A., English, University of North Carolina at Chapel Hill, 1927. 206 pp. H1, p. 229; I2, p. 50.

1667   COLBY, Ann Maurice. An Investigation of the Folksongs of the Mohawk Valley. M.A., Catholic University of America, 1958. 69 pp. I2, p. 273.

1668   CRABTREE, Lillian G. Songs and Ballads Sung in Overton County, Tennessee: A Collection. M.A., English, George Peabody College for Teachers, 1936. H1, p. 229; I2, p. 115.

1669   DANIELL, Martha Louise. Sixteen Play Party Songs from Randolph County, West Virginia. M.A., Ohio State University, 1943. B7 163, p. 23; H1, p. 229; I2, p. 172.

1670   DeBUSK, Clarence Kaiser, Jr. An Appraisal of the Musicological Resources of the Pecos River Focus. M.M., University of Texas, 1963. 204 pp. B18 UT-1963-8, p. 86; I1 4449, p. 77; I2, p. 305.

1671   DUNCAN, Ruby. Ballads and Folk Songs Collected in Northern Hamilton County [Tennessee]. M.A., English, University of Tennessee, 1939. 388 pp. H1, p. 229; I2, p. 140.

Discusses Child ballads, other ballads and folksongs of old-world origin, American ballads and folksongs, children's songs, singing games, songs of wanderers and outcasts, American journalistic ballads, songs of lovers' tragedies, and songs of sentiment. Each song treated includes background information and text, but not music.

1672   GAMBLE, Margaret E. The Heritage and Folk Music of the Cades Cove, Tennessee. M.M., University of Southern California, 1947. 242 pp. B7 242, p. 33; B14 52, p. 25; H1, p. 230; I2, p. 191.

1673   GANNAWAY, Mary Ann. The Singing Games of the Cumberland Mountains in Tennessee. M.A., English, George Peabody College for Teachers, 1935. H1, p. 230; I2, p. 108.

1674 GARRISON, Theodore Roosevelt. Forty-Five Folk Songs Collected from Searcy County, Arkansas. M.A., English, University of Arkansas, 1944. 148 pp. H1, p. 230; I2, p. 178.

1675 GELBER, Mark. Traditional Ballads of Colorado. M.A., English, University of Colorado, 1963. 72 pp. I2, p. 306.

1676 GRANT, Phil Stringham. The Songs of the "Forty-Niners": A Collection and Survey. M.A., English, University of California at Berkeley, 1924. 180 pp. B7 268, p. 36; I2, p. 38.

1677 GREEN, William F. An Edited Collection of Beech Mountain Folksongs. Master's thesis, English, East Tennessee State University, 1968. H1, p. 231.

1678 HARITAN, Michael Elarion. History of the Pittsburgh Folk Festival, 1956-1979. M.M., Duquesne University, 1980. 189 pp. A1 (19/4) 1316564, p. 330.

1679 HAUN, Mildred. Cocke County [Tennessee] Ballads and Songs. M.A., English, Vanderbilt University, 1937. H1, p. 232; I2, p. 125.
"Collection of 206 ballads and songs handed down in the Haun family of Cocke County, Tennessee."

1680 *HELMS, Karen G. The Role and Function of Oral Tradition of Ballad Form as Related to the Society and Culture of Ocracoke Island, North Carolina. M.A., East Carolina University, 1974. 166 pp. illus.

1681 HENDERSON, Eleanor Evelyn. An Ozark Song Book: A Collection of Songs and Ballads from the Fayetteville Area. M.A., English, University of Arkansas, 1950. 135 pp. H1, p. 232; I2, p. 215.

1682 HETH, Edward L. The Southern Mountain Folk Songs and Their Arrangements for Unaccompanied Singing. M.A., Westminster Choir College, 1940. 153 pp. B7 319, p. 42; I2, p. 150.

1683 HOLCOMBE, Julia Irene. Southern Mountain Folk Songs for American Schools. M.M., Eastman School of Music of the University of Rochester, 1941. 116 pp. B14 69, p. 27; I2, p. 159.

1684 HUMMEL, Lynn Ellis. Ozark Folk Songs. M.A., University of Missouri, 1936. 217 pp. B14 72, p. 27; I2, p. 117.

Over 200 Ozark folk songs listed of three types: ballads brought from British Isles, songs of more recent times, and songs for special occasions.

1685 KETTERING, Eunice Lea. Sacred Folk Songs of the Southern Appalachians. M.S.M., Union Theological Seminary, 1933. B8 1023, p. 71.

1686 KNOX, Winifred I. Folksongs from the Olympic Peninsula and Puget Sound. M.S., Juilliard School of Music, 1945. 96 pp.

Discusses settler songs, lumberjack songs, fishermen songs, and a number of pieces under a general heading of "American songs." Includes music and texts.

1687 *KOEHNLINE, William Angus. A Study of Folksongs of the Western United States Reflecting Western Life. M.A., English, University of North Carolina, 1949. 128 pp. I2, p. 208.

Discusses works (includes texts only) of historical interest and importance such as songs relating to events from 1812 to 1849, songs of the gold rush days, Civil War songs, and songs relating to events from 1865 to 1949. Also includes occupational songs, social and humorous songs, and songs about outlaws and supermen.

1688 KOON, William H. Folk Songs of Watauga [North Carolina]. Master's thesis, English, University of Georgia, 1967. 318 pp. H1, p. 232.

1689 LARONGE, Philip V. The Folksong and Folk Music Traditions of the Chippewa-Flambeau Region in NW Wisconsin. Master's thesis, Wayne State University, 1980. A2 5696, p. 256.

1690 LOOMIS, M. Marjorie. Irish Songs and Ballads in New York State. M.A., New York State College for Teachers of the State University of New York at Albany, 1938. K6 1092, p. 90; L6, p. 3.

1691 McDONALD, Grant. A Study of Selected Folk-Songs of Southern Missouri. M.A., University of Iowa, 1939. 100 pp. I2, p. 143.

1692 McHARGUE, Robert Morris. Study in the Popular Music of the American Frontiers. M.A., History, University of California at Berkeley, 1940. 248 pp. H1, p. 233; I2, p. 152.

1693 McINTOSH, David Seneff. Some Representative Southern Illinois Folk-Songs. M.A., University of Iowa, 1935. 374 pp. I2, p. 110.

1694 McMULLEN, Mildred M. The Prairie Songs: Northwest Kansas Folksongs. M.A., University of Kansas, 1946. 182 pp. L15 653, p. 42.

1695 MASON, Robert. Folk Songs and Folk Tales of Cannon County, Tennessee. M.A., English, George Peabody College for Teachers, 1939. 241 pp. H1, p. 233; I2, p. 143.

1696 MILLER, Jeannette. Folk-Songs of California: The History and Significance of Their Collection and Preservation. M.A., Librarianship, University of California at Berkeley, 1937. 81 pp. illus.

Discusses the background for the study, Spanish-Californian songs, songs of the American period, and miscellaneous songs. Includes a list of representative collections of songs.

1697 MILLER, Nellie Louise. Folk Music in Louisiana. M.M., Northwestern University, 1940. 52 pp. B14 112, p. 30; B15 543, p. 21; I2, p. 153.

1698 MOORE, Ethel Perry. An Experiment in Collecting and Classifying the Folk Songs Sung in Oklahoma. M.A., English, University of Oklahoma, 1926. H1, p. 233; I2, p. 46.

1699 NEAL, Mabel Evangeline. Brown County Songs and Ballads Collected and Annotated. M.A., Folklore, Indiana University, 1926. 182 pp.

1700 OWENS, Bess Alice. Some Unpublished Folksongs of the Cumberlands. M.A., English, George Peabody College for Teachers, 1930. 208 pp. H1, p. 234; I2, p. 70.

1701 PAREDES, Americo. Ballads of the Lower Border. Master's thesis, English, University of Texas at Austin, 1953. H1, p. 234.

"Mexican and American Ballads and Songs."

1702 PARR, Annie Ruth. A Study of European Folk Songs Collected in Waukegan, Illinois. M.M., Northwestern University, 1951. 66 pp. B14 127, p. 31; I2, p. 226.

Gives melodies and texts of Finnish, Swedish, Slovenian, Armenian, and Jewish folk songs.

1703 PERRY, Henry Wacaster. A Sampling of the Folklore of Carter County, Tennessee. M.A., English, George Peabody College for Teachers, 1938. 313 pp.

1704 PETITJEAN, Irene Martin. "Cajun" Folk Songs of Southwest Louisiana. M.A., French, Columbia University, 1930. 133 pp. H1, p. 234; I2, p. 70.

1705 PIPPART, Jane T. Pennsylvania Folk Songs: An Addition to an Old Heritage. M.M.E., Holy Names College, 1979. 135 pp. photos.

Includes a discussion of Mary Kunkel and her songs, the Amish, their schools and music, and the Pennsylvania German in Western Pennslyvania.

1706 *REES, Leslie E. A Collection and Analysis of Folk Songs from Wales, Sanpete County, Utah. M.A., Brigham Young University, 1966. 82 pp. B13, p. 74; I2, p. 328.

Forty-five songs are recorded on a tape.

1707 ROBINSON, Carolyn A. Child Ballads in Eastern Kentucky. Master's thesis, English, Vanderbilt University, 1966. H1, p. 235.

1708 *ROOF, Mary Ellen. A Study of the Influence of Elizabethan England on the Folk Music of the Southern Appalachians. M.Ed., Ohio University, 1953. 164 pp. F1 1179, p. 55; I2, p. 242.

1709 SAUCIER, C. L. Louisiana Folk Tales and Songs. M.A., Modern Languages, George Peabody College for Teachers, 1923. 97 pp. H1, p. 235; I2, p. 37.

"Louisiana folk tales and songs in French dialect with linguistic notes."

1710 SCARFF, Frances Beatriz Gonzalez. A Study of the Matachine Dance in Selected Areas of Mexico and Texas. M.Ed., University of Texas at Austin, 1962. B18 UT-1962-16, p. 86.

1711 *SCHROEDER, Rebecca B. Library Collections of Ohio Folksong. M.A., Library Science, Kent State University, 1964. 152 pp. G4, p. 44; G5, p. 198; I2, p. 319.

The libraries include the Library of Congress, Ohio Folklore and Music Archive of Miami University, Cincinnati Historical Society Library, the Martha Kinney Cooper Ohioana Library in Columbus, and the Ohio State Archaeological and Historical Museum Library at Ohio State University. Included are chapters on folksong collecting in Ohio.

1712 SHIELD, Renée Rose. Dine and Dance: Country Music in Helotes, Texas. M.A., University of Texas at Austin, 1973. I4 1887, p. 161; L7 (81), p. 429.

1713 SHORTHILL, Rachel. Variation in Anglo-American Folksong. M.A., American Studies, University of Kansas, 1983.

1714 SIFUENTES, Rodarte Fernando. A Comparative Study of the New Mexican and Mexican Popular Songs. M.A., Spanish, University of New Mexico, 1939. 102 pp. I2, p. 144.

1715 *STEELY, Mercedes. The Folk Songs of Ebenezer Community. M.A., English, University of North Carolina at Chapel Hill, 1936. 289 pp. H1, p. 236; I2, p. 120.
Wake County, North Carolina.

1716 STOKER, Vera Alice. A Study of Louisiana Folk Music. M.A., Stephen F. Austin State College, 1957. 83 pp. B18 SFA-1957-1, p. 46; I2, p. 271.

1717 SWAN, Clara LeGrande. A Collection of Ballads and Folk Songs from Morning Sun, Iowa. M.A., English, University of Iowa, 1929. 178 pp. I2, p. 64.

1718 *TERRY, Elvis B. A Collection of Ballad and Folk-Like Songs of Enterprise, Utah. Master's thesis, Brigham Young University, 1950. 135 pp. I2, p. 219.

1719 VOLLAND, Anita D. Dance in the Pre-Contact Hawaii: A Study of the Inter-relationship of Art, Religion, and Social Organization. Master's thesis, University of Pennsylvania, 1967. I4 2146, p. 184.

1720 WEST, Roy A. Songs of the Mountaineers. Master's thesis, English, George Peabody College for Teachers, 1922. H1, p. 237.

1721 *WHEELER, Mary. Ohio River Folk Songs of the Packet-Boat Era. M.M., Cincinnati Conservatory of Music, 1937. 164 pp. B14 175, p. 35; I2, p. 130.
Includes 68 musical examples.

1722 WILLIAMS, Cratis Dearl. Ballads and Songs of Kentucky and Lawrence County. M.A., English, University of Kentucky, 1937. 437 pp. H1, p. 237; I2, p. 130.

1723 WILLIS, Ninevah J. A Study of the Folklore of a Mountainous Section of Southwestern Virginia. Master's thesis, Education, Radford College, 1955. H1, p 237.

Discusses "folk songs, especially of Carroll County."

1724 WISE, James Edward. Folk Songs and Ballads of East Texas. M.A., English, Stephen F. Austin State College, 1950. 311 pp. I2, p. 220.

1725 *WRIGHT, Maud. Folk Music of Arkansas. M.A., Education, Louisiana State University, 1937. 50 pp. H1, p. 238; I2, p. 131.

1726 WYATT, P. J. "I'm Not Selling Anything"—Some Folklore from Kansas. M.A., Folklore, Indiana University, 1956. 179 pp.

1727 WYLDER, Robert Clay. A Comparative Analysis of Some Montana Folksongs. M.A., English, University of Montana, 1949. 123 pp. I2, p. 211.

ETHNIC GROUPS
Afro-American

1728 ANDERSON, Margaret Bassett. The Treatment of Some of the Bible Stories in Negro Spirituals. M.A., English, Columbia University, 1930. 50 pp. H1, p. 226; I2, p. 64.

1729 *APPREY, Zane Swayzine Ragland. Strategies for Survival through Creativity in the Period of Slavery and in the Black Church Experience, and Their Relevance to Music Therapy. M.M.Ed., University of Kansas, 1976. 94 pp.

1730 BALES, Mary Virginia. Negro Folksongs in Texas: Their Definition and Origin. M.A., English, Texas Christian University, 1927. 190 pp. H1, p. 227; I2, p. 49.

1731 BALLOU, Leonard R. Negroes and Music in Nineteenth Century America: A Survey. M.A., Education, Virginia State College, 1964. 167 pp. I2, p. 312.

1732 BARTLETT, Troy R. Afro-American Influences on Some of the Music of the Americas from 1920-1950. M.A., Education, Alabama State College, 1955. F1 1274, p. 59; I2, p. 251.

1733 BEAVER, Mary Corinne. The Origin and Characteristics of Negro Spirituals. M.A., Claremont Graduate School, 1963. 94 pp. I2, p. 303.

1734 BELTON, Geneva R. The Contributions of Negro Music and Musicians in World War II. M.M., Northwestern University, 1946. 64 pp. B2, p. 116; B7 51, p. 9; B15 47, p. 6.

1735 BENNETT, Carolyn L. African Survivals in the Religious Music Tradition of the United States Negro. Master's thesis, DePaul University, 1968. F1 1612, p. 73.

1736 BIGGERS, Charles Edward. A Comparison of Negro Folksongs with Negro Traditional Verse of the Twentieth Century. M.A., English, Tennessee Agricultural and Industrial State University, 1954. 73 pp. I2, p. 245.

1737 BOGOMOLNY, Michael. A Sociological Interpretation of the Negro Folksong. Master's thesis, English, Ohio State University, 1929. H1, p. 227.

1738 BOYNTON, Madge B. An Evaluation of the Slave Songs as an Historical Source. Master's thesis, History, Texas Women's University, 1970. H1, p. 227; H3 2866, p. 183.

1739 *BROOKS, Sydonia Mae. History of Spirituals in the United States. Master's thesis, DePaul University, 1973. 89 pp.

1740 BROWN, Cecilia Roberta. Afro-American Contribution to Dance in the United States, 1865-1965. M.S., Illinois State University, 1970. 148 pp. C1 42, p. 25.

1741 *BUFORD, Alzada M. Singleton. A Survey of Afro-American Music and Musicians. M.A., Ohio State University, 1938. 195 pp. I3, p. 33.

1742 BURTON, William. The History of the Negro Spiritual and Its Contribution to Sacred Music. M.A., San Francisco Theological Seminary, 1943. B8 8, p. 3.

1743 CARTER, Albert E. The Louisiana Negro and His Music. M.M., Northwestern University, 1947. 72 pp. B7 121, p. 18; B14 29, p. 24; B15 131, p. 9; I2, p. 190.

Includes chapters on the African heritage, occupational songs, blues and hollers, swing, Creole songs, and spirituals. Each song discussed includes background information, text, and music.

1744 CHEEKS, Gertrude Dansby. The Historical Background and Development of the Negro and His Songs. M.M., Millikin University, 1949. 65 pp. I2, p. 205.

1745 CLARKE, Joe E. L. Communal Origins of Songs among the Negroes. Master's thesis, English, Washington University at St. Louis, 1926. H1, p. 229.

1746 CLARY, Inez H. Selected Black Singing Traditions. Master's thesis, Virginia State College, 1972. F1 1281, p. 63.

1747 *COBB, Charles. A Theoretical Analysis of Black Quartet Gospel Music. M.M., University of Wisconsin at Madison, 1974. 2 vols. 619 pp.

1748 *CRAWFORD, Portia Naomi. A Study of Negro Folksongs from Greensboro, North Carolina and Surrounding Towns. M.A., University of North Carolina at Chapel Hill, 1965. 114 pp. H1, p. 229; I2, p. 321.

1749 ENCKE, Elizabeth C. The Contribution of the Negro to American Music. Master's thesis, New Jersey State Teacher's College at Newark, 1955. F1 1143, p. 54.

1750 FITZPATRICK, Newell C. The Origin and Development of the Negro Spirituals. M.M., Syracuse University, 1934. 77 pp. I2, p. 99.

1751 FORREST, Hilda Mae. A Study of Negro Spirituals. M.A., English, University of Illinois, 1931. 134 pp. I2, p. 74.

1752 FOSTER, William P. The Influence of the Negro on Music in America. M.A., Wayne State University, 1950. 128 pp. B7 231, p. 32; B14 50, p. 25; I2, p. 214.

1753 FOWLER, Ona Arlene. Contributions the Negro Has Made to American Music. M.S., Education, Kansas State College, 1936. 101 pp. I2, p. 115.

1754 *GILLUM, Ruth Helen. The Negro Folksong and Its Influence in American Music. M.A., University of Kansas, 1940. 144 pp. B7 255, p. 34; I2, p. 150.

1755 GLAZER, Irving William. Negro Music in Early America, from 1619 to the Civil War. M.A., New York University, 1945. 99 pp. B7 257, p. 35; I2, p. 182.

1756 GREENE, Barbara Joyce. African Musical Survivals in the Songs of the Negro in Haiti, Jamaica, and the United States. M.A., Anthropology, University of Chicago, 1948. B7 272, p. 36; B14 59, p. 26; I2, p. 199; I4 0768, p. 66.

1757 HAIRSTON, Teresa. Stylistic Trends in the Twentieth Century Afro-American Gospel Music. Master's thesis, Southern Illinois University at Edwardsville, 1982. A2 2994, p. 145.

1758 *HILTON, Margaret E. A Selective Study of Negro Worksongs in the United States. M.M., Eastern Illinois University, 1976. 48 pp.

1759 IRVIS, K. Leroy. The Negro in the Civil War Song Ballads. Master's thesis, English, New York State University at Albany, 1939. H1, p. 232; K6 1091, p. 90.

1760 JESSUP, Lynn Elva. African Characteristics Found in Afro-American and Anglo-American Music. M.A., University of Washington, 1971. 179 pp. B5 (19), p. 134.

1761 KERR, Thomas Henderson. A Critical Survey of Printed Vocal Arrangements of Afro-American Religious Folk Songs. M.M., Eastman School of Music of the University of Rochester, 1939. B8 663, p. 48; B14 82, p. 28; I2, p. 142.

1762 *KINSCELLA, Hazel Gertrude. Songs of the American Negro and Their Influence upon Composed Music. M.A., Columbia University, 1934. 43 pp. illus. B14 86, p. 28; H1, p. 232; I2, p. 102.

1763 *LIVENGOOD, Karen Sue. Negro Music and Its Influence on American Music. M.M.Ed., University of Louisville, 1968. 132 pp. F1 1659, p. 75.

1764 LUCAS, John Samuel. Rhythms of Negro Music and Negro Poetry. M.A., University of Minnesota, 1945. 241 pp. B14 98, p. 29.

1765 McADAMS, Nettie F. The Folksongs of the American Negro: A Collection of Unprinted Texts Preceded by a General Survey of the Traits of the Negro Songs. M.A., English, University of California at Berkeley, 1923. 159 pp. I2, p. 36; J4 6188, p. 177.

Discusses traits common to the Negro folk songs and ballads, and reasons for the distinctive traits of Negro verse. Chapter 4 is a collection of unprinted texts of 60 spirituals and 126 secular songs.

1766 McGEE, Daniel Bennett. Religious Beliefs and Ethical Motifs of the Negro Spirituals. Th.M., Southeastern Baptist Theological Seminary, 1960. 117 pp. I2, p. 286; J3 1241, p. 73; J4 6189, p. 177.

1767 *MacLEOD, Bruce Alan. The Role of Flutes in Afro-American Music of the United States: An Historical Survey and Analysis. M.A., University of Pittsburgh, 1976. 97 pp.

Some of his material is restated in his article "Quills, Fifes, and Flutes before the Civil War," *Southern Folklore Quarterly* 42/2-3 (1978): 201-08.

1768 MAYLE, Bessie H. History and Interpretation of the Pre-Reformation Carol and the Negro Spiritual. Master's thesis, Boston University, 1932. J4 6187, p. 177.

1769 *MONTAGUE, James Harold. A Historical Survey of Negro Music and Musicians and Their Influence on Twentieth Century Music. M.Mus., Syracuse University, 1938. 52 pp. illus. B14 115, p. 30.

1770 MORRIS, Ophelia Estelle. Some Characteristics of the Negro American Secular Folk-Songs. M.A., English, Fisk University, 1948. 78 pp. H1, p. 234; I2, p. 201.

1771 *MYERS, William Jackson, Jr. The Syncretism of European and West African Influences in Music of the United States. M.A., Midwestern University, 1962. 113 pp.

1772 NICKERSON, Camille Lucie. Africo-Creole Music in Louisiana: A Thesis on the Plantation Songs Created by the Creole Negroes of Louisiana. M.M., Oberlin College, 1932. 90 pp. H1, p. 234; I2, p. 84.

"The supplement to this thesis contains seven Creole songs collected and harmonized."

1773 PATTON, Leila Elizabeth. The Spirituals of the American Negro. M.A., Education, Columbia University, 1938. 17 pp. H1, p. 234; I2, p. 136.

1774 PEARSON, Boyce Neal. A Cantometric Analysis of Three Afro-American Songs Recorded in the Commerce, Texas Area. M.S., East Texas State University, 1978. 57 pp. A1 (17/3) 1312678, p. 216.

1775 *ROBBINS, Leroy W. Negro Folk Music. M.M., University of Kansas, 1927. 24 pp.

1776 ROBINSON, Mabel L. American Negro Folk Music: The Evolution of Its Structure and Technique. M.A., Boston University, 1940. 103 pp. I2, p. 154.

1777 *SADLER, Cora. Creole Songs. M.A., University of Michigan, 1939. 254 pp. I2, p. 144.

1778 SAIGHOE, Francis A. Kobina. Traditional African Music as Performed by Black Americans. M.M., University of Maryland, 1977. 116 pp. illus.; photos.

This thesis demonstrates why Black Americans became interested in traditional African musical practices and also discusses the reasons why certain elements of their practices betray some forms of modification and adaptation of the original practices. Based on field research.

1779 SEBASTIAN, Linda Jean Chaney. Symbolism in Afro-American Slave Songs in the Pre-Civil War South. M.S., Speech, North Texas State University, 1976. 123 pp. L11, p. 107.

1780 *SHAW, Phyllis S. African Survivals in the Negro Spiritual as Seen in "Nobody Knows the Trouble I See." Master's thesis, Kent State University, 1972. 154 pp. illus.

1781 SLAPPEY, George H. Some Additions to the Study of Negro Folk Songs. Master's thesis, English, Oglethorpe University, 1928. H1, p. 236.

1782 THOMPSON, Elizabeth Azalia Jette. The Origin and the Contribution that Negro Spirituals Have Made in the Area of Folk Music. M.A., Education, Alabama State Teachers College at Montgomery, 1947. H1, p. 236; I2, p. 195.

1783 *THROWER, Sarah Selina. The Spiritual of the Gullah Negro in South Carolina. M.M., Cincinnati Conservatory of Music, 1954. 64 pp. B14 164, p. 34; I2, p. 250.

1784 *TINSLEY, Vallie. Some Negro Songs Heard in the Hills of North Louisiana. M.A., English, Louisiana State University, 1928. 76 pp. illus. H1, p. 236; I2, p. 58.

1785 TOCUS, Clarence Spencer. The Negro Idiom in American Musical Composition. M.M., University of Southern California, 1942. 143 pp. I2, p. 169.

1786 TRANTHAM, Carrie Pool. An Investigation of the Unpublished Negro Folk Songs of Dorothy Scarborough. M.A., English, Baylor University, 1941. 280 pp. H1, p. 236; H2 5380, p. 199; I2, p. 163.

1787 WALDEN, Jean Elizabeth. The History, Development, and Contribution of the Negro Folk Song. M.M., Northwestern University, 1945. 75 pp. B14 170, p. 34; B15 867, p. 30; I2, p. 185.

1788 WALKER, Sammye Mae Sadler. A Study of Negro Folk Songs of Oklahoma. M.A., English, University of Iowa, 1943. 139 pp. I2, p. 176.

1789 WALL, Ruth D. African-American Negro Music. M.A., Education, New Jersey State Teacher's College at Newark, 1957. F1 1128, p. 53; I2, p. 271.

1790 WALMSLEY, Robert. A Comparative Analysis of the Symbolism of Selected Black Spirituals as Reflected in Some Contemporary Gospel Songs and Its Impact upon Black Culture. Master's thesis, Religion, Howard University, 1973. J4 6329, p. 181.

1791 WATSON, Jack McLauren. Negro Folk Music in Eastern South Carolina. M.M., University of Southern California, 1940. 85 pp. I2, p. 155.

1792 WHITE, Lillian Olga. The Folksongs of the American Negro and Their Value Today. M.A., English, University of Idaho, 1925. 73 pp. H1, p. 237; I2, p. 43.

1793 WILLIAMS, Robert Elbert. The Negro Spiritual and Religious Symbolism. S.M.M., Union Theological Seminary, 1950. B8 1256, p. 86.

1794 WILLIAMS, Thelma A. Origin and Analysis of Negro Folk Song. M.S., Wayne State University, 1938. 68 pp. B6 W727, p. 30; B14 177, p. 35; H1, p. 237; I2, p. 138.

1795 WORK, John Wesley. The Folk Songs of the American Negro. M.A., Education, Columbia University Teachers College, 1930. 40 pp. H1, p. 237; I2, p. 71.

Includes a discussion of spirituals and "the origin of the blues."

1796 WRIGHT, Jeremiah A. The Treatment of Biblical Passages in Negro Spirituals. M.A., English, Howard University, 1969. 177 pp. J4 6346, p. 182.

Particularly useful is Appendix A which lists biblical sources of Negro spirituals.

1797 ZANDER, Marjorie T. The Brass Band Funeral and Related Negro Burial Customs. Master's thesis, Folklore, University of North Carolina at Chapel Hill, 1962. H1, p. 238.

Anglo-American

1798 BAILEY, Frederick. The Historical Ballad: Its Tradition in Britain and America. Master's thesis, English, University of Tennessee, 1963. H1, p. 227.

1799 *BARKS, Susan Katherine. Death and a Lady: Echoes of a Mortal Conversation in English and American Folk Song Tradition. M.A., English, University of North Carolina at Chapel Hill, 1967. H1, p. 227.

1800 BROWNE, Earl William. Variant Versions of Scottish and English Humorous Popular Ballads in America. A.M., English, University of Southern California, 1951. 343 pp. B7 99, p. 15; B14 23, p. 23.

1801 COWAN, Clayton Leroy. Irish Folksong Elements in American Popular Music, 1860-1900. M.A., University of Southern California, 1950. 125 pp. B7 150, p. 22; B14 38, p. 24; I2, p. 213.

1802 ELSENHAUS, Ingrid Angeleka. Ten British Traditional Ballads in America. M.A., University of Texas at Austin, 1961. B18 UT-1961-1, p. 84.

1803 HALL, Dorothy C. Comparative Study of the Popular Ballad of England and America. Master's thesis, English, University of Idaho, 1923. H1, p. 231.

1804 *JOINER, James Richard. A Study of the Relationships between the Tunes of American Folk-Hymnody and the Tunes of the General British-American Repertory of Folk Song. M.C.M., Southwestern Baptist Theological Seminary, 1968. 235 pp. illus. B18 SBS-1968-3, p. 45.

1805 *KANNAPEL, Mary Bernard. The Place of the American Folk Ballad in Children's Song Literature. M.Ed., University of Cincinnati, 1945. 64 pp.

Includes "Ballads found in publications in children's song literature, 1922-1943," pp. 51-61, and "Listed recordings of American ballads and closely related folk song," pp. 62-64.

1806 *McCULLOUGH, Lawrence Ervin. The Rose in the Heather: Traditional Irish Music in Its American Cultural Milieu. M.A., University of Pittsburgh, 1975. 107 pp. B5 (20), p. 588.

1807 McTIERNAN, Ellan M. Irish Ballads and Songs in America. M.A., English, Cornell University, 1945. 96 pp. I2, p. 183.

1808 *MATE, Mary Irene. The Child Ballads Revamped. M.S. in Ed., Southern Illinois University, 1964. 99 pp.

1809 MILLER, Minnie M. Tom Clarence Ashley: An Appalachian Folk Musician. Master's thesis, East Tennessee State University, 1973. 64 pp.

This study focuses on the life of Ashley in Mountain City, Tennessee.

1810 PARNELL, Catherine E. The Archive of Folk Song, Library of Congress: A Source of Songs for Use with the Kodaly Concept of Music Education. M.M., Holy Names College, 1977. 56 pp.

Discusses the development of the Archive of Folk Song. Included is a preliminary inventory of songs, each entry listing the AFS catalog number, title, and performer. Also included is a selection of transcriptions of fifteen songs taken from the inventory.

1811 *PORTNOY, Marshall Alan. Jean Thomas' American Folk Song Festival: British Balladry in Eastern Kentucky. M.A., University of Louisville, 1978. 117 pp. illus. A1 (17/2) 1312485, p. 149; A2 3167, p. 137.

Jean Thomas founded the Festival; her papers are located in the University of Louisville.

1812 *STARCHER, Duane B. Introduction to Anglo-American Folk Song: A College Course. Master's thesis, University of Michigan, 1958.

1813 *WALKER, E. C. Some Characteristics of "Barbara Allen" in America. M.A., English, University of North Carolina at Chapel Hill, 1944.

1814 WENKER, Jerome. A Computational Method for the Analysis of Anglo-American Folksongs. M.A., Folklore, Indiana University, 1964. 271 pp. I2, p. 321.

This study is based on the premise that "the problems involved in applying the objective analytical techniques used by ethnomusicologists and folklorists to a statistically significant corpus of Anglo-American folksongs are due primarily to the excessive amount of labor required." Discusses music notation and the use of the computer.

1815 WILSBACH, Thomas Aquinas. Never Was Piping So Gay: Uilleann Piping in the United States. M.M., University of Maryland, 1978. 122 pp. illus.; photos.

A history of the bellows-blown Irish bagpipes in America from approximately 1790 to the present. Includes a good bibliography of sound discs and tapes.

Native-American

1816 ADAMS, Robert H. Songs of Our Grandfathers: Music of the Unami Delaware Indians. M.A., University of Washington, 1977. 193 pp. B5 (22), p. 512; B17 (11/1) 1236, p. 72.

1817 ALBERTSON, Ruthelle Marjorie. The American Indian and His Song. M.M., University of Idaho, 1941. 50 pp. B7 6, p. 3; B14 1, p. 22; I1 3659, p. 5; I2, p. 156.

"Bannock, Shoshoni, mainly at Fort Hall Reservation."

1818 ATER, Elma Louise. A Historical Study of the Singing Conventions of the Indians of Robeson County, North Carolina. M.A., Ohio State University, 1943. B7 28, p. 6; I1 3762, p. 11; I2, p. 170.

1819 BAILEY, Virginia May. An Evaluation of the Musical Expression of the Southern California Indians. M.A., Claremont College, 1934. 91 pp. B7 33, p. 7; B14 9, p. 22.

1820 BARNARD, Herwanna Becker. The Comanche and His Literature with an Anthology of His Myths, Legends, Folktales, Oratory, Poetry, and Songs. M.A., English, University of Oklahoma, 1941. 277 pp. B7 41, p. 8; B14 13, p. 22; H1, p. 227; I1 156, p. 16; I2, p. 156.

1821 BEATTY, John Joseph. Kiowa-Apache Music and Dance. M.A., University of Oklahoma, 1966. 97 pp. I1 3865, p. 21; I4 0136, p. 12.

1822 BECKWITH, Martha Warren. Dance Forms of the Moqui and Kwakiutl Indians. M.A., Anthropology, Columbia University, 1906. 43 pp. B7 50, p. 9; I1 208, p. 21; I2, p. 7.

1823 *BELOFF, Sandra Beth. Music of the Pawnees (with Special Reference to Present Day Oklahoma Practices). M.A., University of California at Los Angeles, 1972. 214 pp. B13, p. 74; B17 (6/1) 952, p. 62.

1824 BENSON, Robert L. Indian Music in Selected Northern Wisconsin Counties. Master's thesis, University of Wisconsin at Platteville, 1973. F1 1252, p. 64.

1825 BLAIR, Leola Ruth. A Study of the Cultural Heritage of the California Children from the Indians. M.M., University of Southern California, 1947. 154 pp. B7 64 p. 11; B14 20, p. 23; I1 270, p. 27.

Includes a list of recordings in the Museum of the University of California at Berkeley. Describes music and dance of each tribe.

1826 BOGAN, Phebe M. The Ceremonial Dances of the Yaqui Indians near Tucson, Arizona. M.A., History, University of Arizona, 1922. 87 pp. B7 70, p. 12; I1 292, p. 30; I2, p. 33.

1827 BROUGH, Rosemary Joy. Lucky, the Opportunist: A Psychobiological Personality Study of the Navaho Singer. M.A., Cornell University, 1953. 158 pp. B7 92, p. 14; I1 381, p. 39; I2, p. 237.

1828 BUESCHEL, Gordon Richard. Indian Song and Dance. M.M., Northwestern University, 1948. 63 pp. B7 106, p. 16; B14 24, p. 23; I1 4086, p. 42; I2, p. 197.

Includes ten Oglala Sioux songs.

1829 *BUSS, Judy Epstein. The Flute and Flute Music of the North American Indians. Master's thesis, University of Illinois at Urbana-Champaign, 1977. 134 pp.

1830 CARRITHERS, Michael B. Raids on the Squaw Dance: Some Sketches. Master's thesis, Wesleyan University, 1971. I4 0294, p. 26.

Concerns dance of the Navajo Indians.

1831 *CASON, Georgie Rees. An Introduction to a Study of California Indian Music. M.A., University of California at Berkeley, 1936. 70 pp. illus. B7 122, p. 18; B14 30, p. 24; I1 4182, p. 52; I2, p. 123.

1832 CHESKY, Jane. The Nature and Function of Papago Music. M.A., University of Arizona, 1943. 137 pp. I1 555, p. 56; I4 0332, p. 29.

1833 *CLIVE, Joseph C. Music of the Pahute Indians. M.S., University of Utah, 1949. 44 pp. B7 136, p. 20; B14 35, p. 24; I1 4257, p. 59; I2, p. 206.

"Musical transcriptions of 21 songs (of southern Utah), no texts."

1834 COINE, Harriet Edythe. The Play Life of Certain Indian Tribes in California. M.A., University of Southern California, 1932. 65 pp. B7 139, p. 20.

1835 COOKE, Frederick A. P. American Indian Music and Dancing. M.M., College of Music of Cincinnati, 1934. B7 144, p. 21; I1 4309, p. 64.

1836 *DAVENPORT, Linda Gilbert. Music among the Contemporary Penobscot Indians. M. Mus., University of Illinois at Urbana-Champaign, 1977. 211 pp.

1837 DRUMMOND, Isabel N. A Study of the Literary and Artistic Elements of the Life of the Sioux. M.A., English, Indiana University, 1930. 137 pp. B7 189, p. 26; B14 43, p. 25.

"Based entirely on published materials by Densmore."

1838 DRUMMOND, Julius L. The Dream and the Dance: A Comparative Study of Ritual Symbolism and Its Relation to Myth and Social Structures in Two American Indian Tribes. Master's thesis, University of Chicago, 1968. I4 0529, p. 46.

1839 *EARLES, Roma. Teaching the Music and Other Cultural Traditions of the Kickapoo and Pottawatomi People in Kansas. M.M.Ed., University of Kansas, 1975. 65 pp. illus.

Includes one sound cassette.

1840   EISLER, David. The Development of the Dancing Societies on the Northwest
        Coast of North America. Master's thesis, Temple University, 1971. I4 0557,
        p. 48.
        Indians of North America.

1841   EMERY, Nedra. A Survey of Navajo Nursery Tales and Songs Written in Navajo
        with English Interpretations. M.A., Northern Arizona University at
        Flagstaff, 1956. 76 pp. I1 4616, p. 94; I2, p. 251.

1842   FISCHER, Ruby Keefauver. Literary and Artist Expression of the Hopi Indians.
        M.A., English, Indiana University, 1930. 141 pp. B7 224, p. 31; B14 47, p. 25.

1843   FLORES, Alonzo J. A Study to Determine the Musical Preference of the Young
        American Indian High School Graduates Attending Haskell Institute,
        Lawrence, Kansas. M.A., University of Kansas, 1966. 96 pp. I1 4732, p. 105.

1844   *FOLTIN, Béla. Continuity and Change in Klamath Indian Music and Musical
        Culture. M.Mus., University of Illinois at Urbana-Champaign, 1971.
        199 pp. illus.

1845   FRISBIE, Charlotte Johnson. Kinaaldá: A Study of the Navaho Girl's Puberty
        Ceremony. M.A., Wesleyan University, 1964. 610 pp. B17 (2/1) 1058, p. 74.

1846   GAMBLE, John Irvin. Kiowa Dance Gatherings and Costumed Dancers. M.A.,
        Washington University, 1952. 78 pp. B7 241, p. 33; I1 1144, p. 115; I4 0690,
        p. 59.

1847   GATES, Charlene Elizabeth. Toward a Stylistic Description of Music in the
        Navajo Enemy Way. M.A., University of Oregon, 1975. 208 pp. B5 (24),
        p. 103.

1848   GELLATLY, Marjorie Gail. Fourteen Northwest Coast Indian Songs Transcribed
        into Musical Notation. M.A., University of Washington, 1940. 79 pp.
        B7 250, p. 34; B14 54, p. 25; I1 1170, p. 117; I2, p. 149.
        "Data from Muckleshoot Reservation: Puyallup, Lummi, Yakima, Snoqualmic."

1849   GOLD, Keo, and Elaine BORESON. An Investigation into a Hypothesis of a
        Cultural Affinity of the Mongols of Northeast Asia and the Sioux Indians
        of North America through a Comparison of the Music. M.A., University
        of Nebraska, 1969. 46 pp. I1 4898, p. 122.

1850 GOODMAN, Linda J. The Form and Function of the Basket Dance of San Juan Pueblo. Master's thesis, Wesleyan University, 1968. I4 0742, p. 63.

1851 GROTTS, Pearl Irene. Sociological Aspects of the Crow Indian Dances. M.A., Physical Education, University of Iowa, 1942. 23 pp. B7 277, p. 37; C2 251, p. 22; I1 1302, p. 130.

1852 GUILD, Elliott William. The Sociological Role of Music in Primitive Cultures. M.A., Stanford University, 1931. I1 1309, p. 130.
Includes a discussion of music of North American Indians.

1853 GUNST, Marie Louise. Ceremonials of the Papago and Pima Indians, with Special Emphasis on the Relationship of the Dance to Their Religion. M.A., University of Arizona, 1930. 73 pp. B7 281, p. 38; I1 1313, p. 131.

1854 HESS, Ralph Edward. Arizona Indian Music and Suggestions for Its Use in the Elementary Schools. M.F.A., University of California at Los Angeles, 1950. 145 pp. B7 318, p. 42; B14 67, p. 27; I1 1470, p. 147; I2, p. 215.

1855 HUENEMANN, Lynn Fredrick. An Historical Survey of the Music of the Winnebago Tribe of Nebraska. M.A., Indiana University, 1970. 143 pp. L1 5820, p. 159; I4 0942, p. 81.

1856 ISBELL, Sarah Rachel. Musical Talent of Indians. M.A., University of Denver, 1928. 81 pp. I1 1606, p. 160.
"Chilocco Indian School, Oklahoma."

1857 JONES, Rosalie May. The Blackfeet Medicine Lodge Ceremony: Ritual and Dance Drama. M.S., Modern Dance and Ballet, University of Utah, 1968. 163 pp. B5 (13), p. 348; C1 106, p. 31.

1858 KAUFMAN, Howard Keva. Cheyenne Indian Music and Its Cultural Background. M.A., Indiana University, 1952. 312 pp. B14 80, p. 28; I1 1716, p. 171; I4 1039, p. 89.
Includes 54 musical examples.

1859 KING, Bernice Margaret. A Study of Form and Expression in American Indian Music, as Exemplified in the Songs of Jémez Pueblo. M.A., University of Minnesota, 1935. 270 pp. B14 85, p. 28; I1 1770, p. 176; I4 1075, p. 92.
Seventy songs are analyzed. Also concerns Indian dances.

1860   KISLING, Joan Falter. A Study of Selected Fort Hall Shoshone-Bannock Indian Dances. M.A., Education, Idaho State University, 1975. 46 pp. K4, p. 19.

1861   LAMM, Charles Alfred. The Relation between Musical Achievement and Music Reading Proficiency of American Indian Instrumental Pupils from Various Cultural Areas. M.A., University of Kansas, 1958. I1 5580, p. 189.

1862   LANE, Laura. Notation and Analysis of Selected Kiowa Songs. M.A., West Texas State University, 1963. 67 pp. I1 5588, p. 190; I2, p. 307.

1863   LEE, Nancy Isabel. Dances Inspired by the Navaho. M.F.A., University of Utah, 1971. C1 117, p. 32.

1864   LINCOLN, Martha Louise. The Cherokee Outlet and Its Music. M.M., University of Southern California, 1949. 117 pp. B14 94, p. 29; I1 1938, p. 192; I2, p. 208.

1865   LOSSING, Laverna Lucy. A Study of the Character and Role of Music among the California Indians. M.A., History, University of Southern California, 1934. 71 pp. I1 1985, p. 196; I2, p. 102.

1866   LOWRY, Ira Pate. The Instrumental Music of the Indians of Robeson County, North Carolina. M.A., Ohio State University, 1942. I1 5733, p. 204; I2, p. 166.

1867   McGEE, Charles Bernard. The Primitive Music of the Alaskan Eskimo. M.M., Northwestern University, 1947. 50 pp. B14 101, p. 29; B15 506, p. 20; I1 5798, p. 211; I2, p. 193.

1868   MARTI, Anna Miller. A History of the Ghost-Dance Religion among the Indians. M.A., University of Oklahoma, 1935. B8 1295, p. 89; I1 2203, p. 217.

1869   MASSA, Gloria. Music and Customs Associated with the Christian Worship among the American Indians. S.M.M., Union Theological Seminary, 1952. B8 1079, p. 75.

1870 *MOHAJERY, Barbara A. The Use of Musical Analysis to Substantiate Patterns of Cultural Interaction among Some North American Indian Tribes. M.A., State University College at Potsdam, New York, 1973. 113 pp.

1871 MOHLING, Virginia Gill. Twana Spirit Power Songs. M.A., University of Washington, 1957. 30 pp. B14 114, p. 30; I1 6019, p. 232; I4 1398, p. 119.

1872 MORENO, Joseph J. A Comparison of the Musical Behavior of Indian and Non-Indian College Students. M.A., University of Kansas, 1966. 81 pp. I1 6044, p. 234.

1873 MURRAY, Eloise. Contribution of the American Indian to Leisure Time. M.A., George Peabody College for Teachers, 1934. 168 pp. I1 2390, p. 235. Discusses dance.

1874 *NETTL, Bruno. Musical Culture of the Arapaho. M.A., Indiana University, 1951. 116 pp. illus. B6 N474, p. 23; B14 123, p. 31; I1 2423, p. 239.

1875 *PALMER, James R. The Uses and Functions of Peyote Music among North American Indians. Master's thesis, Sociology and Anthropology, Kent State University, 1968. 58 pp. illus.

1876 PIETROFORTE, Alfred. Yokuts' and Paiute Folk Songs. M.A., Fresno State College, 1961. 112 pp. I1 6317, p. 262; I2, p. 296.

1877 POLLENZ, Philippa. Some Problems in the Notation of Seneca Dances. M.A., Columbia University, 1947. 89 pp. I1 2636, p. 261; I4 1611, p. 137.

1878 POWERS, William K. Yuwipi Music in Cultural Context. Master's thesis, Wesleyan University, 1971. I4 1622, p. 138. Sioux music.

1879 SCHUBERT, Melvin Frank. An Analysis of Certain Similarities between the City Dionysia and the Fort Hall Sun Dances. M.A., University of Southern California, 1954. 111 pp. D2 (8) 1576, p. 148; I1 2945, p. 291.

1880 SHEFFIELD, Sarah Vantrease. A Study of Indian Dances. M.A., George Peabody College for Teachers, 1930. 176 pp. I1 3003, p. 297.

1881   SHLANTA, Boghdan A. A Comparison of Navaho and Pueblo Indians in Musical Talent. M.A., University of Mexico, 1938. 77 pp. B14 141, p. 32; I1 3019, p. 298.

1882   SMITH, Edna Eveland. Ceremonials of the Papago and Pima Indians, with Special Emphasis on the Relationship of the Dance to Their Religion. M.A., University of Iowa, 1935. 66 pp. B8 311, p. 24; I1 3073, p. 304.

1883   SMITH, Robert L. A Graphic Interpretation of Four Pueblo Indian Corn Dances. M.A., University of New Mexico, 1951. photos. I1 3089, p. 305.

    "Illustrated by Smith's paintings; also 21 plates and 18 photos of dances, dancers, costumes."

1884   SNOW, Ira Jean. A Study of Five Civilized Indian Tribes of Oklahoma: A Unit of Work Integrating Music, Art, English, and Oklahoma History in the Junior High School. M.M., University of California at Los Angeles, 1946. 349 pp. B14 146, p. 33; I1 3098, p. 306.

1885   SNYDER, D. Geraldine. Seneca Indian Songs. M.M., Northwestern University, 1944. 38 pp. B14 147, p. 33; B15 770, p. 27; I1 3102, p. 307.

1886   STAAB, Mary Theresine. Indian Lullabies, and an Analytical Study of Some North American Indian Cradle Songs. M.A., Catholic University of America, 1940. 28 pp. I1 6885, p. 317; I2, p. 154.

1887   TACCONE, Anthony. American Indian Ritual/Drama: A General Introduction to the Pre-History of Dramatic Spectacles in North America. M.A., University of Colorado, 1975. 152 pp.

    Chapter 4 is a discussion of lyrics and music.

1888   *THOMPSON, James William. Selected Studies of Musical Functions in Iroquois Culture. M.M., George Peabody College for Teachers, 1954. 110 pp. B12, p. 139.

1889   TOLLEFSON, Kenneth Dean. A Thematic Analysis of the Crow Indians. M.A., University of Oklahoma, 1965. 84 pp. I1 7067, p. 334.

1890 *TURPEN, Charles. Music in Navaho Ceremonialism. M.M., College-Conservatory of Music of Cincinnati, 1951. 91 pp. B14 168, p. 34; I1 7108, p. 338; I2, p. 228.

1891 VAUGHAN, Portia Loyetta. An Investigation of Music as Taught in a Government Indian School in Oklahoma. M.A., University of Kansas, 1939. 189 pp. B14 169, p. 34; I1 3378, p. 334.
"Tahlequah, Oklahoma."

1892 WALKER, Ouida Merle. Motivation of Song as Illustrated by the Pueblo Indians. M.A., Anthropology, University of Texas, 1931. 144 pp. I1 7194, p. 346; I2, p. 78; I4 2156, p. 184.

1893 WARE, Luella Catherine. Teaching Music in the Junior High School to the Mono Indians of Madera County, California. M.M., University of the Pacific, 1959. 111 pp. I1 7215, p. 348.

1894 *WEISHAAR, Ada Louise. A Study of the Music of the American Indian. M.A., College-Conservatory of Music of Cincinnati, 1946. 63 pp. illus. B14 172, p. 35; I1 7254, p. 352; I2, p. 188.
Also includes American composers who use Indian elements.

1895 WELLS, Willie Scruggs. Indian Music and Its Place in the Curriculum of the Modern School. M.A., West Texas State University, 1952. 100 pp. I1 3477, p. 344.

1896 WILDER, Carelton S. The Yaqui Deer Dance: A Study in Cultural Change. M.A., University of Arizona, 1940. 157 pp. I1 3530, p. 349; I4 2210, p. 189.

1897 WILLIAMS, James R. Tribal Education of the Hopi Indian Child. M.A., Northern Arizona University, 1948. 99 pp. I1 3548, p. 351.
Discusses music.

1898 WILLIAMS, Melda Ann. Historical Background and Musical Analysis of Thirty Selected Nez Percé Songs. M.M., University of Idaho, 1967. 200 pp. I1 7330, p. 360.

1899 *WITMER, Robert Earl. The Musical Culture of the Blood Indians. M.M., University of Illinois at Urbana-Champaign, 1970. 314 pp. B13, p. 32.

Spanish-American

1900 GUERRA, Fermina. Mexican and Spanish Folklore and Incidents in Southwest Texas. Master's thesis, Spanish, University of Texas at Austin, 1941. H1, p. 231.

The appendix provides music and words of some folksongs.

1901 McGIRR, Orvus Kailor. A Survey of Folksongs among the Spanish-Speaking People in Flagstaff and the Surrounding Area. M.A., Education, Arizona State College at Flagstaff, 1946. 160 pp. I2, p. 187.

1902 McKEAN, Mildred Riddle. Native Spanish American Dance Tunes of the San Luis Valley, Colorado. M.A., Education, Arizona State College at Flagstaff, 1940. 40 pp. I2, p. 152.

1903 McPHEETERS, Dean W. A Comparative Study of Some Spanish Songs and Ballads Collected in Tampa, Florida. Master's thesis, Spanish, University of Florida, 1941. H1, p. 233.

1904 MARES, Pablo. Spanish-American Folk Songs and Dances of New Mexico. M.A., Colorado State College, 1946. 66 pp. I2, p. 187.

1905 O'MEARA, Donn Michael. Spanish Folk Songs in Present Day Denver, 1948. M.A., Modern Languages, University of Denver, 1948. 120 pp. I2, p. 202.

1906 *WEST, Patricia Marchand. Hispanic Folk Songs of the Southwestern United States: Applications in Music Education. M.A., University of California at Los Angeles, 1976. 150 pp. B5 (21), p. 496.

See also nos. **837, 1360, 1696.**

Other Ethnic Groups

1907 ADAM, Gaston Eugene. Chansons Françaises en Louisiane. M.A., French, Louisiana State University, 1950. 172 pp. I2, p. 212.

1908 ENGLER, Leo Francis. The German Folk Song in Comal County, Texas. M.A., German, University of Texas at Austin, 1953. 39 pp. H1, p. 230; I2, p. 239.

1909 *GORANOWSKI, Helen. An Analysis of Sixty-Five Polish Folk-Songs, with Conclusions Based on This Analysis concerning the Relation between Language Rhythms and Music Rhythms, and concerning the Evolution and Transplantation of These Songs to America. M.A., Wayne State University, 1951. 218 pp. illus. B6 G661, p. 15; B7 262, p. 35; B14 57, p. 26; I2, p. 223.

1910 HANSON, Henry Endicott. French Influence on the Folksongs of Louisiana. M.A., Education, Stanford University, 1938. 202 pp. H1, p. 231; I2, p. 133.

1911 HÉBERT, Berthe. French Folk Songs of North America. A.M., Boston University, 1938. 89 pp. I2, p. 133.

1912 *KARDAS, Jan Kleeman. Acculturation in the Folk Music of a Polish-American Community in Lackawanna, New York. M.A., Brown University, 1976.

1913 LEVY, Isaac Jack. Sephardic Ballads and Songs in the United States: New Variants and Additions. M.A., Spanish, University of Iowa, 1959. I2, p. 280.

1914 MILAND, Emil Querineau. Portuguese Folk Music in Santa Clara County, California. M.A., Education, Stanford University, 1946. 53 pp. I2, p. 187.

1915 NEWEY, Donald Wesley. A Study of Some Assyrian Folk Songs Performed in the United States. M.M., Northwestern University, 1957. 85 pp. B14 124, p. 31; B15 574, p. 22; I2, p. 269.
Transcription and analysis of nine songs recorded in Chicago.

1916 PAWLOWSKA, Harriet. Polish Folk Songs Gathered in Detroit, with an Analysis of the Music by Grace L. Engel. M.A., Wayne State University, 1940. 57 pp. B14 128, p. 31.
Includes 41 songs.

1917 PHILIPS, Mary K. A Study of the Sources of Welsh Music in America and an Analysis and Evaluation of the Welsh-American Contribution to the Folk and Art Music of This Country. M.A., Claremont College, 1948. 166 pp. B14 130, p. 32; I2, p. 202.

1918 *STRAMLER, Marcus Garvey. The Jewish Community of Pittsburgh: An Ethno-Musicological Study. M.A., University of Pittsburgh, 1975.

1919 *WALDMAN, Deborah Anne. Transcultural Folk Song Survival: Active and Passive Bearers of the French-Canadian Folk Song Tradition in Woonsocker, Rhode Island and Adjacent Towns. M.A., Brown University, 1976.

1920 *WASCHEK, Brownlee. A Study of Czechoslovak Folk Music Translated to the Community of Masaryktown, Florida. M.Mus.Ed., Florida State University, 1959. 154 pp. illus. I2, p. 282.

1921 WHITFIELD, Irène Thérèse. Louisiana French Folk Songs. M.A., French, Louisiana State University, 1935. 226 pp. H1, p. 237; I2, p. 113.

See also nos. **170, 182.**

SPECIAL TOPICS

1922 *BARTIS, Peter. A Preliminary Classification System for Hollers in the United States. M.A., Folklore, University of North Carolina at Chapel Hill, 1974.

1923 BEARD, Anne W. The Personal Folksong Collection of Bascom Lamar Lunsford. Master's thesis, English, Miami University of Ohio, 1959. 317 pp. H1, p. 227.

A study of the variants in the 315 items of folksong recorded in 1935 by Lunsford for the Columbia University Library. Lunsford learned the songs in western North Carolina. The songs are organized in the following categories: ballads, lyrics, popular songs, and songs written by Lunsford. Includes a brief biography of Lunsford and a number of fiddle tunes.

1924 BOKELMAN, Marina. The Coon Can Game: A Blues Ballad Tradition. M.A., Folklore, University of California at Los Angeles, 1968. B5 (14), p. 350.

1925 CANNON, Martin A. Cowboy Song Adaptations. M.A., Texas Tech University, 1966. H1, p. 228; I2, p. 326.

1926 DUNLAP, John M. The Outlaw in Southern Folksong. M.A., English, University of North Carolina at Chapel Hill, 1950. 159 pp. H1, p. 229; I2, p. 213.

1927 FITCH, Margaret. The Cowboy in Verse and Song. Master's thesis, English, New Mexico Highlands University, 1932. H1, p. 230.

1928   KAPLAN, Arlene Esther. A Study of Folksinging in a Mass Society. M.A., Sociology, University of California, 1954. 89 pp.

This study deals with the phenomenon of folk singing in the San Francisco Bay area. Includes a discussion of the history of a folksinging society (unnamed), the thematic content analysis of folk songs, and incipient social organization of the folk-singing groups.

1929   KILPATRICK, Jack Frederick. The Possible Relationship of Content to Form in Certain Gros Ventre Songs. M.A., Catholic University of America, 1946. 46 pp. I1 5496, p. 181.

1930   KIMBALL, Marilyn. George Edwards, Catskill Folksinger. M.A., State University of New York at Oneonta, 1966. 293 pp. illus.; photos.

Information in this biography includes Edwards' musical tradition and career, family background, and places of residence and travel. Includes appendixes of official records, biographies on Edwards, song titles and publications, and texts for his songs from the Camp Woodland Archives, New York.

1931   LUKAS, Victor T. The Traditionally Oriented Urban Folk Musician: Revitalistic Aspects of a Subculture. M.A., Anthropology, University of Illinois, 1967. 100 pp. I4 1244, p. 106.

Discusses problems, method, culture, innovation, and revitalization of the urban folk musician.

1932   *MAYNARD, Loren L. Understanding the Cowboy and His Music. M.A., Wayne State University, 1936. 108 pp. illus. H1, p. 233; I2, p. 118.

1933   POLLAN, Loy. Provenance of Certain Cowboy Ballads. Master's thesis, English, University of Oklahoma, 1939. H1, p. 235.

Cowboy ballads in Texas, Oklahoma, and elsewhere.

1934   SCROGGINS, Sterling. Cowboy Songs. M.M., University of Colorado, 1976. 277 pp. illus.

The two parts of this study consist of "A Survey of Cowboy Song Scholarship" from the 19th century on and an anthology of 110 songs, each of which includes text, music, provenance, and source. The bibliography is recommended for further study of this topic. Some of Scroggins' material has been published in his article "Cowboy Song," *Colorado Music Educator* 23/4 (May 1976): 3-7.

1935 TAYLOR, David L. They Like to Sing the Old Songs: The A. L. Phipps Family and Its Music. Master's thesis, Western Kentucky University, 1979. A2 3199, p. 138.

1936 WESTOVER, A. Elizabeth. Songs and Ballads of the Railroad. Master's thesis, State University of New York at Albany, 1939. K6 1093, p. 90.

1937 WRIGHT, Arthur M. Songs of Our Armed Forces Viewed as Folk Songs. M.A., English, University of North Dakota, 1959. 145 pp. I2, p. 282.

1938 YOUNG, Merle. Chivalry in the Cowboy Ballads. Master's thesis, Texas College of Arts and Industries, 1955. F1 1216, p. 57.

FIDDLERS AND FIDDLE TUNES

1939 *BENNETT, David Parker. A Study in Fiddle Tunes from Western North Carolina. M.A., University of North Carolina at Chapel Hill, 1940. 90 pp. B7 54, p. 9.

Includes a discussion of the cultural, historical, and geographical background of fiddle music in the area studied, a biographical sketch of "Fiddlin' Bill Hensley," and a style analysis, including music, of eighteen fiddle tunes transcribed by the author from recordings of Hensley.

1940 *CARTER, Thomas Robert. Joe Caudill: Traditional Fiddler from Alleghany County, North Carolina. M.A., Folklore, University of North Carolina at Chapel Hill, 1973. 70 pp. B5 (22), p. 512.

1941 HOWARD, Gilbert W. Fiddle Songs and Banjo Songs: A Description and Index. Master's thesis, Western Kentucky University, 1982. A2 3006, p. 145.

1942 *LEIVERS, George Kenneth. Structure and Function of an Old-Time Fiddlers' Association. M.A., California State University at Chico, 1974. 126 pp.

1943 LINN, Karen E. The Fiddle Styles of Northern New York State. Master's thesis, Brown University, 1982. A2 3025, p. 146.

1944 *MOSER, Dorothea Joan. Instrumental Folk Music of the Southern Appalachians: A Study of Traditional Fiddle Tunes. M.A., University of North Carolina at Chapel Hill, 1963. 214 pp. H1, p. 234.

See also nos. **1658, 1923**.

COMMERCIAL COUNTRY MUSIC AND BLUEGRASS

1945 BOLGER, Margaret Ann. The Carter Family: Sources for Song. M.A., International Studies, Western Kentucky University, 1976. B5 (24), p. 284.

1946 CHILCOTE, Wayne L. The Evolution of Bluegrass Music: From Early Appalachian Mountain Folk Music to a Commercial Art. Master's thesis, East Tennessee State University, 1973. H3 2867, p. 183.

1947 CRAWFORD, Barbara. Ballad Characteristics in Modern Popular Country Music. Master's thesis, English, East Tennessee State University, 1969. H1, p. 229.

1948 *GOODNATURE, Paul. Woody Guthrie: Folk Music Transcendentalist. M.S., Mankato State University, 1975. 61 pp.
Woodrow Wilson Guthrie, 1912-67.

1949 PATTERSON, John S. The Folksong Revival and Some Sources of the Popular Image of the Folksinger, 1920-1963. M.A., Folklore, Indiana University, 1963. 97 pp.
Includes a discussion of Burl Ives and Woodie Guthrie.

1950 POLK, Linda Sue. An Analysis of Country-Western Music as a Communicative Art Form. M.A., Murray State University, 1970. 184 pp. L14, p. 353.

1951 PUGH, Ronnie Floyd. The Texas Troubadour: Selected Aspects of the Career of Ernest Tubb. M.A., Stephen F. Austin State University, 1978. 150 pp. A1 (17/2) 1312372, pp. 149-50.
"An assessment of the historical significance of Tubb's career within the larger framework of country music history."

1952   RUMBLE, John W. Commercialism in American Bluegrass Music: A Survey of Stylistic Change in Its Institutional and Cultural Context, 1965-1975. Master's thesis, Vanderbilt University, 1978. A2 3500, p. 148.

1953   SALASSI, Otto. That Good Old Country Music. Master's thesis, University of Arkansas at Fayetteville, 1978. A2 3501, p. 148.

1954   SALMONI, Fabrizio. American Country Music: Codes and Community. M.A., University of Texas at Austin, 1981. 87 pp. A2 3060, p. 148.

1955   SMITH, Lloyd Mayne. Bluegrass Music and Musicians: An Introductory Study of a Musical Style in Its Cultural Context. M.A., Folklore, Indiana University, 1964. 94 pp. I2, p. 319.

1956   STRICKLIN, David B. The Development of the Musical Career of Bob Wills, 1929-1938: Folk Forces and Commercialization. Master's thesis, Baylor University, 1979. A2 3196, p. 138.

1957   VANDERLAAN, David James. Country Music as Communication: A Comparative Content Analysis of the Lyrics of Traditional Country Music and Progressive Country Music. M.S., North Texas State University, 1980. 83 pp. A1 (19/1) 1314985, p. 76.

See also no. **2035**.

THESES **5** *Organology*

1958 *BARKER, John Sidney. Organ Design in Selected Southern Baptist Churches, 1960-1974. M.C.M., Southern Baptist Theological Seminary, 1975. 163 pp. illus.

1959 *BRAKKE, Jerome T. The Vogelpohl Firm of New Ulm, Minnesota: Organ Builders for Midwestern America, 1890-1921. M.A., Mankato State University, 1973. 95 pp.

1960 CALLEN, William M. A Brief History of the Saxophone with Emphasis on Its History and Use in Bands of the United States. Master's thesis, Central Missouri State College, 1966. F1 1622, p. 68.

1961 CASE, Del Williams. George Donald Harrison: His Influence on and Contribution to American Organ Building. Master's thesis, University of Southern California, 1968. B13, p. 34.

1962 CREECH, Delton Troy. Piano Technology in the United States as Applied to the Blind. M.M., Northwestern University, 1955. B15 161, p. 9.

1963 DAY, Gladys Christena. A Study of Pipe and Electronic Organs in 165 Public High Schools in the United States. M.M., University of Texas at Austin, 1952. B12, p. 144.

1964 DOMMER, Robert V. A Study of the Influences of the Theatre Organ on the Church Organs of Eau Claire, Wisconsin. M.A., University of Wisconsin, 1971. 86 pp. F1 1492, p. 70.

1965 GREGORY, George Ronald. A Study of the Carillons in the Southwest Area of the United States. M.M., University of Texas at Austin, 1961. B18 UT-1961-3, p. 84.

1966 HAGAN, Dan. A Study of the Henry Erben Organ in Grace Episcopal Church, Clarkesville, Georgia. M.F.A., University of Georgia, 1967. 44 pp. B6 H141, p. 16.

1967 HARRISON, Joan Elaine. A Study of Contemporary American Violins. M.Mus., Eastman School of Music of the University of Rochester, 1944. 82 pp.

1968 HERMAN, William. An Historical Study and Analysis of the Production of Music and Musical Instruments in the Buffalo Area. Master's thesis, Canisius College, 1952. F1 1307, p. 60.

1969 HORNDON, Doris Arlene. The Appalachian Dulcimer: Its Origins and History. M.A., University of North Dakota, 1967. 55 pp. illus. B5 (12), p. 138; B17 (1/1) 405, p. 34.

The author also discusses early Swedish and Norwegian immigration to the United States.

1970 HUFF, Floyd D. A History of the Organ in Texas. Master's thesis, Baylor University, 1976. A2 2769, p. 114.

1971 *KEHL, Roy Frederic. Ernest M. Skinner and the American Romantic Organ: A Critical Survey of Tonal Characteristics. M.A., Ohio State University, 1960. 57 pp.

1972 LORD, Jewel W. The Trumpet: Its History, Literature and Place in the Public School. M.Mus., University of Southern California, 1949. B3 326, p. 172.

1973 *LOVELESS, Don James. The History and Authenticity of the Musical Instruments of the Van Buren Collection. M.A., Brigham Young University, 1956. 66 pp. photos.

Lotta Van Buren.

1974 McDONALD, Donald Gordon. The Mormon Tabernacle Organ. S.M.M., Union Theological Seminary, 1952. B8 1061, p. 74.

1975 *MARTINEZ, Anna Marie. The Development of the American Organ as Influenced by Those of the European Countries. M.M., Midwestern University, 1960. 55 pp.

1976 MAYNARD, William J. Dayton C. Miller: His Life, Work, and Contributions as a Scientist and Organologist. Master's thesis, Library Science, Long Island University, 1971. B9 24, p. 4; G3, p. 45; G4, p. 60.

The Dayton C. Miller instrument collection is located in the Library of Congress.

1977 ORR, Freeman E., Jr. Twentieth-Century Organ Design in America. M.M., Northwestern University, 1954. B8 222, p. 18; B15 594, p. 22.

1978 PARKS, Edna Dorintha. A History of the Building Techniques and Liturgical Uses of the Organ in the Churches of Boston. M.A., Boston University, 1944. B8 420, p. 31.

1979 PERRIN, Irma Cooper. History of Organ and Organ Builders in America before 1900. M.M., Northwestern University, 1953. B8 225, p. 18; B15 619, p. 23.

1980 REIST, Lloyd Arthur. The Slide Trombone, Its History, Literature and Use in American Schools. M.Mus., University of Southern California, 1948. B3 360, p. 174.

1981 SHARP, James R. Tonal Design of the American Organ, 1910-1969. Master's thesis, Michigan State University, 1970. 172 pp. B13, p. 34.

1982 SMITH, Philip M. A History of the Reuter Organ Company, 1917-1975: An Evolution of Taste. M.A., Musicology, University of Kansas, 1976. 313 pp. illus.

Discusses various church and theater organs. Included is a brief history of the organ in the U.S. Various appendices list specific organ specifications.

See also no. **1815**.

THESES **6** *Special Topics*

PHILOSOPHY, AESTHETICS, AND CRITICISM

1983 *BECKWITH, Natalie Bowen. Two American Critics: Richard Aldrich and James Gibbons Huneker. M.A., Brown University, 1955.

1984 *FEINSTEIN, Martin. An Analysis of Musical Criticism in New York since 1822. M.A., Wayne State University, 1943. 100 pp.

1985 *FRENCH, Gilbert Gregory. Aesthetical Thoughts of Aaron Copland. A.M., Washington University at St. Louis, 1970. 65 pp. B13, p. 35.

1986 *GAMMILL, Ellen Reed. The Transcendental Philosophy of Charles E. Ives. M.M., Southern Methodist University, 1975. 38 pp.

1987 GEERTSEMA, Anita. The Correlation between the Aesthetic Writings of Elliott Carter and His Second String Quartet. M.Mus., University of South Africa, 1980. A1 (19/4), p. 330.

1988 GEPPERT, Eunice Claire Peevy. A Comparative Study of the Reviews of Olin Downes and Virgil Thomson. M.M., University of Texas at Austin, 1950. B18 UT-1950-9, p. 71.

1989 *HANSEN, Basil. An Historic Account of Music Criticism and Music Critics in Utah. Master's thesis, Brigham Young University, 1933.

1990 *HILL, James Richard. The Music Educational Implications of Leonard B. Meyer's Theories on Aesthetic Responses to Music. M.A., Brigham Young University, 1963. 77 pp.

1991 *MANGAN, Ruthmary. Music and Time: A Search for Relationships. M.A., Eastern Michigan University, 1979.

Included is a discussion of John Cage's *4'33''*.

1992 MARKOW, Robert. The Music Criticism of Philip Hale: The Boston Symphony Orchestra Concerts, 1889-1933. Master's thesis, McGill University, 1982. A2 3028, p. 146.

1993 MORPHOS, Paul. An Exploratory Study of the Jazz Critic. M.A., Communications, University of Pennsylvania, 1978. 88 pp. illus.

1994 *OAKERSON, Elizabeth Axtell. Paul Rosenfeld and American Music. M.M., Indiana University, 1975. 107 pp.

1995 PALADES, Stephen P. An Investigation of the Attitude of Certain New York City Music Critics toward the Music of the American Musical Stage. M.A., American University, 1962. 118 pp.

The following critics are discussed in this order: Olin Downes, Robert A. Simon, Douglas Watt, Howard Taubman, and Winthrop Sargeant. Also includes a bibliography of the articles and reviews by the critics studied, pp. 109-16.

1996 POE, John E. A Comparative Study of Reviews of Classical Music Recordings in Five Periodicals during 1963. Master's thesis, Emory University, 1963. G2, p. 176.

1997 SCHERMER, Richard. The Aesthetics of Charles Ives in Relation to His String Quartet No. 2. M.A., California State University at Fullerton, 1980. 184 pp. A1 (18/4) 1314856, p. 304; A2 3674, p. 164.

1998 *SHERWIN, Michael. The Classical Age of New York Musical Criticism, 1880-1920: A Study of Henry T. Finck, James G. Huneker, W. J. Henderson, Henry E. Krehbiel, and Richard Aldrich. M.A., City College of New York, 1972. 99 pp.

1999 *STAEBLER, Roger Allen. Charles Ives: An Evaluation of His Aesthetic Philosophy. M.M., University of Cincinnati, 1959. 75 pp.

2000 *STAEBLER, Ronald Milton. The Influence of the Critical Writings of Aaron Copland upon American Music. M.M., University of Cincinnati, 1959. 107 pp.
Includes a complete chronological listing of Copland's works, pp. 103-07.

2001 *TEASLEY, Elizabeth Kincaid. An Analysis and Comparison of the Critical Works of Virgil Thomson and Olin Downes. M.A., North Texas State University, 1947. 37 pp. B18 NTSU-1947-19, p. 14.

2002 *THOMPSON, Donald Prosser. Stravinsky and the Press: Performances and Reviews of Stravinsky's Works in New York City, 1910-1954. M.A., University of Missouri-Columbia, 1954. 326 pp.

2003 *YEAGER, Cynthia H. The Musical Ideas of the Futurists and Similar Expressions by American Composers in the First Half of the Twentieth Century. M.M., University of Cincinnati, 1979. 135 pp. illus.

COMMUNICATIONS MEDIA.
RADIO, TELEVISION, RECORDING, FILM, AND PUBLISHING

2004 ADELS, Robert Mitchell. Specialization of Popular Music Radio Stations in the Philadelphia Metropolitan Area: A Study of Disc Jockey Behavior. M.A., Communications, University of Pennsylvania, 1971. 52 pp.
Includes discussions of "specialized radio music and the specialized listener" and "differential approach to music and commercial messages."

2005 BAUERLEIN, Charles R. Origins of the Popular Music Press in America. Master's thesis, Pennsylvania University, 1979. A2 565, p. 23.

2006 *BECK, Julia Riley. An Analysis of Transition Music in Radio Programs. M.A., Wayne State University, 1945. 46 pp. illus.

2007 *BOUDREAUX, Peggy Cecile. Music Publishing in New Orleans in the Nineteenth Century. M.A., Louisiana State University, 1977. 112 pp. A2 3393, p. 144.

2008 *BRIGHAM, Anna E. A History of Music Education by Radio. M.A., University of Kansas, 1947.

2009 CHITWOOD, J. R. Development of Music Bibliography in the United States. M.A., University of Chicago, 1954. 63 pp.

2010 DAVIS, Richard Harding. A Series of Scripts for Educational Radio Programming, Based on American Folk Songs from 1775 to 1890. M.A., University of California at Los Angeles, 1954. D2 (8) 1703, p. 152.

2011 *DUDECK, Helen Clapp. Presentation of Musical Instruments in Radio Broadcasting. M.A., Wayne State University, 1940. 62 pp. illus.

2012 *EPSTEIN, Dena Julia Polacheck. Music Publishing in Chicago Prior to 1871: The Firm of Root & Cady, 1858-1871. M.A., Library Science, University of Illinois, 1943. 175 pp.
Epstein's thesis has been published in a revised edition under the following title: *Music Publishing in Chicago before 1871: The Firm of Root & Cady, 1858-1871.* Detroit Studies in Music Bibliography, 14 (Detroit: Information Coordinators, 1969).

2013 FLANDORF, Vera S. Music Periodicals in the United States: A Survey of Their History and Content. M.A., University of Chicago, 1952. 221 pp. B4, p. 38.

2014 FOSTER, James Michael. An Audiography of and an Investigation into the Recorded Performances of John Powell. 62 pp. M.A., University of Virginia, 1978.

2015 FRIEDMAN, Robert. Development of an Educational Recording of American Folk Music. M.S., Education, University of Southern California, 1954. 36 pp. I2, p. 246.

2016 *GEORGE, Lee. Aspects of Industrial Film Music. M.A., Wayne State University, 1964. 90 pp. illus.

2017 *HERSHBERGER, Mable I. The History and Development of the Processes of Music Printing. Master's thesis, Library Science, Kent State University, 1958. 344 pp. illus.
One section is on music printing in North America.

2018 *HOLMES, James R. *The Musical Quarterly:* Its History and Influence on the Development of American Musicology. M.A., University of North Carolina at Chapel Hill, 1967. 83 pp. B13, p. 33; B17 (2/1) 92, pp. 9-10.
Traces the journal's history to 1967.

2019 HOULIHAN, Marc. An Analysis of Three Examples of the Technicolor Musical. M.A., University of California at Los Angeles, 1953. E2 0543, p. 40.

2020 KELLY, Stephen K. Arthur Farwell and the Wa-Wan Press. M.A., Rutgers University, 1969. 89 pp. B13, p. 32.
Includes chapters on the life of Farwell, his attitude concerning American musical nationalism, and his musical contributions to the press. There is also a catalog of the Wa-Wan Press, pp. 75-79.

2021 LARSEN, Steven Leroy. Some Aspects of the Album *Out of the Woods* by the Chamber Ensemble "Oregon." M.A., University of Oregon, 1981. 154 pp. A1 (20/3) 1317665, p. 298.

2022 LEBOW, Marcia Wilson. A Systematic Examination of the *Journal of Music and Art* Edited by John Sullivan Dwight 1852-1881, Boston, Massachusetts. Master's thesis, University of California at Los Angeles, 1969. B13, p. 72.

2023 *McKNIGHT, Mark Curtis. The Development of Music for the American Silent Film. M.A., Louisiana State University, 1975. 77 pp.

2024 McMILLAN, Knox M. The Effective Use of Music in Radio and Television Commercials. Master's thesis, University of Georgia, 1976. A2 2801, p. 115.

2025 MILLEN, Irene. American Musical Magazines, 1786-1865. M.L.S., Carnegie Institute of Technology, 1949. B4, p. 38.

2026   PECK, Gregory L. A Survey Study of the Self-Described All Jazz Radio Station on the Frequency Modulated Band. M.A., Bowling Green State University, 1976. 182 pp. A2 2816, p. 115.

2027   PECK, Mariol R. Music Periodicals in Portland, Oregon, 1879-1925. Master's thesis, University of Oregon, 1980. A2 3647, p. 163.

2028   POLLOCK, Louis I. Bridge and Mood Music for Radio Drama. M.A., University of Michigan, 1953. D2 (7) 1355, p. 159.

2029   *POWELL, Paul Richard. A Study of A. E. Blackmar and Brother, Music Publishers of New Orleans, Louisiana, and Augusta, Georgia: With a Check List of Imprints in Louisiana Collections. M.L.S., Louisiana State University, 1978. 113 pp. illus.

2030   PROCTOR, David P. A Critical History of American Rock Journalism. Master's thesis, University of Utah, 1981. A2 630, p. 30.

2031   REDD, Lawrence. The Impact of Radio, Motion Pictures, and Television on the Development of Rhythm and Blues and Rock and Roll Music. M.A., Michigan State University, 1971. E2 1010, p. 56.

2032   SIMINOSKI, Ted. Moving through Air: The Role of Dance in the Musical Films of Gene Kelly. M.A., University of Southern California, 1976. E2 1177, p. 61.

2033   SPOTH, Doris M. An Analysis of Music for Radio Dramatic Shows, including a Handbook of Musical Bridges, Transitions, and Backgrounds. M.A., Michigan State College, 1949. D2 (3) 144, p. 148.

2034   STEPHEN, C. Descriptive Bibliography of American Musical Magazines, 1866-1886 Available in the Carnegie Library of Pittsburgh. M.L.S., Carnegie Institute of Technology, 1954. 55 pp.

2035   STOCKDALE, Richard P. The Development of the Country Music Radio Format. M.A., Kansas State University, 1979. 114 pp. A2 4914, p. 216.

An historical approach to country music as heard on radio from its first documented broadcasting on WSB, Atlanta, in 1922 to 1978 when, according to the Country Music Association, there were 1150 all-country radio stations. Cited in *Journalism Abstracts* 17 (1979): 116.

2036   SUTTON, M. The Hollywood Musical Film. M.A., Exeter University, 1976.

2037   VOLGER, George. A Comparative Analysis of the Uses of Music and Sound Effects in Motion Picture and Radio Drama. M.A., University of Southern California, 1939. E2 1319, p. 66.

2038   *WHITELOCK, Kenly Wilson. The Musigraph, a Graphic Music Recorder. M.A., University of Utah, 1949. 50 pp. plates.

2039   WILSON, Michael. Musical Accompaniment during the Silent Film Era, Circa 1890-1930. M.A., University of Southern California, 1977. E2 1386, p. 69.

2040   WINTERSOLE, William Richard. Production of a Series of Radio Scripts Written for Children and Based on American Folk Songs from 1775 to 1890. M.A., University of California at Los Angeles, 1959. 125 pp. D2 (13) 3029, p. 130; I2, p. 282.

2041   WRZESINSKI, Janice L. Music Programming at Contemporary Music Radio Stations. Master's thesis, Miami University of Ohio, 1979. A2 3213, p. 139.

ARTS MANAGEMENT AND PATRONAGE

2042   AMUNDSON, Kristen J. Of Poetry and Power: Major Policy Decisions of the National Cultural Center, 1958-1965. M.A., Arts Administration, American University, 1978. 171 pp. B9 5, p. 1.

A history of the John F. Kennedy Center for the Performing Arts.

2043   COLEMAN, Margaret E'Vonne. CETA and the Arts. M.A., American University, 1979. 46 pp.

The Comprehensive Employment and Training Act was a federal program under which artists and musicians could find jobs as public service employees.

2044   FITZHUGH, Lynne. Introducing the Audience: A Review and Analysis of Audience Studies for the Performing Arts in America. M.A., Arts Management, American University, 1982. 101 pp.

Directed primarily to the arts manager. Discusses audience profiles for theater, orchestral music, opera, and dance, and marketing behavior in relation to economic, technological, demographic, political, and social factors.

2045 McGUIRE, Mary Lee. U.S. Government Support for the Arts: The First Two Hundred Years. M.A., American University, 1979. 61 pp.

Examines government actions relating to the arts from 1800 to 1976.

2046 METZGER, Richard Lee. The Role of Foundations in the Recording of American Music. Master's thesis, Library Science, University of Chicago, 1972. G3, p. 46.

2047 *NEWMAN, Richard Michael. Culturelations — A Review of Business Support and the Arts. M.A., Journalism, Syracuse University, 1969. 95 pp. illus.

2048 NOWLIN, Miles Jackson. A Survey of Artist Series Sponsored by Concert Associations in Texas. M.M., University of Texas at Austin, 1951. B12, p. 145.

2049 REFIOR, Everett L. The American Federation of Musicians: Organization, Policies and Practices. Master's thesis, University of Chicago, 1955.

2050 RIEBE, Charmette. UNESCO and Intercultural Music Education: Folk Music Teaching in Europe and in the United States under UNESCO Teacher-Exchange Basis. M.A., University of Michigan, 1950. I2, p. 217.

2051 *TAFERNER, Theodore A. Agencies for the Advancement of Music Appreciation in the United States. Master's thesis, Columbia University, 1927. 30 pp.

2052 YOUNG, Milton B. A Study of the Los Angeles Bureau of Music with Implications for Civic Music in the United States. M.M., University of Southern California, 1950. B12, p. 80.

LIBRARIES, MUSEUMS, AND SPECIAL COLLECTIONS

2053 ANDERSEN, E. L. Study of Recordings in Sixty Municipal Public Libraries Serving Populations of Seventy-Five Thousand and Over as of 1948. A.M., University of Chicago, 1950. 133 pp.

2054 ANHALT, Lenore. The History, Development, and Organization of the Record Collection of the Great Neck (New York) Library. M.A., Palmer Graduate Library School of Long Island University, 1969. 106 pp. A1 (10/1) 13-02866, p. 103; G2, p. 5.

2055 BALDWIN, M. I. Music Librarianship: An Annotated Bibliography of Periodical Literature, 1942 - June 1952. M.S.L.S., Drexel Institute of Technology, 1953. 54 pp.

2056 BENIGSOHN, Shirley B. A Study of Resources, Services and Policies of Record Collections in Public Libraries in Nassau County (New York). Master's thesis, Long Island University, 1968. G2, p. 15.

2057 BENNETT, J. P. The Music Library Association, 1931-1956. Master's thesis, Western Reserve University, 1957. G1 2556, p. 166.

2058 BLAIR, Amy Jean Glenney. A Survey of Cylinder and Disc Music Box Collections in a Selected Group of United States Museums. M.M., University of Texas at Austin, 1967. B13, p. 34; B18 UT-1967-1, p. 90.

2059 *BROWN, Dorothy Oshern. Civil War Songs in the Harris Collection of American Poetry and Plays at Brown University. M.A., Brown University, 1959. 192 pp. B7 96, p. 15; I2, p. 277; H1, p. 364.

2060 CAPLAN, Francine M. The Phonograph Record Collection, John Herrick Jackson Music Library, Yale University — A Study, 1969. Master's thesis, Long Island University, 1970. G3, p. 10.

2061 COLEMAN, Dorothy Mae. An Analysis of the Literature Dealing with Music Libraries and Librarianship as Listed in *Library Literature*. Master's thesis, Atlantic University, 1963. G2, p. 45.

2062 COOK, Verla R. A History and Evaluation of the Music Division of the District of Columbia Public Library. M.A., Catholic University of America, 1952. 87 pp. B9 13, p. 2; G1 1106, p. 72.
      Includes a brief history of music divisions in public libraries in America.

2063 GRAY, Patsy Barbee. A Survey of Sound Recordings Collections in North Carolina Public Libraries. Master's thesis, University of North Carolina, 1965. G2, p. 84; G4, p. 45.

2064 HAVILAND, P. J. Musical Fund Society of Philadelphia and Its Library. M.S.L.S., Drexel Institute of Technology, 1955. 48 pp.

2065 *HELVERN, Sue Frances. A Handbook of Procedure for Music Libraries. Master's thesis, Kent State University, 1955. 140 pp. illus.
Contains a short history of music libraries in the United States.

2066 *HENDERSON, George Robert, Jr. A Union List of Musical Literature in North Texas Regional Libraries, 1946. M.Mus., North Texas State University, 1949. 75 pp.

2067 JOHNSON, E. M. Music Libraries in Music Departments and Conservatories. A.M.L.S., University of Michigan, 1949. 75 pp.

2068 JONES, Wilson E. An Historical Study of the Music Collection in the Newark, New Jersey, Public Library. Master's thesis, Long Island University, 1969. G2, p. 114.

2069 *LAURENT, David. Secular Music Published in America before 1830 in the Harris Collection of American Poetry at Brown University. M.A., Brown University, 1953.

2070 *LORD-WOOD, June. Musical Americana in the Hunt-Berol Collection at the Columbia University Libraries. M.A., Columbia University, 1975. 390 pp.

2071 *MAYES, Curtis S. A Descriptive Catalogue of Historic Percussion, Wind, and Stringed Instruments in Three Pennsylvania Museums. M.Mus., Florida State University, 1974. 247 pp. illus.; 95 plates. B17 (10/4) 8028, p. 490.

2072 MONROE, Anita Fletcher. Tune Books in the Irving Lowens Musical Americana Collection: An Historical and Bibliographical Study. Master's thesis, University of North Carolina at Chapel Hill, 1966. G2, p. 155; G4, p. 450.

2073 MOORE, Daniel T. Oscar G. Sonneck and His Contributions to Music Librarianship and Bibliography. Master's thesis, Library Science, Southern Connecticut State College, 1973. G3, p. 47.

2074 MORRONI, June Rose. The Music Library Association, 1931-1961. Master's thesis, University of Chicago, 1968. G1 2646, p. 170; G2, p. 157; G4, p. 429.

2075 QUAIN, Mildred. A History and Descriptive Study of the Music Division of the Library and Museum of the Performing Arts, the New York Public Library at Lincoln Center, New York, N.Y. Master's thesis, Long Island University, 1969. G2, p. 181.

2076 SHAMP, B. K. The Music Section of the Cleveland Public Library. Master's thesis, Western Reserve University, 1954. G2 1446, p. 91.

2077 SLOAN, (Mrs.) R. M. History of the Phonograph Record in the American Public Library. M.S.L.S., Western Reserve University, 1950. 56 pp.

2078 SNODGRASS, Wilson David. Music Libraries and Collections in Texas. M.L.S., University of Texas, 1954. B18 UT-1954-26, p. 76.

2079 SNYDER, E. B. The History and Development of the Music Collection and Department of the Public Library of Des Moines. Master's thesis, Western Reserve University, 1958. G1 1185, p. 76.

2080 THOMAS, Jean W. A Pittsburgh Collection of Nineteenth Century Household Music. M.A., University of Pittsburgh, 1981.

This study focuses on a five-volume collection of sheet music, 1840s through 1880s, belonging to a mother and daughter who resided in Pittsburgh. Discussed are local music dealers and stage entertainment presented by visiting European artists.

2081 WADSWORTH, R. W. Notes on the Development of Music Collections in American Academic Libraries. Master's thesis, University of Chicago, 1943. 140 pp. G1 1638, p. 105.

2082 WETZEL, Richard Dean. The American Hymn and Tune Books from 1800 to 1865 in the Warrington Collection of the Pittsburgh Theological Seminary Library. Master's thesis, University of Pittsburgh, 1966. B13, p. 33.

2083 *WOHLFORD, Mary Kathryn. Study of Record Collections in Public Libraries of the United States and Canada. Master's thesis, Library Science, Kent State University, 1950. 63 pp.

THESES 7 Related Fields

THEATER. TOPICAL STUDIES

2084 BATTAGILA, Mary Jane. The London Comedians in Colonial America. M.A., University of Kansas, 1950. D2 (13) 2995, p. 129.

2085 BELLANCA, Horace V. A History of Stagecraft in America from 1798 to 1820 and Its Relation to the Drama of the Period. M.A., Speech and Drama, Catholic University of America, 1954. 56 pp. D2 (8) 1493, p. 145.

2086 *BOYD, Sharon. Sounds of the Stage: The Use of Music and Sounds as an Expressionistic Technique in Modern American Drama. M.A., Mississippi College, 1966. 58 pp.

2087 BROWNING, Robert Eugene. The Showboat Theatre of America's Rivers: Its Birth, Growth and Decline. M.A., University of Southern California, 1953. D2 (7) 1260, p. 156.

2088 BURDICK, Don P. The American Company of Comedians: Social and Artistic Problems, 1752-1792. M.S., University of Wisconsin, 1959. D2 (13) 2996, p. 129.

2089   CALVIN, Judith. A History of the Showboat Theatre on the Northern Rivers. M.A., Pennsylvania State University, 1960. D2 (14) 2262, p. 167; D3 1099, p. 123.

2090   CREEL, Richard Lowell. The Effect of the Civil War on Nineteenth-Century American Theatre. M.A., Theater, California State University at Long Beach, 1973. 161 pp. A1 (11/4) 13-04978, p. 501.

2091   DUGDALE, Mattie W. Travelers' Views of Louisiana before 1860. Master's thesis, History, University of Texas at Austin, 1938. H1, p. 266.
        Discusses "floating theaters, theaters in New Orleans, and slave dances."

2092   FRIEDMAN, Madgel D. An Historical Study of the Contributions of the Lewis Hallam Company to American Drama. M.A., University of Southern California, 1949. D2 (3) 201, p. 150.

2093   GUSTAVSON, Phoebe Jane. The Negro Character in American Drama before 1865. M.A., University of Wisconsin, 1949. D2 (3) 268, p. 152.

2094   HISZ, Evelyn. History of the Theatre Collection, New York Public Library at Lincoln Center. M.S., Palmer Graduate Library School, 1969. 84 pp. A1 (10/1) 2871, p. 87; G2, p. 100.

2095   JOHNSTON, Roy J. Social Concepts in the Early American Drama to 1825. M.A., University of Tennessee, 1950. D2 (4) 535, p. 153.

2096   JUSTICE, Edward C. The Attitude of Eighteenth Century America towards Its Theater and Actors. M.A., Speech and Drama, Catholic University of America, 1952. 78 pp.
        The author approaches this subject by the following regions: the South, New York and Philadelphia, and New England. The major theatrical companies of the day are examined.

2097   McCOSKER, Susan. The American Company, 1752-1791, Founders of the American Theatre. M.A., Speech and Drama, Catholic University of America, 1968. 96 pp. B9 57, p. 7; B17 (10/4) 10107, p. 588.

2098 MERING, Yolla. The San Francisco Theatrical Career of Dr. D. G. Robinson. M.A., Theater, California State University at Long Beach, 1977. 166 pp. A1 (15/2) 13-9584, p. 126.

Research encompasses the years 1849-59. An appendix contains a list of Robinson's songs.

2099 *NUGENT, Beatrice L. Benedict DeBar's Management of the St. Charles Theatre in New Orleans, Louisiana, 1853-1861. Master's thesis, Speech, Louisiana State University, 1967.

2100 PETTIT, Paul B. The Showboat Theater: The Development of the Showboat on the Mississippi River and on the Eastern Waterways. Master's thesis, Cornell University, 1943. H1, p. 249.

2101 ROANE, Andrea Theresa. The Showboat as a Theatrical Institution in New Orleans, 1831-1940. M.A., University of New Orleans, 1973. 35 pp. D3 460, p. 54.

2102 SINNOTT, Cynthia Mary. The Nature of the American Drama, 1787-1820. M.A., History, University of Virginia, 1971. 143 pp.

2103 SOLDO, Betty Lougaris. The Feminine Favorites of the Virginia City Stage, 1865-1880. M.A., Theater, California State University at Fullerton, 1975. 94 pp. A1 (13/1) 13-06741, p. 48.

2104 *STEPHENSON, Nan L. The Charleston Theatre Management of Joseph George Holman, 1815 to 1817. M.A., Speech, Louisiana State University, 1976.

2105 WITHAM, Floyd Deland. Early American Melodrama, 1795-1882. M.A., Stanford University, 1958. D2 (12) 2492, p. 131.

THEATER. STATES AND CITIES

2106 ANDERSON, Evelyn C. A History of the Theatre in St. Peter, Minnesota, from Its Beginning to 1930. M.A., University of Minnesota, 1946. D3 703, p. 78.

2107   ASP, Bjarne M. A Record of the Professional Theatre Activity in Fargo, North Dakota from 1921 through 1960. M.A., North Dakota State University, 1961. D2 (15) 2615, p. 176.

2108   BAGLEY, Russell Elmer. An Historical Study of Theatrical Entertainment in Pensacola, Florida, 1882-1892. M.A., University of Florida, 1949. D2 (3) 96, p. 147; D3 223, p. 26.

2109   BAILEY, Frances M. A History of the Stage in Mobile, Alabama, 1824-1850. Master's thesis, Dramatic Art, University of Iowa, 1934. H1, p. 244.

2110   BELL, William Campton. A History of the Theatrical Activities of Cheyenne, Wyoming, from 1867 to 1902. M.A., Northwestern University, 1935. 2 vols. D3 1389, p. 155.

2111   BIGELOW, Edwin L. A Record of the Professional Theatre Activity in Fargo, North Dakota from 1889 through 1903. M.A., North Dakota State University, 1955. D2 (9) 1952, p. 150; D3 923, p. 105.

2112   *BITZ, Nellie Edith. A Half-Century of Theater in Early Rochester: A Record of the Struggle to Establish a Permanent Theater. M.A., Syracuse University, 1941. 161 pp. plates.

2113   BLACK, Mary Childs. The Theatre in Colonial Annapolis. M.A., George Washington University, 1952. 139 pp. B9 36, p. 5; D2 (4) 965, p. 155; D3 529, p. 60; L3, p. 11; L10, p. 58.
       Contains a "Daybook of Recorded Performances, 1752-1773" of both operas and plays.

2114   BRADEN, Edwina Coltharp. A History of Theater in Corsicana, Texas, 1875-1915. M.A., East Texas State University, 1969. D3 1203, p. 135; L7 (78), p. 314.

2115   BRENEMAN, Lucille Nix. A History of the Theatre in Honolulu during the Second World War (1941-1946). M.A., University of Hawaii, 1949. D2 (3) 100, p. 147.

2116   BRIAN, George. A History of Theatrical Activities in Baton Rouge from 1900 to 1923. M.A., Louisiana State University, 1951. D2 (5) 913, p. 176.

2117 BRISTOW, Eugene K. Look Out for Saturday Night: A Social History of Professional Variety Theater in Memphis, Tennessee, 1859-1880. Master's thesis, University of Iowa, 1956.
Discusses variety entertainment having music accompaniment.

2118 BRODNAX, Margaret O. The Theatre in Fort Worth, 1901-1962. Master's thesis, English, Texas Christian University, 1959. H1, p. 245.

2119 BROWN, Lawrence Robert. Frontier Dramatic Criticism, St. Louis, 1835-1839. M.S., University of Wisconsin, 1949. D2 (3) 272, p. 152.

2120 BROWNING, Richard J. A Record of the Professional Theatre Activity in Fargo, Dakota Territory, from 1880 through 1888. M.S., North Dakota State University, 1958. D2 (12) 2707, p. 137; D3 922, p. 105.

2121 CHESTER, Violet Lercara. The History of the Theatre in San Francisco from the Gold Rush to the Conflagration of 1906. M.A., Stanford University, 1930. D3 69, p. 10.

2122 CLARK, Linda Sue Kidd. A Theater History of Texarkana [Texas] from 1876 through 1924. M.A., East Texas State University, 1972. D3 1239, p. 138; L7 (78), p. 314.

2123 CLARKE, Mitchell. The Early Theatre in Kentucky. M.A., English, Western Kentucky University, 1947. D3 424, p. 50; H1, p. 245.

2124 COLE, Marion. Theatrical and Musical Entertainment in Early Cleveland, 1796-1854. M.A., Case Western Reserve University, 1958. 170 pp. D3 957, p. 108.

2125 DALTON, Donald B. The History of Theatre in Asheville, North Carolina, 1832-1972. M.A., University of North Carolina, 1972. D3 900, p. 102.

2126 DAY, Myrle. The History of the Theatre of Chicago. M.A., University of Northern Colorado, 1942. D3 285, p. 34.

2127 DEVIN, Ronald Boyd. The History of the Theatre in Enterprise, Oregon, from 1901 through 1920. M.A., University of Oregon, 1961. D2 (15) 2618, p. 176.

2128 DREXLER, Ralph Duane. A History of Theatre in Bloomington, Illinois, from Its Beginning to 1873. M.S., Illinois State University, 1963. 134 pp. D3 276, p. 33.

2129 EGGERS, Robert Franklin. A History of Theatre in Boise, Idaho, from 1863 to 1963. M.A., University of Oregon, 1963. D3 266, p. 31.
Mentions an unfavorable reception for a minstrel troupe, p. 24.

2130 EYSSEN, Donald Chester. The Theatre in Ohio, 1800-1890. M.A., Ohio Wesleyan University, 1934. D3 980, p. 111.

2131 FAY, Barbara Carleen Brice. The Theatre in South-Eastern Iowa, 1864-1880. M.A., University of Iowa, 1947. 176 pp. D3 370, p. 43.
A good account which gives the history of, the popularity of, and the pro and con reaction to minstrelsy, pp. 130-45.

2132 FORT, Ronald Claire. The Theater and Entertainment in Fort Worth, Texas, 1903-1904. M.A., Texas Christian University, 1969. L7 (79), p. 456.

2133 FREBAULT, Hubert. Professional Theatre in Athens, Ohio, since 1897. M.F.A., Ohio University, 1953. D2 (7) 1464, p. 162.

2134 GAFF, Lilyan Zaro. The Development of the Theatre on the American Frontier to 1850. M.A., University of Southern California at Los Angeles, 1940.
Discusses Negro minstrelsy, pp. 161, 164-65.

2135 GARTNER, David. A Detailed History of the Theatre in Santa Fe, New Mexico, 1847-1881, Containing, in Addition, an Outline of the Theatrical Activities in This City from 1881-1891. M.A., Washington University, 1951.
Discusses the Montgomery Minstrels, pp. 13-14, 21-23.

2136 GEARY, Elmo G. A Study of Dramatics in Castle Valley from 1875 to 1925. M.A., University of Utah, 1953. D2 (7) 1267, p. 156.

2137 *GRAY, Wallace Allison. An Historical Study of Professional Dramatic Activities in Alexandria, Louisiana, from the Beginning to 1920. M.A., Speech, Louisiana State University, 1951. D2 (5) 914, p. 176; D3 425, p. 50.

2138   GREENFIELD, Mildred Albert. Early History of the Theatre in Baltimore. M.A., Johns Hopkins University, 1953. B9 50, p. 7; L3 p. 12.

2139   GRIFFIN, Evelyn. Early Theatres and Theatrical Events in Denver. M.A., University of Denver, 1923. D3 152, p. 18.

Mentions minstrelsy, melodrama, light opera, and extravaganza.

2140   GROVES, William McDonald, Jr. A History of the Professional Theatre in Marshall, Texas, from 1877 to 1915. M.A., Stephen F. Austin State University, 1976. A1 (15/1) 13-09255, p. 61; D3 1233, p. 138.

2141   HAMIL, Linda Virginia. A Study of Theatrical Activity in Natchez, Mississippi from 1800-1840. M.A., University of Mississippi, 1976. D3 718, p. 80.

2142   HAMILTON, Robert T. A History of Theatre in Keokuk, Iowa, from 1875-1900. M.A., University of Michigan, 1954. D2 (8) 1497, pp. 145-46; D3 379, p. 44.

2143   HARDIN, Wylie Audrain. A History of Theatre in Terrell, Texas, from 1890 through 1910. M.A., East Texas State University, 1971. D3 1240, p. 139; L7 (78), p. 315.

2144   HARRIS, Geraldine Caroline. A History of the Theatre in Ohio, 1815-1880. M.A., Ohio State University, 1937. D3 981, p. 111.

Discusses minstrelsy, especially T. D. Rice, pp. 66-74.

2145   *HEIDT, Patsy Ruth. The History of the Theatre in Lake Charles, Louisiana, from 1920 to 1950. M.A., Speech, Louisiana State University, 1951. D2 (5) 916, p. 176.

2146   HOOLE, William Stanley. A History of the Charleston Theatres, 1800-1875. M.A., North Texas State University, 1941. D3 1149, p. 128.

2147   JONES, Jane E. History of the Stage in Louisville, Kentucky, from Its Beginning to 1845. M.A., Dramatic Arts, University of Iowa, 1932. D3 407, p. 48; H1, p. 247.

Title page of *The Crow Quadrilles*
(New York: George Willig, Jr., ca. 1837).
The title page was likely printed in Baltimore, Maryland.

A piano arrangement of "Jim Crow," No. 4 in a set of 6 pieces in *The Crow Quadrilles* (New York: George Willig, Jr., ca. 1837),
based on the original music by Thomas Dartmouth Rice.

2148   KAISER, Louis H. A Theatrical History of Laramie, Wyoming, 1868-1880. M.A., University of Wyoming, 1950. D2 (4) 574, p. 155; D3 1392, p. 156.
Discusses minstrel shows, pp. 17-18, 26-27, 29-30, 77-78, and 96-97.

2149   KAISER, Norman J. A History of the German Theatre of Milwaukee from 1850 to 1890. M.A., University of Wisconsin, 1954. D2 (8) 1499, p. 146; D3 1379, p. 154.

2150   KELLER, Helen B. The History of the Theater in Columbus, Georgia, from 1828 to 1865. Master's thesis, English, University of Georgia, 1957. H1, p. 247.

2151   KENNEDY, Mary A. The Theater Movement in Washington, 1800-1835. M.A., English, Catholic University of America, 1933. 49 pp. B9 21, p. 3; D3 207, p. 24; H1, p. 247.
Includes three parts: "Background and History to 1804," "The First Washington [D.C.] Theatre, 1804-1821," and "The Second Washington Theatre, 1821-1835." Based, in part, on contemporary newspapers and diaries.

2152   KER, Minnette. The History of the Theatre in California in the Nineteenth Century. M.A., University of California at Berkeley, 1924. D3 61, p. 9; L2 (44) 16.137, p. 143.

2153   LAND, Robert Hunt. Theatre in Colonial Virginia. M.A., University of Virginia, 1936. 135 pp. D3 1337, p. 149.

2154   LANE, Morgan Jackson. Commercial Theatre in San Diego with Special Emphasis, 1892-1917. M.A., San Diego State College, 1969. 178 pp. L13, p. 5.

2155   LANGLEY, William Osler. The Theatre in Columbus, Georgia, from 1828-1878. Master's thesis, Auburn University, 1937. 215 pp. D3 236, p. 28; H1, p. 248.
Mentions minstrel performances, pp. 37, 52, 55-56, 61, and 63.

2156   LANGWORTHY, Helen. The Theatre in the Lower Valley of the Ohio, 1797-1860. M.A., University of Iowa, 1926. D3 932, p. 106.

2157 LEWISON, Agnes O. A Theatrical History of Des Moines, Iowa, 1846-1890. M.A., University of Iowa, 1931. 277 pp. D3 372, p. 43.

Lists minstrel performances, pp. 14, 22, 27, 64, 79, and 102.

2158 *LINDSEY, Henry Carlton. A History of the Theatre in Shreveport, Louisiana to 1900. M.A., Speech, Louisiana State University, 1951. D2 (5) 919, p. 176; D3 514, p. 58.

2159 *LUTTRELL, Wanda Melvina. The Theatre of Memphis, Tennessee, from 1829 to 1860. M.A., Speech, Louisiana State University, 1951. D2 (5) 920, p. 176; D3 1179, p. 132.

2160 *LYLE, Beverly B. A Detailed Survey of the New Orleans Theatre from 1800 to 1825 (English Productions). Master's thesis, Speech, Louisiana State University, 1938. H1, p. 248.

2161 LYON, Dyanne Stricklin. The Professional Theatre in Baltimore from Its Beginning in 1782 to 1799. M.A., English, University of Maryland, 1976. 168 pp. B9 56, p. 7; B17 (10/4) 10095, p. 588.

Discussed are the Baltimore Company of Comedians: Thomas Wall, Adam Lindsay, and Dennis Ryan, 1782-86; the Old American Company: Lewis Hallam and John Henry, 1786-90; and the Philadelphia Company: Thomas Wignell and Alexander Reinagle.

2162 McDAVITT, Elaine Elizabeth. A History of the Theatre in Milwaukee, Wisconsin, from Its Beginnings to 1865. M.A., Northwestern University, 1935. D3 1377, p. 154.

Briefly mentions minstrelsy, p. 69.

2163 McKEE, Edna Hollingsworth. A Study of the Theatrical Entertainments in Jackson, Mississippi, before the Civil War or between the Years 1836-1863. M.S., Florida State University, 1959. D2 (13) 3002, p. 129; D3 714, p. 80.

Mentions minstrelsy, p. 38.

2164 MATHER, Patricia Ann. The Theatrical History of Wichita, Kansas, 1872-1920. M.A., University of Kansas, 1950. D2 (4) 438, p. 151; D3 396, p. 47.

2165   MEEK, Beryl. A Record of the Theatre in Lexington, Kentucky, from 1799-1850. Master's thesis, Dramatic Arts, University of Iowa, 1930. D3 403, p. 48; H1, p. 248.

2166   MEGARITY, Shirley Ann. The Theatre in Fort Worth, 1870-1899. M.A., Texas Woman's University, 1971. D3 1211, p. 135; L7 (80), p. 320.

2167   MERRICK, Mary Louise. A History of the Theatre of Zanesville, Ohio, between the Years of 1831 and 1866. M.A., Ohio State University, 1941. D3 979, p. 111.

2168   MILLER, Dale. A Record of the Theatrical Activity in Bismarck, Dakota Territory from January 1873 to June 1886. M.A., North Dakota State University, 1960. D2 (14) 2266, p. 167; D3 921, p. 104.

2169   *MORRIS, Alfred S. Music History of the Salt Lake Theatre: The Formative Years, 1862-1870. M.A., Brigham Young University, 1957. 172 pp. illus.

2170   MORROW, Marguerite H. A History of the English Stage in New Orleans from 1817-1837. M.A., Dramatic Arts, University of Iowa, 1933. D3 448, p. 53; H1, p. 249.

2171   *MULLINS, Charles G. A History of Theatrical Activities in Three Florida Parishes of Louisiana, 1925-1940. Master's thesis, Speech, Louisiana State University, 1972.

2172   OMAN, Richard J. Chicago Theatre 1837-1847: Reflections of an Emerging Metropolis. M.A., University of Florida, 1970. 112 pp. D3 286, p. 34.

2173   PECK, Phoebe. The Theater in Kansas City. M.A., University of Kansas City, 1940. D3 734, p. 83.
          Notes that the minstrel Tom Mac came from Kansas City.

2174   *PICKETT, C. H. A History of the Non-Commercial Theatre in New Orleans from 1835 to 1860. M.A., Speech, Louisiana State University, 1959. D3 464, p. 54.

2175 PRIMEAUX, Beverly. Annals of the Theatre in Lafayette, Louisiana, 1920-1940. M.A., University of Mississippi, 1955. D2 (9) 1954, p. 150.

2176 PROBSTFIELD, Evelyn. A Record of the Professional Theatre Activity in Fargo, North Dakota, from 1904 through 1913. M.A., North Dakota Agricultural College, 1958. D2 (12) 2713, p. 138.

2177 QUIGLEY, Bernard J. First Seasons in Philadelphia: A Study of the Philadelphia Stage, 1682-1767. M.A., Drama, Catholic University of America, 1951. 107 pp. illus.; plates. D2 (5) 922, p. 176.

2178 RABKE, Barbara. Theater in San Antonio, 1886-1891. M.A., Drama, Trinity University, 1964. H1, p. 249; L7 (80), p. 422.

2179 REED, Charles E., Jr. An Historical Study of Professional Dramatic Entertainment in Little Rock, Arkansas, 1889-1899. M.A., University of Florida, 1949. D2 (3) 97, p. 147.

2180 REEVES, Ann Taylor. Nineteenth Century Theatre in Northeast Texas. M.F.A., University of Texas, 1962.

Discusses minstrel performers, troupes, and performances, pp. 41-43, 53-55, 58-59, 62, 67, 70, 73-74, 81, and 83-84.

2181 ROBERTS, Rosalie Du Val. A History of the Professional Legitimate Theatre and Opera in Honolulu, 1910-1920. M.A., University of Hawaii, 1958. D2 (14) 2267, p. 167.

2182 SCOTT, Kathleen S. The Professional Legitimate Theatre in Honolulu, 1900-1910. M.A., University of Hawaii, 1953. D2 (14) 2269, p. 167.

2183 SEMENZA, Edwin S. The History of the Professional Theatre in the State of Nevada. M.A., University of Southern California, 1934. D3 827, p. 93.

Lists minstrel performances, pp. 53, 70, 88, 95, and 98.

2184 SHAFFER, Virginia M. The Theatre in Baltimore (from Its Beginnings to 1786). Master's thesis, English, Johns Hopkins University, 1926. B9 61, p. 8; D3 532, p. 61; H1, p. 250.

2185   SHANK, Phillip James. A History of the Early Variety Theatres and Legitimate Theatres in Waco, Texas, from the Beginnings to 1928. M.A., Theater, Baylor University, 1977. 305 pp. A1 (15/4) 13-9893, pp. 249-50.

An appendix contains a chronological listing of performances in Waco theaters in 1876-1928.

2186   SHERMAN, Susanne. Post-Revolutionary Theatre in Virginia, 1784-1810. M.A., College of William and Mary, 1950. L4, p. 75.

2187   SIMPSON, Mary Pius. The Williamsburg Theatre, 1716-1774. M.A., Speech and Drama, Catholic University of America, 1948. 106 pp. D3 1322, p. 148.

2188   *SINNETT, Alice Rosemary. A Selective Survey of the Syracuse Theater, 1823-1915. M.A., Syracuse University, 1949. 257 pp. illus. D2 (6) 1217, p. 162; D3 897, p. 101.

2189   SMITH, Tallant. The History of the Theatre in Santa Barbara, 1769-1894. M.A., University of California at Santa Barbara, 1969. 191 pp. D3 107, p. 13.

2190   SPARKS, Andrew H. A History of the Theatre in Savannah, 1800-1836. M.A., English, University of Georgia, 1940. D3 240, p. 28; H1, p. 250.

2191   SPEAR, Richard E. The Theatre in Detroit, 1887-1895, as Revealed by the Dramatic Criticism of George P. Goodale. M.A., Wayne State University, 1955. D2 (9) 1770, p. 144; D3 673, p. 75.

2192   STEVENS, Eva. The History of the Theatre in Nashville, Tennessee, 1871-1875. M.A., English, Vanderbilt University, 1934. D3 1195, p. 134; H1, p. 250.

Lists minstrel performances and notes that minstrel productions increased from five in 1871 to twenty in 1875: pp. 4, 27, 65, 72, 75, 87, 89-90, 111-15, 120-21, 129, 131, and 134-35.

2193   STEVENS, Katharine Bell. Theatrical Entertainment in Jackson, Mississippi, 1890-1910. M.A., University of Mississippi, 1953. D2 (7) 1279, p. 157; D3 715, p. 80.

2194   *TEAGUE, Oran B. The Professional Theater in Rural Louisiana. M.A., Speech, Louisiana State University, 1952. D3 516, p. 59.

Discusses minstrel troupes, pp. 36-37, 39, 43, and 135.

2195 THOMPSON, Florence L. The Theatre in Cincinnati, Ohio, 1860-1883. M.A., University of Iowa, 1928. D3 946, p. 107.

2196 TOPHAM, Helen A. A History of the Theatre in Honolulu, 1891-1900. M.A., University of Hawaii, 1950. D2 (14) 2271, p. 167; D3 261, p. 30.

2197 TRULSSON, Berton E. A Historical Study of the Theatre of the Mother Lode during the Gold Rush Period. M.A., College of the Pacific, 1950. D2 (4) 508, p. 153; D3 126, p. 15.

2198 VAN KIRK, Gordon. The Beginnings of the Theatre in Chicago, 1837-1839. M.A., Northwestern University, 1934. 72 pp. D3 284, p. 34.

2199 *VARNADO, Alban F. A History of Theatrical Activity in Baton Rouge, Louisiana, 1819-1900. M.A., Speech, Louisiana State University, 1947. D3 426, p. 51.

Lists minstrel performances, pp. 14, 16-21, 23-24, 26, and 29.

2200 VINEYARD, Hazel. Trails of the Trouper: A Historical Study of the Theatre in New Mexico from 1850 to 1910. M.A., University of New Mexico, 1942. D3 861, p. 97.

Mentions a minstrel performance which included a buck and wing dance which ended in a cakewalk, p. 62.

2201 WALDERA, Jean. A Record of the Professional Theatre Activity in Fargo, North Dakota from 1914 through 1920. M.A., North Dakota Agricultural College, 1959. D2 (13) 3008, p. 129.

2202 WATSON, Margaret G. History of the Theatre of Virginia City, Nevada, from 1849-1865. M.A., University of Nevada at Reno, 1940. 215 pp. D3 819, p. 92.

2203 WEST, William Russell. An Historical Study of Professional Theatre Activities in Tallahassee, Florida, from January, 1874 to November, 1893. M.A., Florida State University, 1954. D2 (8) 1688, pp. 151-52.

Mentions minstrel performances and includes some comments on them from local newspapers, pp. 2, 18, 31, 35, 46, 48, 50-51, 53, 56-57, 62-64, 74, 77, 82, and 86-87.

2204   WILLSON, Claire Eugene. A History of the Theatrical Activities of Tombstone, Arizona, from 1880-1918. M.S., Northwestern University, 1934.

One of the best discussions of minstrelsy in graduate research. Gives accounts of performances and notes what highlighted each performance, pp. 46-47, 54-55, 63-65, 67-68, 75, 77, 79-80, 82-85, 93, 101, 110-11, 120, and 131-32.

2205   WILSON, Bertha Amelia. A History of the Theatre in Youngstown, Ohio. M.A., University of Michigan, 1945. D3 978, p. 111.

2206   YONICK, Cora Jane. A History of the Theatre in Springfield, Illinois, from 1855 to 1876. M.A., University of Wyoming, 1952. 120 pp. D3 332, p. 39.

THEATERS AND OPERA HOUSES

2207   AVERETT, Richard A. The History of the Auditorium Theater in Pocatello, Idaho, from 1893 to 1939. M.A., Speech and Drama, Idaho State University, 1970. 249 pp. D3 272, p. 32; K4, p. 2.

2208   BARBE, Lucille. A History of the Boyd Opera House in Omaha, Nebraska (1881-1889). M.A., Municipal University of Omaha, 1963. 202 pp. L1 2506, p. 253.

2209   *BARELLO, Rudolph Valentino. A History of the New Orleans Academy of Music Theatre, 1887-1893. M.A., Speech, Louisiana State University, 1967. D1 17755, p. 368; D3 510, p. 58.

2210   BARTON, Henry. A History of the Dallas Opera House, with a Day Book for the Seasons, 1901-02 to 1910-11. Master's thesis, English, Southern Methodist University, 1935. H1, p. 244.

2211   BEEGLE, Joanne Pangonis. A History of Kaier's Grand Opera House. M.A., Pennsylvania State University, 1964. D3 1019, p. 116.

2212   BENDER, Lorelle C. The French Opera House of New Orleans, 1859-1890. M.A., English, Louisiana State University, 1940. D3 490, p. 56; H1, p. 244.

2213   BENOFF, Stephen Michael. The Jenny Lind Theatre. M.A., University of California at Los Angeles, 1966. D3 71, p. 10.

2214   BERGSTROM, Lois Mildred. The History of the McVicker's Theatre, 1857-1861. M.A., University of Chicago, 1930. 313 pp. D3 297, p. 35.

2215   BOND, Roger B. Wilmington's Masonic Temple and Grand Opera House. M.A., University of Delaware, 1969. D3 198, p. 23.

2216   BOUSTKEON, Lindy. History of the Laramie Theatre (1881-1890). M.A., University of Wyoming, 1961. D2 (15) 2616, p. 176; D3 1393, p. 156.
       Lists minstrel performances, pp. 2, 42, 74, 81, 103, 110, 118, 130-32, and 137.

2217   BOYCE, Monique D. The First Forty Years of the Augusta, Georgia, Theatre. Master's thesis, English, University of Georgia, 1957. H1, p. 245.

2218   *BOYD, Theodore Edward. A History of the New Orleans Academy of Music Theatre, 1869-1880. M.A., Speech, Louisiana State University, 1965. D3 499, p. 57.

2219   BOYER, Robert Downer. A History of the National Theatre, Washington, D.C. M.A., Speech and Dramatic Arts, University of Maryland, 1963. 121 pp. B9 9, p. 2.
       Also discusses opera, minstrel troupes, and various virtuosos.

2220   BROCK, Richard Barrett. A Study of the Greencastle, Indiana, Opera House, 1875-1912. M.A., DePauw University, 1963. D3 341, p. 40.

2221   BROWN, Edward Devereaux. A History of Theatrical Activities at the Mobile Theatre, Mobile, Alabama from 1860-1875. M.A., Michigan State College, 1952. D2 (6) 966, p. 155.

2222   BROWN, William Langdon. A History of the Leland Opera House, Albany, New York, under the Management of John W. Albaugh, 1873-1881. M.A., State University of New York at Albany, 1972. D3 872, p. 99; K6 1321, p. 109.

2223   BUSH, Karen E. The Oxford Opera House, Oxford, Michigan, in Its Hour, 1891-1914. M.A., Michigan State University, 1966. D3 680, p. 76.

2224   CHIDSEY, Martha Ann. The West Street Theatre, Annapolis, Maryland, 1771-1774. M.A., American University, 1977. 82 pp. A1 (15/3) 13-09852, p. 177; B9 41, p. 6; B17 (11/2) 2590, p. 170.

2225 CLAY, Lucille N. The Lexington [Kentucky] Theatre from 1800 to 1840. Master's thesis, English, University of Kentucky, 1930. D3 404, p. 48; H1, p. 245.

2226 CONN, Arthur Leslie. The History of the Loring Opera House, Riverside, California. M.A., University of California at Los Angeles, 1970. D3 53, p. 8.

2227 CORY, Joyce Burke. The Dallas Theater Center: A History. M.A., Drama, Trinity University, 1968. H1, p. 245; L7 (80), p. 418.

2228 COX, James Rex. The History of the Newberry, South Carolina, Opera House, 1880-1973. M.A., University of South Carolina, 1974. 108 pp. D3 1162, p. 130.

2229 CRAWFORD, Robert. Piper's Opera House, Virginia City, Nevada. M.A., University of California at Los Angeles, 1950. D2 (4) 325, p. 148; D3 824, p. 93.

States that minstrel shows were always popular on the Comstock and that the shows came regularly during the 1890s, pp. 39, 52, and 64.

2230 CROWLEY, Elmer S. History of the Tabor Grand Opera House, Denver, Colorado, 1881-1891. M.A., University of Denver, 1940. D3 158, p. 19.

2231 DAVIS, K. L. A Chronicle of the Savoy Theatre, Louisville, Kentucky. M.A., University of Louisville, 1980. 99 pp. A1 (19/2) 1315472, p. 198.

2232 DEGITZ, Dorothy M. History of the Tabor Opera House, Leadville, Colorado, from 1879 to 1905. M.A., Western State College of Colorado, 1935. D3 173, p. 20.

2233 EAGLE, Robert J. The Charles Playhouse: An Investigation of the Historical and Artistic Development of the Resident Theatre in Boston. M.A., Drama, Catholic University of America, 1967. 85 pp.

Presents critical reviews of the musicals, *The Fantasticks* (presented December 1961) and *The Boys from Syracuse* (presented December 1963) at the Charles Playhouse.

2234 EATON, Robert Crawford. The Dallas Little Theater: The Maple Avenue Days, 1927-1943. M.A., Trinity University, 1972. L7 (80), p. 419.

2235 FLANDERS, Reuben H. A History of the Boyd Theatre in Omaha, Nebraska. M.A., University of Nebraska, 1963. 240 pp. D3 812, p. 92; L1 2508, p. 253. Lists productions from 3 September 1891 to 2 February 1920.

2236 FOWLER, Larry. History of the Stevens Opera House, Garden City, Kansas, 1886-1929. M.A., Emporia State University, 1969.

2237 *FRANCIS, Mark S. The Mankato Opera House: Music on the Frontier, 1872-1885. M.M., Mankato State College, 1975. 57 pp. illus. D3 686, p. 76.

2238 GERN, Jesse William. Colorado Mountain Theatre: History of Theatre at Central City, 1859-1885. M.A., Ohio State University, 1960. D2 (14) 2263, p. 167.

2239 GIGLIO, Mary Elena. The Terre Haute Grand Opera House, 1897-1898. M.A., Indiana State University, 1974. D3 358, p. 42.

2240 GOSSAGE, Forest Donald. A History of the Funke Opera House in Lincoln, Nebraska. M.A., University of Nebraska, 1961. D2 (15) 2619, p. 176; D3 807, p. 91; L1 2510, p. 253. The period covered is 1884-1902.

2241 GOURD, E. William. A Study of the Henry Opera House, Rockville, Connecticut. M.F.A., Ohio University, 1964. D3 191, p. 22.

2242 GREINER, Tyler L. A History of Professional Entertainment at the Fulton Opera House in Lancaster, Pennsylvania, 1852-1930. M.A., Pennsylvania State University, 1977. 2 vols. 859 pp. A2 938, p. 40; D3 1015, p. 115.

2243 GRIFFITH, Max Eugene. The Delaware, Ohio, City Opera House and Its Nineteenth Century Activities. M.A., Ohio State University, 1968. D3 968, p. 109.

2244 *HAINES, Peggy A. The History of the City Opera House, Traverse City, Michigan, from 1891 until July of 1897. M.A., Eastern Michigan University, 1971. 57 pp. illus. D3 681, p. 76.

2245 *HAMILTON, M. L. The Lyceum in New Orleans. M.A., Speech, Louisiana State University, 1948. D3 476, p. 55.

2246 *HARGETT, Sheila Ann. A Daybook and a History of the St. Charles Theatre, 1864-1868. M.A., Speech, Louisiana State University, 1971. D3 497, p. 57.

2247 HEMMING, Mary Ruth. The History of the Grand Opera House of St. Paul, Minnesota from 1883 to 1889. M.A., Speech and Drama, Catholic University of America, 1951. D2 (5) 917, p. 176.

2248 HENDERSON, Jerry E. A History of the Ryman Auditorium in Nashville, Tennessee, 1892-1920. M.A., Louisiana State University, 1961. D2 (15) 2622, p. 176.

2249 HILL, Raymond Scott. A History of the Princess Theatre of Des Moines, Iowa. M.F.A., University of Iowa, 1949. D2 (3) 114, p. 147.

2250 JOHNSON, Genevieve Goodman. A History of the Chicago Theater, October 21, 1871-1872. M.A., University of Chicago, 1932. D3 310, p. 36.
Lists minstrel performances and plays, pp. 3, 12, 24, 46-47, 52, 89-90, 98-100, and 148.

2251 JONASON, Marvin G. A History of the Junction City Opera House in Junction City, Kansas, 1880-1919. M.S., Emporia State University, 1970. D3 392, p. 46.

2252 KELLY, Martin P. The Albany, New York, Theatre from 1900-1910. M.A., Catholic University of America, 1954. D2 (8) 1500, p. 146.

2253 KEMMERLING, James. A History of the Whitley Opera House in Emporia, Kansas, 1881-1913. M.S., Kansas State Teachers College, 1967. D1 17724, p. 367; D3 388, p. 46.
This study is published in *The Emporia State Research Studies* 18/3 (March 1970), 72 pp., illus. Includes a chronological listing of entertainments such as minstrel performances, band concerts, and operas.

2254 KEMPLIN, Carolyn Ann. The History of the Granbury Opera House, 1886-1978. 96 pp. M.A., Theatre, North Texas State University, 1978. A1 (17/1) 1312108, p. 96.

2255 KENNEDY, Lucile B. A History of the Dallas Opera House (A Record of the Plays and Their Reception), with a Day Book for Seasons, 1911-1912 through 1921. Master's thesis, English, Southern Methodist University, 1940. H1, p. 247.

2256 KHEEL, Pearl Lee. A Survey of the Rochester Theater from 1900 to 1910. M.A., University of Rochester, 1947. L5, p. 247.

2257 *KLING, Esther. The New Orleans Academy of Music Theatre, 1853-1861. M.A., Speech, Louisiana State University, 1960. D2 (14) 2264, p. 167; D3 486, p. 56.

2258 KNIGHT, Virginia D. The New Opera House of Athens, Georgia, 1887-1932. M.F.A., University of Georgia, 1970. D3 231, p. 27.

2259 KRAAI, Menno John M. The Landers Theatre, 1906-1970. Master's thesis, Southwest Missouri State College, 1971. L8 (66), p. 303.

2260 *KRESTALUDE, James A. A Daybook and a History of the St. Charles Theatre, 1868-1872. M.A., Speech, Louisiana State University, 1972. D3 498, p. 57.

2261 KUEMMERLE, Clyde Victor, Jr. A History of Ford's Grand Opera House, Baltimore: From Its Origin in 1871 to Its Demise in 1964. M.A., Speech and Dramatic Arts, University of Maryland, 1965. B9 55, p. 7; D3 544, p. 62; L3, p. 29.
Also includes a discussion of theater in Baltimore prior to 1871.

2262 LAMBERT, Marlene Kalbfleisch. The Terre Haute Opera House from 1869 until 1874. M.A., Indiana State University, 1972.

2263 LANE, Doris A. A History of the Fort Worth Theater from 1880-1888. Master's thesis, English, Texas Christian University, 1948. D3 1214, p. 136; H1, p. 249.

2264 *LAWLOR, Jo Ann. History of the St. Charles Theatre of New Orleans, 1888-1899. M.A., Speech, Louisiana State University, 1966. D3 511, p. 58.

2265 McCULLOUGH, Mary Jean. Dallas Theater Center: Artist vs. Audience. M.A., Trinity University, 1974. L7 (80), p. 421.

2266   McCURDY, Evelyn Mary. The History of the Adelphi Theatre, San Francisco, California, 1850-1858. M.A., Stanford University, 1953. 96 pp. D2 (7) 1274, p. 157; D3 70, p. 10.

2267   MACKEY, Alice Jeanette. A History of the Coates Opera House, Kansas City, Missouri, 1870-1901. M.A., Central Missouri State College, 1963. D3 735, p. 83; L8 (59), p. 252.

2268   MARTIN, Mary Lou. A History and Evaluation of the Dallas Theater Center. M.A., West Texas State University, 1970. L7 (81), p. 446.

2269   MERRILL, Patricia Ellene. A History of the Tootle Opera House, St. Joseph, Missouri. M.A., University of Missouri, 1973. D3 741, p. 83.

2270   MIESLE, Frank L. A History of the Opera House at Fremont, Ohio, from 1890 to 1900. M.A., Bowling Green State University, 1948. D3 969, p. 109.

2271   *NELSON, Deda L. A Daybook and a History of the Jefferson Theater, 1900-1905. M.A., Speech, Louisiana State University, 1976. A2 4789, p. 196.

2272   *NESBITT, Robert Dowds. Early Concert Life at the Wieting Opera House in Syracuse, N.Y. M.Mus., Syracuse University, 1947. 92 pp. plates.

A chronological survey of many of the more important musical events which took place in the successive Wieting halls and opera houses.

2273   NICHOLS, Kenneth L. In Order of Appearance: Akron's Theaters, 1840-1940. M.A., University of Akron, 1968. 138 pp. D3 927, p. 105.

2274   NIEDICK, Arthur E. A Sketch of the Theaters of Ithaca, 1842-1942. M.A., Cornell University, 1942. L5, p. 242.

2275   *O'NEAL, Aaron Burwood. History of the St. Charles Theatre of New Orleans, 1880-1888. M.A., Speech, Louisiana State University, 1965. D3 505, p. 57.

2276   PARRAMORE, Annie Elaine. An Historical Study of Theatrical Presentations at the Jacksonville (Florida) Opera House, 1883-1887. M.A., University of Florida, 1954. D2 (8) 1686, p. 151; D3 219, p. 26.

2277   POWELL, Carolyn. The Lyceum Theatre of Memphis, Tennessee, 1890-1900. M.A., University of Mississippi, 1953. D2 (7) 1276, p. 157; D3 1188, p. 133.

2278   PRICE, Joyce Dyer. A History of the King Opera House in Greenville, Texas. M.A., East Texas State University, 1967. D1 17513, p. 360; D3 1222, p. 136; L7 (78), p. 315.

2279   RADOW, Rhoda Kirschner. A History of the Burlew Opera House, Charleston, West Virginia from 1891-1920. M.A., Marshall University, 1964. D3 1364, p. 152.

2280   REED, Carole Fay. A History of the Grand Opera House in Peoria, Illinois. M.S., Illinois State University, 1963. D3 328, p. 38.

2281   *REYNOLDS, Ina Christeen. A History of the New Orleans Academy of Music Theatre, 1861-1869. M.A., Speech, Louisiana State University, 1964. D3 494, p. 56.

2282   RIDGE, Patricia. A History of the Cheboygan Opera House, Cheboygan, Michigan, from 1891 to 1920. M.A., Michigan State University, 1963. D3 659, p. 73.

2283   *ROSS, Allan Sutphin. The New Orleans Academy of Music Theatre, 1880-1887. M.A., Speech, Louisiana State University, 1965. D3 507, p. 58.

2284   SCHAUB, Owen W. A History of the Grand Opera House Stock Company of Indianapolis, 1898 to 1900. M.A., Indiana University, 1968. D3 352, p. 41.

2285   SHAW, Bertha Louise. History of the Wheeler Opera, Aspen, Colorado, 1889-1894. M.A., Western State College of Colorado, 1965. D3 137, p. 17.

2286   SHERIDAN, Charles H. The History of "Music Hall" Opera House, Flint, Michigan, 1883-1893. M.A., Wayne State University, 1951. D2 (5) 923, p. 176; D3 678, p. 75; L9 998, p. 78.

        Includes a discussion of minstrelsy, the troupes which played there, and their popularity, pp. 54-57.

2287   SIENA, Marcia Ann. The History of the Great Southern Theater, Columbus, Ohio. M.A., Ohio State University, 1957. D2 (11) 2434, p. 151; D3 965, p. 109.

2288   SMITH, Larry A. The History of the Barton Opera House, Fresno, California, 1890-1914. M.A., California State University at Fresno, 1970. D3 39, p. 6.

2289   SOZEN, Joyce Chalcraft. Annals of the Opera House in Beardstown, Illinois from 1872 to 1900. M.A., University of Illinois, 1957. D2 (11) 2322, p. 148; D3 275, p. 275.
       Lists minstrel performances and other information about the troupes, pp. 69-78.

2290   STEENROD, Spencer. A History of Stuart's Opera House, Nelsonville, Ohio. M.A., Ohio University, 1973. D3 970, p. 110.

2291   STEPHENSON, Robert Rex. The Premier Season of Wysor's Grand Opera House, 1892-1893. M.A., Indiana State University, 1972. D3 360, p. 42.

2292   THORSON, Lillian Theodore. A Record of the First Year of McVicker's Theater, November 7, 1857-November 7, 1858. M.A., University of Michigan, 1946. 122 pp. D3 298, p. 35.

2293   TULK, Jere Stevens. History of the Laramie Theatre (1900-1910). M.A., University of Wyoming, 1967. D1 18447, p. 391.

2294   TYLER, Pamela. The Los Angeles Theatre, 1840-1900. M.A., University of Southern California, 1942. D3 40, p. 6; L2 (45) 22.159, p. 155.
       Minstrel performances mentioned in passing, pp. 17, 32-33, and 39.

2295   WADDELL, Richard Eugene. Theatre in Charlottesville, 1886-1912: The Levy Opera House and the Jefferson Auditorium. M.A., Speech and Drama, University of Virginia, 1972. 128 pp. D3 1296, p. 145.

2296   WALTON, William. A History of Professional Theatre at "The Oliver" in Lincoln, Nebraska (1897-1918). M.A., University of Nebraska, 1956. D2 (10) 2205, p. 148; D3 809, p. 91.

2297   WILSON, Jack A. A History of the Belding Opera House, Belding, Michigan, from 1889-1915. M.A., Michigan State University, 1965. D3 658, p. 73.

2298 WRIGHT, James W. The Chicago Auditorium Theatre, 1866-1966. M.A., Michigan State University, 1966. D3 305, p. 35.

DANCE

2299 BALKUS, Mary Patricia. History and Development of the Modern Dance Group of the Texas Woman's University from 1936 through 1965: Its Scope of Influence and Contributions to the Understanding and Appreciation of Dance as a Contemporary Art Form. M.A., Texas Woman's University, 1965. L7 (80), p. 316.

2300 *BATES, Barbara Claire. The Growth of Dance in the American Music Theater. M.S., Smith College, 1969. 148 pp.

2301 BATTERSON, Victor R. A Comparative Study of Some Dances of Latin America and of the United States and Their Common Origin. M.A., Ohio State University, 1947. C2 31, p. 8.

2302 BECHT, Donna. Theater Dance Today in the U.S.S.R., U.S.A. and Great Britain. M.A., Mills College, 1960. 52 pp. C2 36, p. 8.

2303 BECKER, Howard Saul. The Professional Dance Musician in Chicago. M.A., University of Chicago, 1949. 140 pp. B7 49, p. 9; B14 16, p. 23.
"Based on interviews with over 100 musicians."

2304 BETTS, Anne. An Historical Survey of the New Dance Group of New York City. M.A., New York University, 1945. C2 47, p. 9.

2305 *BRALY, Shairrie Lynne. A Choreographer's Approach to Stephen Sondheim's *Company*. M.A., Theater Arts, California State University at Long Beach, 1978. 58 pp. illus.

2306 BROOME, Estelle M. Contributions of Elizabeth Burchenal to Folk Dancing in the U.S. M.A., Physical Education, Smith College, 1954. 107 pp. C2 77, p. 11; I2, p. 245.

2307 BUBRICK, Pauline. An Historical Survey of Folk Dance Festivals, Groups, and Societies Active in the United States of America. M.A., New York University, 1943. C2 83, p. 11.

2308 *BUCALSTEIN, Paul. The Antecedents and Development of American Dramatic Ballet. M.A., California State University at Fullerton, 1973. 100 pp. illus.

2309 BYWATER, Shirley Gay. Choreography to the Sounds of Harry Partch. M.F.A., University of Utah, 1972. 23 pp. C1 45, p. 25.

2310 CAIN, Mary Jo. The Dance Element in Musical Comedy since 1943. M.A., North Carolina University, 1949. D2 (3) 150, p. 148.

2311 CARRUTH, Wincie Ann. The Significance of Religion in the Dance. M.A., Louisiana State University, 1937. I1 515, p. 52.
Discusses "Dance of the North American Indian."

2312 CHAPMAN, Beverly Armstrong. New Dance in New York, 1911-1915. M.A., American University, 1977. 225 pp. A1 (16/2) 1310918, p. 129.

2313 COLE, Diana Muriel. Utah Ballet — A Unique Development in the World of Dance. M.A., University of Utah, 1971. 89 pp. C1 52, p. 26.

2314 CORNWELL, Elizabeth. Regional Variations in Characteristics of American Square, Contra and Round Dances in Certain Regions of the United States. M.A., Physical Education, Wellesley College, 1943. 161 pp. B7 146, p. 21; C2 130, p. 15; I2, p. 172.

2315 COSTA, Mazeppa King. Dance in the Society and Hawaiian Islands as Presented by the Early Writers, 1767-1842. M.A., Drama, University of Hawaii, 1951. 151 pp. B7 147, p. 21; D2 (5) 729, p. 171; I2, p. 221.

2316 CRABTREE, Mary. A Survey of the Dance in Eastern Massachusetts. M.A., New York University, 1938. C2 134, p. 15.

2317 CRANE, Anne Helene. A Study of the Integration of the Dance in the Musical Theater as Illustrated by Works of Balanchine, De Mille, and Robbins. M.A., Catholic University of America, 1959. D2 (13) 2832, p. 124. 63 pp. Includes a "History of Dance in American Musical Theater."

2318 CROMIE, Andrea. Twentieth Century Popular American Dance: A Symbol of Society. M.S., University of Colorado, 1972. C1 55, p. 26.

2319 *CUMMINGS, Janice Marie. Cultural Significance of Black Religious Dance: Towards an Understanding of Vodu Dance in New Orleans. M.A., University of Illinois at Urbana-Champaign, 1977. 62 pp.

2320 DAVIDSON, Robert Nathaniel. A Study of the Ghost Dance of 1889. M.A., Stanford University, 1952. 49 pp. I1 742, p. 75.

2321 DAVIS, Ouid Pauline. A Study of the Terminology of American Country Dances. M.Ed., Physical Education, University of Texas, 1940. 134 pp. B7 170, p. 24; H1, p. 229; I2, p. 149.

2322 DRAUT, Linda L. The Louisville Ballet Company: A History, 1951-1965. Master's thesis, University of Louisville, 1981. A2 2541, p. 120.

2323 DUVALL, Mirian R. Contemporary Attitudes and Habits in Social Dancing. M.A., George Peabody College for Teachers, 1937. 87 pp. C2 176, p. 18.

2324 ELLIS, Kathryn Gladney. The Life and Contributions of Ruth Lovell Murray to Dance and Dance Education. M.Ed., Wayne State University, 1972. 150 pp. C1 64, p. 27.

2325 ELLIS, Merrill L. An Evaluation of the Oklahoma Federal Music Project. M.M.Ed., University of Oklahoma, 1940. L12, p. 85.

2326 EVANS, Marilyn Rae. The History of the San Francisco Ballet Company from Its Beginning through 1951. M.F.A., University of Utah, 1960. D2 (14) 2110, p. 162.

2327 FAINSTADT, Mirianne Elizabeth Jirgal. Dances of India in U.S.A., 1906-1970. M.A., University of California at Los Angeles, 1970. C1 69, p. 28.

2328 FLEMING, Jessica. Study of the Hawaiian Hula. M.A., New York University, 1946. C2 197, p. 19.

2329 *FORREST, John Alexander. Matachin and Morris: A Study in Comparative Choreography. M.A., Folklore, University of North Carolina at Chapel Hill, 1977.

2330 FRIEDMAN, Edna. American Opinions on Dance and Dancing from 1840-1940. M.A., New York University, 1940. C2 209, p. 20.

2331 GOODE, Elizabeth. Dance Research Completed in the Colleges and Universities of the United States of America. M.A., New York University, 1946. C2 235, p. 21.

2332 *GRUEN, Naomi Frances. The Choreography of Martha Graham: Matter into Meaning. M.A., University of Wisconsin at Madison, 1975. 116 pp.

2333 HARPER, Jean E. A Comparative Study of American Country Dance with Foreign Folk Dance in Colleges and Universities of the U.S. M.S., Physical Education, Smith College, 1949. 111 pp. B7 296, p. 39; C2 273, p. 24; I2, p. 207.

2334 HAUGER, Janet Vaksdal. Avant-Garde Choreography of the Sixties: A Lecture-Demonstration. M.S., Illinois State University, 1970. 32 pp. C1 89, p. 29.

2335 HINES, Sharon Rosa. Historical Study and Adaptation of Hawaiian Folk Dances for Physical Education Classes. M.A., University of the Pacific, 1960. I2, p. 285.

2336 HOYT, Mary Joann. A Look at the Modern Dance Material of the Museum of Modern Art in New York City. M.A., New York University, 1951. C2 308, p. 26.

2337 JAROSSZ, Lillian M. Popular Ballroom Dances in the United States and the American Scene from 1850-1950. M.A., New York University, 1950. C2 325, p. 27.

2338 JEHLE, Ruth Amanda. American Square Dancing in the Three Sections of Maryland and the District of Columbia. M.A., Education, University of Maryland, 1943. 73 pp. B9 1, p. 1; I2, p. 173.

2339 KENEFICK, Ruth Maureen. The Power and Position of the Spanish and Mexican Folk Dance in Southern California. M.A., Physical Education, Claremont College, 1936. 69 pp. C2 343, p. 28; I2, p. 117.

2340 KLYM, Maryanne. Four Major Choreographers of Musical Comedy Films. Master's thesis, Texas Woman's University, 1979. A2 3447, p. 146.

2341 KRIEHN, Ruth. Lecture Demonstration in Dance: A History of Dancing in American Theater. M.S., University of Wisconsin, 1937. C2 359, p. 29.

2342 *LEWIS, Geraldine Olga. A Study of the Professional Status of Private Dance Studios in Broome County, New York. M.A., Dance, University of Illinois at Urbana-Champaign, 1962. 174 pp.

2343 LEWIS, Marilyn. A Study of Modern Dance as a Means of Worship in the United States with Emphasis upon the History Development and Contributions of the Social Dance Guild and of Rhythmic Choirs. M.A., Texas Woman's University, 1965. C1 269, p. 48.

2344 LITTLE, Velma Mary Lois. A Study of the Significance of Folk Dances of Three National Dance Groups in Los Angeles. M.A., University of California at Los Angeles, 1943. C2 390, p. 31.

2345 LOMAX, Mary Helen. Folk Dances from Selected Areas of Texas. M.A., Texas Woman's University, 1956. 201 pp. C2 394, p. 32; I2, p. 262.
Health, physical education, and recreation.

2346 MOORE, Claudia. An Historical Survey of Selected Dance Repertories and Festivals in the United States since 1920. M.A., New York University, 1942. C2 445, p. 35.

2347 NARDERER, Evelyn. History of Social Dancing in California, 1848-1900. M.A., San Diego State College, 1968. 122 pp. C1 135, p. 34.

2348 O'HARA, Ruth Virginia. A Study of Dances of Early California. M.A., Education, University of Southern California, 1938. 139 pp. C2 483, p. 37; I2, p. 135.

2349 OLSON, Beth. Origin of Square Dance in California. Master's thesis, Mills College, 1949. 34 pp. C2 486, p. 38.

2350 *OLSON, Orvid Raymond. A History of the Development of Square Dancing as a Recreational Activity in the State of Illinois from the Early 1940's to the Present. M.S., Recreation, University of Illinois at Urbana-Champaign, 1961. 77 pp.

2351 PARRISH, Elizabeth. A Study of the Modern Dance in the Cultural Setting of the United States. M.A., University of California at Berkeley, 1933. C2 494, p. 38.

2352 *PARSONS, Kathleen Anne. The Dancers Company of Brigham Young University: Its Organization and Management. M.A., Physical Education, Brigham Young University, 1976. 68 pp.

2353 PETERSON, Barbara. A Bibliographical Essay on the Adult Literature of the Folk Dance of Southern Appalachia. Master's thesis, Library Science, Long Island University, 1972. G3, p. 53.

2354 PITKIN, Ronald. History of the New England Contra Dance. Master's thesis, Goddard College [no date cited]. C2 512, p. 39.

2355 PRATHER, Priscilla. The Dance in the United States: Its Development and Implications from 1890 to 1950. M.A., Ohio State University, 1950. C2 523, p. 40.

2356 RIEGEL, Ruth Ann. The Historical Development of American Folk Dances. M.A., Physical Education, University of Iowa, 1942. 163 pp. C2 544, p. 41; I2, p. 168.

2357 ROBERTSON, W. Grace. The Customs, Costumes, and Origins of the Folk Dances of Early California. M.S., Education, University of Southern California, 1941. 124 pp. I2, p. 162.

2358 SCHNEIDER, Gretchen Adel. Dance as an Expressive Response to Frontier Life in the Mining Camps of California, 1848-1855. M.A., University of California at Los Angeles, 1968. C1 161, p. 36.

2359 SMITH, Dorothy P. The Role of the Dance in the Samoan Primitive Culture Contrasted with the Role of Dance in Our Colonial American Culture. M.A., New York University [no date cited]. C2 601, p. 45.

2360 STOCK, Pier Ashley. Dance in the Theaters of Washington, 1810-1840. M.A., Dance, American University, 1980. 162 pp. A1 (19/1) 1315, p. 99.

The two theaters discussed are the Washington and National. Includes a list of dance performances during those years, based on contemporary newspapers.

2361 TERRY, Terlene D. A Survey of Black Dance in Washington, 1870-1945. M.A., American University, 1982. 104 pp. photos.

Includes a chapter on minstrel and vaudeville shows in Washington, D.C. from 1865 to 1900.

2362 TRAVER, Shirley M. The Development of Ballet on the Concert Stage in the United States of America between 1940 and 1946. M.A., Texas State College for Women, 1946. 287 pp. C2 648, p. 48.

2363 TRINITY, Joseph. George Balanchine's Contribution to Musical Comedy. M.A., Catholic University of America, 1957.

2364 TU, Yeh-Ko. American Folk Dances. M.A., Ohio State University, 1948. C2 652, p. 49.

2365 WARE, Bettie A. A Historical Study of Dance at Wellesley College. M.S., Wellesley College, 1949. C2 672, p. 50.

2366 WARREN, Lawrence. Lester Horton, California Dance Pioneer. M.A., University of California at Los Angeles, 1968. 126 pp. C1 184, p. 38.

2367 *WEBER, Thomas Edmund. A Historical Analysis of the Place of Dance in Undergraduate Men's Professional Physical Education in the United States. M.S., Physical Education, University of Illinois at Urbana-Champaign, 1965. 82 pp. illus.

2368 *WESSON, Karl E. Dance in the Church of Jesus Christ of Latter-Day Saints, 1830-1940. M.A., Brigham Young University, 1975. 136 pp. illus.

2369 WILLIAMS, Frances Sellers. American Dances for the American Secondary Schools. M.A., Education, Temple University, 1933. 184 pp. I1 3544, p. 350.
"Dances of the American Indian along the Frontier." Indians discussed include Blackfoot, Makah, Pueblo, Algonquin, and Sioux.

2370 YASHKO, Ruth E. An Historical Study of Pioneer Dancing in Utah. M.S., Physical Education, University of Utah, 1947. 61 pp. C2 700, p. 52; I2, p. 196.

*A*uthor *Index*

Barton, Henry **2210**
Basham, Rosemary **1249**
Basse, Albert, Jr. **224**
Bastin, Wilton James Bruce **762**
Bates, Barbara Claire **2300**
Bates, Carol Henry **225**
Battagila, Mary Jane **2084**
Batterson, Victor R. **2301**
Bauer, Joyce Griffin **1389**
Bauer, Margaret Spearly **599**
Bauer, Raymond Miles **763**
Bauerlein, Charles R. **2005**
Bauman, Dick **764**
Baver, Marlene Jeannette **1082**
Bayreuther, Florence **1390**
Beard, Anne W. **1923**
Beatty, John Joseph **1821**
Beaver, Mary Corinne **1733**
Becht, Donna **2302**
Beck, Emily Johnson **120**
Beck, Julia Riley **2006**
Becker, Howard Saul **2303**
Beckett, Elizabeth **1143**
Beckwith, Martha Warren **1822**
Beckwith, Natalie Bowen **1983**
Beegle, Joanne Pangonis **2211**
Beesley, Dorothy Hills **226**
Beiswanger, Barbara Page **1**
Belfy, Jeanne M. **1391**
Bell, William Campton **2110**
Bellanca, Horace V. **2085**
Belliston, Bona **457**
Beloff, Sandra Beth **1823**
Belsom, John A. **687**
Belt, Byron Harold **480**
Belton, Geneva R. **1734**
Bender, Lorelle C. **2212**
Benigsohn, Shirley B. **2056**
Bennett, Barbara **1314**
Bennett, Carolyn L. **1735**
Bennett, David Parker **1939**
Bennett, J. P. **2057**
Bennington, Billy D. **765**

Benoff, Stephen Michael **2213**
Benowitz, Zelda **688**
Benson, David Paul **959**
Benson, Robert L. **1824**
Benton, Franklin Frederick **1083**
Bergstrom, Lois Mildred **2214**
Berman, Mitchell Alan **227**
Bestor, Charles Lemon **1392**
Betts, Anne **2304**
Bickley, Thomas F. **1042**
Bigelow, Edwin L. **2111**
Biggers, Charles Edward **1736**
Bilhartz, Patty A. **228**
Billings, Melvin D. **481**
Billups, Kenneth Brown **1144**
Bingham, Carl W. **1145**
Bingham, Joanne L. **1101**
Bird, Mary Faber **986**
Bird, Robert Atkinson **766**
Birkhead, Carole Caudill **482**
Bishop, Frances Blackburn **643**
Bishop, John J., Jr. **483**
Bissmeyer, Mary Carolyn **229**
Bittner, Robert E. **153**
Bitz, Nellie Edith **2112**
Black, Mary Childs **2113**
Black, Nell Woods **942**
Black, Timuel K. **767**
Blackwelder, Harold Gene **589**
Blaha, Pamela Jane **230**
Blair, Amy Jean Glenney **2058**
Blair, Leola Ruth **1825**
Blanchard, Marguerite S. **2**
Bland, Lewis Horace **231**
Blanding, Mary Catherine **3**
Blankenship, Adele Jean **232**
Blankenship, Gay Grace **458**
Blanton, Mary Jacqueline **121**
Blitch, Lila Marie **459**
Bobbitt, Paul Rogers, Jr. **960**
Boelzner, David Ernest **1393**
Boette, Marie D. **1653**
Boewe, John Frederick **233**

Bueschel, Gordon Richard **1828**
Buffaloe, Bonnie Gail **1103**
Buford, Alzada M. Singleton **1741**
Buford, Mary Elizabeth **1656**
Bullington, Ailcy Josephine **53**
Bundy, Orrin Richard, Jr. **486**
Burchak, Jay Wilbur **1401**
Burdick, Don P. **2088**
Burdick, Virginia **54**
Burgess, Eleanor **1150**
Burkhard, Samuel Theodore **1037**
Burnett, Madeline Land **859**
Burnham, Ray G. **123**
Burns, Deborah A. **1038**
Burt, George W. **124**
Burton, William **1742**
Burts, Richard C. **645**
Bush, Karen E. **2223**
Bush, Michael **1657**
Buss, Judy Epstein **1829**
Bynum, James Louis **860**
Byrd, William Clifton **691**
Bywater, Shirley Gay **2309**

Cain, Mary Jo **2310**
Cairns, Holly A. **692**
Calderwood, R. D. **1151**
Caldwell, George O. **1402**
Caldwell, Kenneth V. **487**
Calhoun, Cecil Warner **1658**
Callen, William M. **1960**
Calmer, Charles E. **241**
Calvin, Judith **2089**
Camara, Joseph Anthony **1152**
Camp, Virgil H. **242**
Campbell, Jay J. **1153**
Campbell, Richard R. **646**
Cannon, Martin A. **1925**
Caplan, Francine M. **2060**
Card, Edith Bryson **861**
Carden, Joy C. **155**
Cardullo, Karen Mandeville **243**

Carey, Kathryn M. **1319**
Carlisle, Irene Jones **1659**
Carlson, Roy **1154**
Carney, Margaret Earls **693**
Carpenter, James F. **1155**
Carr, Bruce A. **862**
Carratello, John D. **863**
Carrithers, Michael B. **1830**
Carroll, Elizabeth Woodruff **156**
Carrow, Catherine Ikard **125**
Carruth, Mildred L. **1636**
Carruth, Wincie Ann **2311**
Carson, Bobby Joe **864**
Carter, Albert E. **1743**
Carter, Marva Griffin **244**
Carter, Thomas Robert **1940**
Case, Del Williams **1961**
Casey, L. D. **963**
Caso, Fernando H. **205**
Cason, Georgie Rees **1831**
Castleton, Don Bernard **1063**
Cates, Jesse Howard **964**
Cather, George D. **1250**
Cavalieri, Louise T. **1156**
Cavallero, Joseph **55**
Cepin, Caroline Coker **245**
Chadwick, Muriel Ann **1403**
Chamberlain, William Woodrow
    1660
Chambers, V. Blaine **717**
Chan, Jse Him **831**
Chan, Wing-Chi **246**
Chancy, James Melvin **1367**
Chandler, George W., Jr. **1661**
Chang, Songsri **1251**
Chapman, Beverly Armstrong **2312**
Chapman, Mary Helen **247**
Chapman, Roger E. **601**
Charles, Norman **56**
Chasteen, Jo Beth **832**
Cheeks, Gertrude Dansby **1744**
Chesky, Jane **1832**
Chester, Nancy Claire **248**

Crabtree, Lillian G. **1668**
Crabtree, Mary **2316**
Craig, Barbara Peterson **1411**
Crain, Martha **257**
Crane, Anne Helene **2317**
Crawford, Barbara **1947**
Crawford, Katharine Elizabeth
　1412
Crawford, Loren Brown **1255**
Crawford, Portia Naomi **1748**
Crawford, Robert **2229**
Crawford, Sylvia Lee **694**
Creech, Delton Troy **1962**
Creel, Richard Lowell **2090**
Creigh, Robert Hugh **1413**
Cressman, Herbert Detweiler **1025**
Crim, Jack Smith **1414**
Crockett, Charlotte Gwen **258**
Cromie, Andrea **2318**
Crook, Charles Ernest **651**
Crook, J. Don **1321**
Crook, Stewart Johnson **1160**
Crooks, Greta Lee Bardsley **259**
Crosman, Max W. **7**
Crowley, Elmer S. **2230**
Crutchfield, Mary Elizabeth **869**
Cullins, Ella Webb **60**
Cummings, Janice Marie **2319**
Cutler, Flory Fenton **1638**

Dabney, Ray F. **490**
Dahlberg, Susan J. **695**
Dalke, Jacob J. **1256**
Dallas, George M., Jr. **1161**
Dalton, Donald B. **2125**
Daniell, Martha Louise **1669**
Dannemiller, Joanne Dilley **605**
Darter, Thomas Eugene **260**
Daugherty, Edward B. **158**
Daum, Glen Allen **719**
Daum, John LaVern **261**
Daun, Glenn Shields **561**

Davenport, Linda Gilbert **1836**
Davidson, Caroline Richards **652**
Davidson, Marilyn M. **1415**
Davidson, Robert Nathaniel **2320**
Davies, Katherine Currie **262**
Davis, Audrey Hennen **61**
Davis, Elaine **720**
Davis, Harvey Owen **62**
Davis, K. L. **2231**
Davis, Ouid Pauline **2321**
Davis, Richard Allen **1416**
Davis, Richard Harding **2010**
Davis, Virginia Lucile **870**
Day, Gladys Christena **1963**
Day, Myrle **2126**
Day, Robert L. **1162**
Days, Grace Eleanor **263**
Dean, Harry A. **264**
DeBusk, Clarence Kaiser, Jr. **1670**
DeCharms, Desiree **265**
Degitz, Dorothy M. **2232**
Deibert, William Edward Ellis **266**
Del Monaco, John **491**
Delvin, Robert Carlton **653**
Demming, Lanson Frederick **606**
Dempsey, Harry J. **773**
Dempsey, Karen **8**
Demus, Mary Helen **607**
Den, Marjorie Freilich **267**
Denniston, Robert James **833**
Denton, Floyd Chandler **1163**
DeSimone, Carol M. **1417**
DeTar, Francis Edward **1418**
Devin, Ronald Boyd **2127**
Devine, George John **654**
Devore, Richard O. **1369**
Dew, Phoebe Yan-Chee **268**
Dewey, James William **1419**
DiBiase, Mildred **159**
Dickey, Judy Ruth **126**
Dillon, Clarissa F. **63**
Dobbyn, Freddie Phyllis **269**
Dommer, Robert V. **1964**

Ewing, Crystal **127**
Ewing, Roberta Louise **67**
Eyssen, Donald Chester **2130**

Fabrizio, Mark **1168**
Fahey, John Aloysius **775**
Fainstadt, Mirianne Elizabeth
   Jirgal **2327**
Falcone, Patricia Jane **162**
Fanta, Karen Lee **776**
Farber, Daniel Lewis **278**
Farrier, Walter **1260**
Fassino, Frederick Joseph **1430**
Fasthoff, Henry J. **12**
Fay, Barbara Carleen Brice **2131**
Feinstein, Martin **1984**
Feldman, Mitchell Evan **777**
Felton, Walter Wiest **873**
Felts, Jack H. **496**
Ferlan, David J. **836**
Ferris, John Raymond **279**
Fertig, Judith Pinnolis **1431**
Field, George Franklin **1261**
Finaldi, Edmond T. **280**
Finucan, Doreen **591**
Firnhaber, Oscar Ernst **1323**
Fischer, Ruby Keefauver **1842**
Fisher, Helen D. **989**
Fisher, Nevin W. **1004**
Fisher, Suzanne M. **13**
Fiske, Judy Mayberry **1432**
Fitch, Margaret **1927**
Fitzhugh, Lynne **2044**
Fitzpatrick, Newell C. **1750**
Flaherty, Avellina **1105**
Flanders, Reuben H. **2235**
Flandorf, Vera S. **2013**
Fleisher, Gerald **1433**
Fleming, Frances **1262**
Fleming, Jessica **2328**
Flerlage, Alice **1434**
Flinn, Wesley C. **1435**

Flores, Alonzo J. **1843**
Floyd, Annette Rahm **1436**
Foltin, Béla **1844**
Forbes, Douglas L. **1437**
Forbes, Kenneth V. A. **128**
Forque, Charles E. **497**
Forrest, Hilda Mae **1751**
Forrest, John Alexander **2329**
Fort, Ronald Claire **2132**
Foster, (Mrs.) Henry **129**
Foster, James Michael **2014**
Foster, Paul Stephen **1438**
Foster, William P. **1752**
Fowler, Larry **2236**
Fowler, Ona Arlene **1753**
Fox, Charles Clayton **498**
Fox, Ellen Mousseau **943**
Francis, Mark S. **2237**
Frank, Emmet A. **1019**
Fraser, Violet Lennie **1439**
Frebault, Hubert **2133**
Fredrick, Robert **499**
Freitag, Marvin August **837**
French, Carol Ann **874**
French, Gilbert Gregory **1985**
Frey, Eugene Victor **464**
Friedberg, Ruth Crane **281**
Friedman, Edna **2330**
Friedman, Madgel D. **2092**
Friedman, Robert **2015**
Frisbie, Charlotte Johnson **1845**
Frkovich, William Michael **282**
Frye, Daniel W. **283**
Fulford, William Douglas **1440**
Fulkerson, Noel W. **284**
Fuller, Marion Kendall **163**
Fulton, Alvin W. **285**
Furlan, Kenneth R. **286**

Gaber, Deborah R. **875**
Gach, Christine **112**
Gaff, Lilyan Zaro **2134**

Green, William F. **1677**
Greene, Barbara Joyce **1756**
Greene, Mary Hermana **1264**
Greenfield, Mildred Albert **2138**
Greer, Leslie Kathleen **1106**
Gregory, George Ronald **1965**
Gregory, Thomas B. **1332**
Greiner, Tyler L. **2242**
Grettie, Donald V. **1265**
Grier, Marion Janet **880**
Griesman, Robert J. **1107**
Griffin, Evelyn **2139**
Griffith, Margaret Kathryn
    Blackman **465**
Griffith, Max Eugene **2243**
Griffiths, Philip Ray **466**
Grotts, Pearl Irene **1851**
Groves, William McDonald, Jr.
    2140
Grubbs, Baalis **992**
Gruen, Naomi Frances **2332**
Gruman, Eleanor Weeks **881**
Guerra, Fermina **1900**
Guild, Elliott William **1852**
Gunnison, John S. **725**
Gunst, Marie Louise **1853**
Gustavson, Phoebe Jane **2093**
Gutowski, Lynda Diane **69**

Haas, Eugene Joseph **1445**
Haas, William Dan **1068**
Hackney, C. R. **1300**
Hafner, James T. **502**
Hagan, Dan **1966**
Hahn, Katherine **297**
Haid, Maris Stella **1301**
Haines, Peggy A. **2244**
Hairston, Teresa **1757**
Halbrook, Mamie S. **298**
Haldeen, Alfred L. **1446**
Halfpenny, Rowland Barnes **840**
Hall, Dorothy C. **1803**

Hall, James Ramsey **299**
Hall, Lindley Lawrence **660**
Hall, Stephen Frederic **882**
Hall, Vilvin Susan Buckholts **164**
Hall, William **883**
Hallock, Norman Everett **300**
Halpern, Kathryn D. **16**
Hamil, Linda Virginia **2141**
Hamilton, Christine A. **1447**
Hamilton, M. L. **2245**
Hamilton, Robert T. **2142**
Hammer, Eleanor Ray **1108**
Hammer, Mari Sweeney **566**
Hammond, Paul Garnett **884**
Hammond, Stella Lou **1639**
Hampsher, Harry Frank **966**
Hanke, Arline Marie **301**
Hanks, Sarah Elizabeth **1448**
Hanlon, Gloria **783**
Hansen, Barret Eugene **784**
Hansen, Basil **1989**
Hansen, Harald Alvin **134**
Hanson, Henry Endicott **1910**
Hantz, Mary Jane **1449**
Haralambos, Michael **785**
Harbinson, William Grady **1450**
Harbison, David **135**
Hardee, Lewis J., Jr. **726**
Harden, Timothy Don **967**
Hardie, Thomas C. **661**
Hardin, Wylie Audrain **2143**
Harer, Carolyn Bertha **1451**
Hargett, Sheila Ann **2246**
Haritan, Michael Elarion **1678**
Harkins, Suzanne MacLean **1452**
Harloff, Steven **786**
Harms, Paul A. **662**
Harper, Jean E. **2333**
Harrell, Donald Robert **1085**
Harris, Charlene Diane **302**
Harris, Dana Douglas **503**
Harris, Frederick A. **504**
Harris, Geraldine Caroline **2144**

Holcombe, Julia Irene **1683**
Hollander, Goldye **1110**
Holliman, Marcia Pelton **506**
Hollman, Jenette H. **315**
Holmes, Annette Cecile **71**
Holmes, James R. **2018**
Holvik, Karl M. **1268**
Hood, Sebron Yates **1012**
Hooks, Sylvia Marquita Cartwright **1045**
Hoole, William Stanley **2146**
Hoover, Richard Lee **1464**
Hopps, Gloria Lorraine **995**
Horn, Dorothy Duerson **887**
Horn, Leroy Bernard **1070**
Hornbuckle, William R. **968**
Horndon, Doris Arlene **1969**
Horner, Mary Katherine Hall **316**
Hottenroth, A. Elaine **731**
Houck, Elizabeth Stephenson **317**
Houlihan, Marc **2019**
House, Elizabeth Gaines **1465**
Houston, Clark A. **568**
Howard, Gilbert W. **1941**
Howard, Laura Pratt **790**
Howard, Lucinda Elizabeth **72**
Howell, Lillian Pope **318**
Howenstein, Marshall C. **507**
Hoyle, Stephen Edwin **319**
Hoyt, Mary Joann **2336**
Hribar, Mary P. **320**
Hu, Janice S. **1466**
Hubbard, Charles M. **888**
Huber, John Elwyn **1467**
Huenemann, Lynn Fredrick **1855**
Huff, Floyd D. **1970**
Huffman, June Hood **1468**
Huggins, James Leon **969**
Hughes, Ola Irene **1179**
Huhn, Robert Erwin **321**
Hummel, Lynn Ellis **1684**
Hunter, Boyd M. **1302**
Hunter, David S. **610**

Hunter, Michael Rolland **1111**
Hurt, William Jackson **1336**
Hutchinson, Mary Ann **1469**
Hutchinson, Robert B. **732**
Hutchison, Merilyn Kae **1470**

Iacoboni, Ricci E. **791**
Ibberson, John B. **1471**
Ingalls, Janyce Greenleaf **1112**
Ingalls, David M. **467**
Ingalls, Marjorie Stone **889**
Inglefield, Howard Gibbs **1472**
Ingraham, James Leslie **1473**
Inserra, Lorraine **890**
Irvis, K. Leroy **1759**
Isbell, Sarah Rachel **1856**
Iseminger, George **20**
Isquith, Aaron **1079**

Jabbour, Alan A. **1641**
Jackson, Arthur Wesley **1474**
Jackson, Eileen Stanza **1475**
Jackson, Frances Helen **170**
Jackson, Richard Hammel **700**
Jackson, Sam Oliver **1476**
Jacobs, Henry Switzer **1020**
Jacobs, Mark Dennis **733**
Jacobson, Roger F. **1477**
James, Hobert Lee **73**
Jarboe, Ruth A. **891**
Jarossz, Lillian M. **2337**
Jarrett, Alfred Roosevelt **322**
Jasen, David **21**
Jaynes, R. Leiland **1478**
Jeffrey, Valeta **22**
Jehle, Ruth Amanda **2338**
Jenkins, Gwendolyn N. **1479**
Jenkins, Kathleen D. **665**
Jensen, Ginger Anne **1480**
Jensen, Jack A. **734**
Jensen, Robert **792**

Kerr, Thomas Henderson 1761
Kesson, Jane Haines 334
Kettering, Eunice Lea 1685
Key, Jimmy Richardson 971
Keyton, Robert 335
Kezer, Claude D. 736
Kheel, Pearl Lee 2256
Kidd, Wayne 793
Kidder, David Harwell 946
Kielty, Patricia M. 737
Kierman, Marilois Ditto 336
Kilpatrick, Jack Frederick 1929
Kimball, Marilyn 1930
King, Bernice Margaret 1859
King, Carl Darlington 1116
King, William E. 738
Kinney, Mary Gene 78
Kinney, Sally J. 1183
Kinscella, Hazel Gertrude 1762
Kinsey, Mary Etta 337
Kirby, Linnie Sue 947
Kirchoff, Kim Allyson 1269
Kisling, Joan Falter 1860
Klein, Frances Ann 667
Klein, Stephen Tavel 794
Kline, Mary Francella 1340
Kling, Esther 2257
Klym, Maryanne 2340
Knafel, Stephen Robert 702
Knautz, Philip Frederick 1028
Knight, Virginia D. 2258
Knobloch, Ann-Lee 1341
Knox, Carol Ruth 613
Knox, Robert Erskine, Jr. 703
Knox, Winifred I. 1686
Kobart, Ruth 704
Kodish, Debora Gail 1642
Koehnline, William Angus 1687
Kooi, Ray C. 79
Koon, William H. 1688
Korey, Judith A. 1370
Kozlowski, Marianne Clare 172
Kraai, Menno John M. 2259

Kraiss, Barbara A. 897
Krause, David 1029
Krestalude, James A. 2260
Kriehn, Ruth 2341
Kring, William G. 1030
Krummer, Randolph F. 1487
Krupsky, Shannon Harry 80
Kubach, William Raymond 1305
Kuchenmeister, Mary Jeanne 1488
Kudo, Elmer Takeo 1489
Kuemmerle, Clyde Victor, Jr. 2261
Kultti, Karl R. 114
Kushner, David Z. 338
Kushner, David Zakeri 339
Kvapil, Otto Arthur 739

Labrecque, Candida Piërina Marsella 1490
Lackey, Sue Andra 1270
Ladabouche, Paul Arthur 842
Ladd, Charles T. 795
LaDue, George William 1271
Laetsch, Florence Gardner 1184
Lambach, Mona 1185
Lambert, Georgia P. 1491
Lambert, Marlene Kalbfleisch 2262
Lambrecht, Clarence Julius 512
Lamm, Charles Alfred 1861
Land, Robert Hunt 2153
Lane, Doris A. 2263
Lane, James William 1186
Lane, Laura 1862
Lane, Morgan Jackson 2154
Laneer, Larry 513
Laney, Helen Cunningham 898
Langille, Edward D. 1492
Langley, William Osler 2155
Langosch, Marlene 340
Langsford, Harry M. 81
Langworthy, Helen 2156
Lansford, Julia Ann 341
Lantz, Russell Audley 342
Laque, Rosemarie S. 470

Lupo, Gloria Nell **671**
Luscombe, Robert H. **741**
Luttrell, Wanda Melvina **2159**
Lyle, Beverly B. **2160**
Lyman, David H. **900**
Lyon, Dyanne Stricklyn **2161**
Lyons, Joseph C. **1509**
Lyons, Nick Louis **516**

McAdams, Nettie F. **1765**
McBean, Bruce Parker **350**
McCann, June **351**
McCarty, Diane **1192**
McCarty, Rex Byron **972**
McClain, Charles Sharland **352**
McCleery, Carolyn **1072**
McCorkle, Donald Macomber **1055**
McCormick, Elizabeth Marie **26**
McCosker, Susan **2097**
McCowen, Edward Reginald **1193**
McCoy, Robert Charles **353**
McCuen, Joseph Molina **517**
McCullough, Lawrence Ervin **1806**
McCullough, Mary Jean **2265**
McCurdy, Evelyn Mary **2266**
McDaniel, Walter H. **615**
McDavitt, Elaine Elizabeth **2162**
McDonald, Ann **354**
McDonald, Donald Gordon **1974**
McDonald, Gail Faber **355**
McDonald, Grant **1691**
McElrath, Hugh Thomas **973**
McElroy, William Wiley **1510**
McElwain, Juanita **1194**
McFarland, Anne A. **518**
McGee, Charles Bernard **1867**
McGee, Daniel Bennett **1766**
McGill, Lynn D. **1345**
McGilvray, Byron Wendell **175**
McGirr, Orvus Kailor **1901**
McGovern, Mary Immaculate **1195**
McGrath, Roberta Mary **1276**

McGuire, Ann Calhoun **519**
McGuire, Mary Lee **2045**
McHargue, Robert Morris **1692**
McHenry, Donna K. **1277**
Machles, Leonard **1196**
McHorse, Claud Denison **1511**
McIntosh, David Seneff **1693**
MacKay, John W. **1512**
McKean, Gary Franklin **1040**
McKean, Mildred Riddle **1902**
McKee, Edna Hollingsworth **2163**
McKewen, Robert William **520**
Mackey, Alice Jeanette **2267**
McKinley, Frank Arnold **901**
McKinney, Janeen E. **1513**
McKissick, Marvin Leo **844**
McKnight, Mark Curtis **2023**
Mackowitz, Phyllis Ruth **356**
McKown, Catherine **1197**
Macleod, Bruce Alan **1767**
McMillan, Knox M. **2024**
McMullen, Mildred M. **1694**
McMurray, Sue Ellen Zank **1514**
McNatt, Mary R. **1198**
McNerney Famera, Karen **616**
Macomber, Jeffrey R. **1515**
McPheeters, Dean W. **1903**
McRae, William Duncan, Jr. **845**
McTiernan, Ellan M. **1807**
McTyre, Maurine Robles **571**
Madsen, Jean **1516**
Magee, Noel Howard **357**
Mahder, William Carl **1517**
Maher, Mary Annata **948**
Mair, Brian **1518**
Malek, Michael Paul **902**
Maltby, Marc S. **84**
Malyc'kyj, Andrij **1519**
Manfredini, Harry **1520**
Mangan, Ruthmary **1991**
Mangler, Joyce Ellen **358**
Manning, Carroll **521**
Manor, Harold Carl **139**

Miller, Samuel Dixon 1121
Miller, Terry Ellis 1122
Minarik, Sharon Lee 906
Minear, Carolyn Cockrum 370
Minor, Andrew C. 472
Minter, William John 975
Mitchell, Charlie H. 1123
Mitchell, Johnlyn G. 1529
Mitchell, Josephine Gray 140
Mitchell, Margaret Penelope 371
Mitchell, Rosanne 674
Mohajery, Barbara A. 1870
Mohling, Virginia Gill 1871
Mollahan, Elizabeth T. 87
Momany, Sharon 1086
Monagham, Francis Borgia 372
Money, Mary Grace 1280
Monroe, Anita Fletcher 2072
Montague, Glenn Adwin 675
Montague, James Harold 1769
Montague, Stephen Rowley 1530
Montgomery, John Marvin 526
Moody, William 572
Moomaw, Charles Jay 1531
Moon, Kathleen 1348
Moon, Wallace G. 373
Moore, Alicia Y. 374
Moore, Claudia 2346
Moore, Daniel T. 2073
Moore, Douglas 1124
Moore, Ethel Perry 1698
Moore, Gary Winston 1532
Moore, James Edward 375
Moore, Katrina Lee 1202
Moore, Muriel Payne 1008
Moorehouse, Vera 743
Moran, John E. 141
Moran, Mary Anita 676
Moreno, Joseph J. 1872
Morgan, Richard Sanborn 527
Morin, Margaret Fleming 88
Morphos, Paul 1993
Morris, Alfred S. 2169

Morris, Arthur Corwin, Jr. 142
Morris, Ophelia Estelle 1770
Morris, Robert Bower 1281
Morris, Robert Othello 1203
Morrison, Donald Eugene 1282
Morrison, Rheta H. 1073
Morroni, June Rose 2074
Morrow, Marguerite H. 2170
Morse, Susan K. 1533
Mortensen, Randy 376
Moser, Dorothea Joan 1944
Motyl, Jeanne Marie 949
Mucci, Ferdinand Rudolph 377
Mueller, Robert E. 1534
Muilenburg, Harley W. 378
Mullins, Charles G. 2171
Munn, John H. 528
Muradian, Thaddeus George 1125
Murase, Natsuko 379
Murphy, Catherine Amt 573
Murphy, Charles Robert 1349
Murphy, Rose Marie 1306
Murray, Carol J. 1535
Murray, Eloise 1873
Murray, Martha M. 380
Murray, Sterling E. 381
Muskrat, James Bruce 1536
Myers, Betty Dustin 382
Myers, Howard Leo 383
Myers, William Jackson, Jr. 1771
Myracle, Kay Ferree 176

Nagel, Richard J. 529
Narderer, Evelyn 2347
Nash, Dennison James 530
Nash, Ellen B. 706
Nash, Nancy Lee 1537
Neal, Mabel Evangeline 1699
Neil, Lantha-Dale 1350
Nelson, Carl Leonard 1283
Nelson, Deda L. 2271
Nelson, Edwin L. 744

Peach, Lynda Coffman **620**
Peachy, Burt Haines **710**
Pearce, Eva F. **389**
Pearlman, Blanche **1351**
Pearson, Boyce Neal **1774**
Pease, Rhenda Ronfeldt **1546**
Pebworth, James R. **29**
Peck, Gregory L. **2026**
Peck, Mariol R. **2027**
Peck, Phoebe **2173**
Peckman, John L. **910**
Peek, Richard Maurice **1087**
Pellman, Samuel Frank **1547**
Pembrook, Randall G. **1548**
Penner, Marilyn Ruth **1074**
Perkins, Laurence **390**
Perrin, Irma Cooper **1979**
Perrin, Phil D. **1549**
Perry, Henry Wacaster **1703**
Peters, Damaris Porter **391**
Peterson, Barbara **2353**
Peterson, Milo **534**
Peterson, Ronald Dale **1550**
Petitjean, Irene Martin **1704**
Petree, Colbert G. **1287**
Petry, Delano Lee **1208**
Pettit, Paul B. **2100**
Petz, Weldon **91**
Philips, Mary K. **1917**
Phillips, Jean Ann **745**
Phillips, Wendell B. **535**
Pickard, Dorothy Selden **1551**
Pickett, C. H. **2174**
Pietroforte, Alfred **1876**
Pilcher, Diane L. **711**
Pine, Mary Louise **144**
Pippart, Jane T. **1705**
Pirret, Bruce Alan **1552**
Pisciotta, Louis V. **1553**
Pitkin, Ronald **2354**
Plyler, Esther Petre **1048**
Poe, John E. **1996**
Pohly, Linda L. **179**

Point, Phil **180**
Politco, Jeromine **1209**
Polk, Linda Sue **1950**
Pollan, Loy **1933**
Pollenz, Philippa **1877**
Pollock, Louis I. **2028**
Pool, Evelyn Ivora **392**
Poole, Robert Wade **977**
Pooler, Marie **1554**
Pope, Mary Bhame **393**
Portnoy, Marshall Alan **1811**
Postma, Frank **1555**
Potthast, Anne Colette **473**
Powell, Carolyn **2277**
Powell, Clifford Elizabeth **92**
Powell, Paul Richard **2029**
Powers, William K. **1878**
Prather, Priscilla **2355**
Pratz, Kathryn Hester Darnielle **1556**
Prentiss, Barbara G. **680**
Prescott, Marjorie **1210**
Preston, Katherine K. **181**
Price, Joyce Dyer **2278**
Priest, Jimmie Ray **1288**
Primeaux, Beverly **2175**
Pringle, Margaret Ann **1557**
Probstfield, Evelyn **2176**
Proctor, David P. **2030**
Pruett, James Worrell **394**
Pugh, Ronnie Floyd **1951**
Purdy, William Earl **395**
Putnam, Howard Hoggan **396**
Putnam, Maxine Schunnep **1211**
Pyke, L. Allen **1558**

Quackenbush, Margaret Diane **1559**
Quade, Robert Milton **1014**
Quain, Mildred **2075**
Queen, James L. **1352**
Quigley, Bernard J. **2177**
Quistorff, Lynda **397**

Roof, Mary Ellen **1708**
Root, Deane Leslie **593**
Rose, Charles **594**
Rosenblum, Denise L. **1574**
Ross, Allan Sutphin **2283**
Ross, Carolyn W. **1093**
Ross, Jean Esther **912**
Ross, Sylvia Lucy **1575**
Rossomando, Fred Edward **1576**
Rothert, Harold Hanson **1354**
Rouse, Christopher Chapman **1577**
Rowe, Jack Calvin **410**
Royce, Letha M. **1218**
Rubinstein, Lucille **1355**
Ruckert, George **411**
Rudina, Rima **808**
Ruff, Edwin E. **412**
Ruhl, Jacqueline Gordon **913**
Rumble, John W. **1952**
Runkle, Aleta M. **574**
Russell, Clyde **95**
Ryan, Jean F. **413**
Ryan, Mary Grace **849**

Sabin, John T. **1578**
Sacca, Vincent John **1356**
Saclausa, John **1579**
Sadler, Cora **1777**
Safane, Clifford J. **1580**
Saighoe, Francis A. Kobina **1778**
Salassi, Otto **1953**
Sallee, James Edward **914**
Salmoni, Fabrizio **1954**
Salmons, Lee Allen **96**
Sanderson, Alice Louise **1357**
Sanger, Paul Bowman, Jr. **1006**
Saribalas, George Michael **1219**
Satterfield, Jacqueline Creef **1581**
Saucier, C. L. **1709**
Scanlon, Mary Browning **1131**
Scarff, Frances Beatriz Gonzalez
1710

Scarpato, Robert Hagen **747**
Schaefer, Donald George **1291**
Schalk, Carl Flentge **1582**
Schaub, Owen W. **2284**
Scheid, Paul **575**
Schermer, Richard **1997**
Schilling, Arnold J. **1023**
Schleis, Thomas Henry **713**
Schmalz, Robert Frederick **915**
Schmid, Roy Ralph **1088**
Schmitt, Robert J. **1001**
Schmoyer, Helen Cecelia **576**
Schneider, Betty M. **539**
Schneider, Gretchen Adel **2358**
Schneider, Theodore Jacob **1032**
Schoepko, Alfred A. **577**
Schoning, Fred P. **809**
Schraeder, Marilyn Joyce **578**
Schroeder, Pollyanna Tribouillier
32
Schroeder, Rebecca B. **1711**
Schroeder, Vernon Paul **187**
Schubert, Melvin Frank **1879**
Scott, Kathleen S. **2182**
Scott, Ruth Holmes **1058**
Scott, Sheila Lane McAferty **916**
Scroggins, Sterling **1934**
Sebastian, Linda Jean Chaney **1779**
Sedore, Robert N. **540**
Seelenbinder, Ray Lee **146**
Segale, Virginia Jean **1646**
Seitz, Barbara Joan **579**
Semenza, Edwin S. **2183**
Seymour, Margaret R. **188**
Shackelford, Lucy Evelyn **1220**
Shaffer, Virginia M. **2184**
Shamp, B. K. **2076**
Shank, Carl Dean, Jr. **414**
Shank, Phillip James **2185**
Shapp, Elizabeth Irene **541**
Sharp, James R. **1981**
Sharp, Mary Elizabeth **1583**
Sharrock, Barry Roger **917**

Souder, Marian Jo 1292
Soules, Lillian Lohmeyer 100
Southern, Eileen Stanza Jackson 1592
Southwick, Lynda Meredith Miller 116
Sowell, Brady O. 1308
Sozen, Joyce Chalcraft 2289
Sparger, A. Dennis 422
Sparks, Andrew H. 2190
Sparrow, Danny R. 1593
Speaker, Lucy Lee 1362
Spear, Richard E. 2191
Specht, Robert John, Jr. 924
Speck, Frederick A. 1594
Spell, (Mrs.) Lota 1094
Spielman, Earl V. 423
Spier, Ronald Michael 1595
Spigener, Tommy Ray 951
Spoth, Doris M. 2033
Spottswood, Richard Keith 34
Sprunger, Orlo Omer 682
Squares, Roy 714
Staab, Mary Theresine 1886
Staater, H. Ray 191
Stackhouse, Margaret Elise 683
Staebler, Roger Allen 1999
Staebler, Ronald Milton 2000
Staiger, John Norman 582
Stallings, Valdemar Lee 424
Stalvey, Kenneth Dorrance 812
Stanek, Ethel Lou 1596
Stanley, Hildegard Jo 1597
Stanley, John W. 813
Stanley, Jonathan J. 35
Stanton, Charles Kenny 952
Stanton, Royal Waltz 925
Starcher, Duane B. 1812
Starks, Laura Geralee 425
Starling, Earl Alvin 926
Stearns, Gordon Woodburn 1009
Stebbins, Robert Alan 814
Steel, David Warren 953

Steele, Algernon Odell 927
Steele, Charlotte L. 1293
Steelman, Gloria Geren 192
Steely, Mercedes 1715
Steenrod, Spencer 2290
Steese, Ruth Zimmerman 684
Stein, Karen S. 750
Stein, Richard 815
Steiner, Stephen Merritt 954
Stephen, C. 2034
Stephens, Norris Lynn 1076
Stephenson, Mary Lee 426
Stephenson, Nan L. 2104
Stephenson, Robert 1598
Stephenson, Robert Rex 2291
Stevens, Eva 2192
Stevens, Katharine Bell 2193
Steward, Ronald Maurice 751
Stewart, Johnathan 101
Stewart, Marilyn 427
Stewart, Roger Dean 955
Stewart, Rose Belle 928
Stigberg, David Kenneth 929
Stock, Patricia Gail 545
Stock, Pier Ashley 2360
Stockdale, Richard P. 2035
Stogsdill, Thomas M. 1599
Stoker, Vera Alice 1716
Stokes, Cloyce 193
Stoll, Robert J. 428
Stoltenberg, Margaret Mary 1226
Stoneburner, Bryan C. 546
Storck, John W. P. 36
Stork, George Frederick 429
Stowe, William McFerrin, Jr. 752
Stramler, Marcus Garvey 1918
Stranlund, Virginia 1227
Strauss, Barbara 37
Stricklin, David B. 1956
Struss, Janet Sue 930
Sublette, Richard Horace 595
Sucoff, Herbert 430
Suehs, Hermann C. 1133

Trawick, Fawn Grey 629
Trible, Bruce Clarence 433
Trinity, Joseph 2363
Trone, Dolly G. 104
Trottier, Muriel 1609
Trout, Philip Edwin 1297
Trulsson, Berton E. 2197
Tu, Yeh-Ko 2364
Tucker, Wayne G. 434
Tulk, Jere Stevens 2293
Tull, Fisher Aubry, Jr. 1610
Turek, James John 435
Turk-Roge, Janet Louise Coulson 1298
Turner, Beatrice Seberia 933
Turpen, Charles 1890
Tvrdy, Helen 198
Tweed, Myron 1091
Tye, James E. 934
Tyler, Pamela 2294
Tyler, Virginia June 1235
Tyska, Theodore Charles 630

Ungrodt, Judith Joan 436
Unrau, Mary Anne 1611

Van Brocklin, Allan John 935
Van Citters, Mary Lavina 631
Van Cott, Frank A. 199
Van Fossan, Kathryn R. 1612
Van Kirk, Gordon 2198
Vanderlaan, David James 1957
Vantilburg, David E. 437
Varnado, Alban F. 2199
Vars, Dianne 1613
Vaughan, Portia Loyetta 1891
Vega, Hector 206
Velcich, Mary Imelda 1236
Verret, Mary Camilla 1003
Vineyard, Hazel 2200
Vinquist, Mary 438

Voight, Ruth Marie 584
Volger, George 2037
Volland, Anita D. 1719
Vollstedt, Don August 1017
Volonts, John George 821
Von Der Heide, Henry J. 1237
Von Haupt, Lois 822
Voorhees, Anna Tipton 39
Voorhees, Larry Donald 439
Vosburgh, Theodore 200

Waddell, Richard Eugene 2295
Wadsworth, R. W. 2081
Waggoner, William L. 1035
Wagner, John W. 440
Wagner, Marjorie K. 40
Wakeland, Myrtle 105
Walden, Jean Elizabeth 1787
Waldera, Jean 2201
Waldman, Deborah Anne 1919
Waldroff, Kenneth 1238
Walgren, Carol L. Nelson 441
Walker, E. C. 1813
Walker, Laddie Leo 980
Walker, Marvin Ray 442
Walker, Ouida Merle 1892
Walker, Robert Gary 981
Walker, Sammye Mae Sadler 1788
Walker, Vanessa G. 823
Wall, Ruth D. 1789
Wall, Woodrow Wilson 982
Walls, Brian Scott 585
Walmsley, Robert 1790
Walter, Vincent P., Jr. 41
Walton, William 2296
Ward, Charles Wilson 1614
Ward, Tom Robert 443
Ware, Bettie A. 2365
Ware, Luella Catherine 1893
Ware, Mary Anne 1239
Wargelin, Carol Grace 117
Warren, Lawrence 2366

Wilson, Norman Gerald 633
Wincenciak, Sue Lockhart 109
Windecker, Anita F. 1624
Winter, Elizabeth Harrell 149
Wintersole, William Richard 2040
Wise, James Edward 1724
Wiseman, Steven Gayle 634
Witham, Floyd Deland 2105
Witmer, Robert Earl 1899
Witt, Raymond C. 940
Witucki, Alan Philip 1625
Woeppel, Louise B. W. 451
Wohlford, Mary Kathryn 2083
Woicikowfski, John F. 1626
Wolbert, Nancy 474
Wolfe, A. D. 203
Wolfe, A. Edward 852
Wolfe, Curtis Scott 1627
Wolfe, Lucy Louise 1060
Wolter, Richard Arthur 635
Wolverton, Josephine 1364
Wolz, Larry R. 150
Wong, Mary Ruth 46
Woodings, Terry G. 1061
Woodruff, Jean 554
Woods, Genevieve 587
Woodson, Craig DeVere 824
Wooten, William Chapman 555
Work, John Wesley 1795
Worthen, Ellis Clayton 1628
Worthington, Thomas Howard
    1244
Wragg, Eleanor Newton 110
Wright, Arthur M. 1937
Wright, James W. 2298
Wright, Jeremiah A. 1796
Wright, Josephine Rosa Beatrice
    452

Wright, Kittye Sneed 596
Wright, Marilyn Jean 1245
Wright, Mary Louise 588
Wright, Maud 1725
Wrzesinski, Janice L. 2041
Wunderlich, Joyce C. 1365
Wyatt, P. J. 1726
Wylder, Robert Clay 1727
Wynn, Virginia S. 453
Wyrick, Charles R. 204

Yashko, Ruth E. 2370
Yates, Beverly L. 556
Yeager, Cynthia H. 2003
Yeary, David Maurice 1629
Yonick, Cora Jane 2206
Young, John Joseph 1630
Young, John Walter 454
Young, Merle 1938
Young, Milton B. 2052
Young, Pamela Fensch 557
Young, Pauline 1135
Yousling, Richard S. 1631
Yu, Grace Shui-Chi 111
Yudkin, Jacqueline Joy 1246
Yuen, Janice Shan-Chen Hu 1632
Yune, Kuija Lee 1633
Yungton, Alvin H. 455

Zachman, Robert F. 558
Zander, Marjorie T. 1797
Zeller, Frederick R. 151
Zenor, Mina L. 759
Zielke, Dorothy Helen Meyer
    1036
Zimmerman, Karen Voci 1081
Zirner, Ludwig Ernst 636

Geographic Index

*S*ubject *Index*

Afro-American music **3, 820,**
  1165, 1228, 1315, 1728-97.
  See also Black music
Aiken, Jesse B. **884**
Ainsworth, Henry **890**
Aldrich, Richard **1983, 1998**
Almand, Claude Marion **239**
American Catalogue of Books **10**
American Federation of Musicians
  2049
American Guild of Organists **456**
Anderson, Leroy **896**
Antheil, George **322**
Anthems **239, 295, 655, 853, 868,**
  889, 899-900, 908, 912, 928,
  1030, 1078
Arlen, Harold **739**
Armstrong, Louis **806**
Ashley, Tom Clarence **1809**
Auld, Alexander **1122**
Austin, Larry **1390**

Babbitt, Milton **1383, 1509**
Bacon, Ernst **1423**
Bacon, Thomas **266**
Baldwin, Ralph Lyman **1105**
Ballads **95, 190, 1353, 1649-51,**
  1653-57, 1659, 1662-63, 1668,
  1671, 1675, 1679-81, 1684,
  1690, 1699, 1701, 1707,
  1717-18, 1722, 1724, 1759,
  1765, 1798, 1800, 1802-03,
  1805, 1807-08, 1811, 1903,
  1913, 1923-24, 1933, 1936,
  1938. *See also* Folk songs
Ballou, Esther Williamson **1568**
Balzer, Charles **999**
Band music **261, 325, 434, 442,**
  454, 502, 513, 635, 1404, 1408,
  1410, 1430, 1493
Barber, Samuel **218, 245, 277,**
  341, 351, 362, 367, 439, 608,
  611, 635, 1406, 1427, 1494-95,

Gideon, Miriam 397, 1431
Gilbert, Henry F. 1439
Gillespie, John Birks ("Dizzy") 806
Glanville-Hicks, Peggy 216
Goldman, Richard F. 545, 896
Gordon, MacKenzie 176
Gordon, Robert W. 1642
Gospel Hymns 906
Gospel music 45, 832, 858, 860, 866, 871-72, 878, 901, 909, 914, 919, 922, 930-31, 935, 1747, 1757, 1790. *See also* Spirituals
Gottschalk, Louis Moreau 24, 437, 524, 599
Gould, Morton 1430
Gould, Nathaniel Duren 1112
Green, John ("Johnny") 763
Griffes, Charles Tomlinson 213, 236, 262, 282, 304, 312, 335, 351, 428, 444, 453, 676, 1435, 1502, 1537, 1612
Grimm, Carl Hugo 1587
Grobe, Charles 330
Guitar music 431
Guthrie, Woodrow Wilson 1948-49

Hagemann, Richard 676
Hagen, Francis Florentine 394
Haieff, Alexei 1490
Hale, Philip 1992
Hammerstein, Oscar, II 409, 722, 737-38, 758
Hanson, Howard 287, 451, 635, 1503, 1525, 1531, 1544, 1571, 1625
Hardison, Janis 1652
Harkness, Georgia 347
Harp music 216
Harris, Joel Chandler 647

Harris, Roy 287, 334, 630, 1379, 1381, 1389, 1409, 1412, 1465
Harrison, George Donald 1961
Hastings, Thomas 874
Hawthorne, Alice. *See* Winner, Septimus
Heim, Norman 454
Heinrich, Anthony Philip 374, 425
Helm, Everett 634
Henderson, W. J. 1998
Hensley, Bill 1939
Henson, B. R. 460
Herbert, Victor 220, 1437
Hewitt, James 440, 896
Hewitt, John Hill 209
Heyward, DuBose 647
Hillegas, Michael 195
Hodgdon, William Augustus 1133
Holden, Oliver 896
Hommann, Charles 215
Hopkinson, Francis 71, 268, 377, 436, 652-53
Hovhaness, Alan 608, 1382, 1473, 1484, 1536, 1570, 1610
Howard, Alton H. 1089
Howard, Mittie Banks 259
Howard, Sidney 756
Hughes, Langston 820
Huneker, James Gibbons 1983, 1998
Husa, Karel 1460
Hutcheson, Ernest 1266
Hymnody 16, 318, 347, 410, 653, 855, 859, 861, 871-73, 877-79, 881, 887, 891, 893-95, 899, 902-04, 906-10, 915, 917, 919, 921, 923-25, 931-32, 938, 941-42, 946-47, 952, 954, 963-64, 966, 969, 971, 979, 982, 987-88, 1003-04, 1011, 1013, 1021, 1024-26, 1033, 1040, 1044, 1046-49, 1071, 1073, 1078-79, 1089. *See also* Psalmody

Loesser, Frank **739, 756**
Loewe, Frederick **741, 755**
Lombardo, Carmen **763**
Lorenz, Edmund S. **955**
Lovelace, Austin D. **1382**
Luening, Otto **322**
Lund, Anthony C. **1129**
Lunsford, Bascom Lamar **1923**
Lynn, George **1429**
Lyon, James **879**

McClellan, John J. **461**
McCurry, John G. **864**
McDonald, Harl **1397**
MacDowell, Edward **24, 426,**
 1424, 1500
McGrath, Joseph J. **1483**
McKay, George F. **454**
Maekelberghe, August **1393**
Maennorchor **176, 182**
Malcolm, Alexander **168**
Marches. *See* Band music
Marshall, John Bromell **513**
Marshall, John Bromell, Jr. **513**
Mason, Daniel Gregory **355**
Mason, Lowell **318, 326, 624, 879,**
 944, 1103-04, 1109-10, 1124-26,
 1131, 1328, 1590
Mason, Luther Whiting **1134**
Mason, William **1128**
Matterling, George **1382**
Matthews, Thomas **1382**
Mencken, H. L. **98**
Mendelssohn Society **176**
Mennin, Peter **333, 608, 1266,**
 1582
Menotti, Gian Carlo **255, 348,**
 359-60, 399, 692, 1375,
 1416-17, 1572, 1579, 1607
Meyer, Henry E. **952**
Meyer, Leonard B. **1990**
Michael, David Moritz **297, 443**

Miessner, W. Otto **1121**
Military music **103, 1330**
Miller, Albert **1130**
Miller, Dayton C. **1976**
Minstrelsy **35, 176, 466, 721, 725,**
 727, 2129, 2131, 2134-35,
 2139, 2144, 2148, 2155, 2157,
 2162-63, 2173, 2180, 2183,
 2192, 2194, 2199-2200, 2203-04,
 2219, 2223, 2229, 2250, 2253,
 2286, 2289, 2294, 2361
Modern Jazz Quartet **804**
Moller, John Christopher **624**
Monk, Thelonious **811**
Montani, Nicola A. **948, 956**
Moore, Douglas S. **287, 704, 726**
Moore, Mary Carr **404**
Moore, Undine S. **375, 1602**
Moran, Robert Leonard **1370**
Morton, Ferdinand "Jelly Roll"
 803
Moving-picture music **6, 2016,**
 2036
Mozart Society **176**
Mueller, Carl F. **295**
Mueller, George Godfrey **445**
Mullen, Frances **579**
MUSART **41**
Music
 —in industry **50, 81, 572, 2016.**
  See also **79**
 —in mental institutions **66**
 —in paintings **90**
 —in penal institutions **48, 83**
 —of blind musicians **465, 1357**
Music camps **58, 112, 114-15**
Music competitions **118, 144, 151,**
 1153, 1163, 1201, 1224, 1234,
 1237-38, 1346. *See also*
 Music festivals
Music education **2, 22, 41, 94,**
 166, 1092-1366
Music Educators Journal **1198**

Phipps, A. L. **1935**
Piano music **24, 211, 216, 225,**
228, 234, 245, 247-48, 277,
286, 288, 300, 303, 312-13,
323, 327, 330, 333, 338, 345,
349, 354-55, 357, 361-62,
367-68, 385-86, 397, 405,
413-14, 416, 423, 425, 428,
432, 437, 441, 444, 448, 453,
599, 604-05, 607-09, 611, 614,
617, 619-20, 624, 633-34,
636, 763, 803, 1347, 1376,
1379, 1386, 1397, 1400, 1405,
1413, 1415, 1424, 1443, 1447,
1448-49, 1451-52, 1456, 1459,
1466-67, 1470-71, 1480, 1482,
1490, 1500, 1520, 1526, 1529,
1539, 1542, 1556, 1565, 1570,
1574, 1580, 1589, 1606, 1611,
1617, 1624, 1632
Pinkham, Daniel **1432, 1464, 1474**
Piston, Walter **408, 415, 630,**
1449, 1485, 1507, 1535, 1561,
1627, 1629
Popular music **55, 84, 761, 780-81,**
784, 786, 791, 795, 799, 801-02,
818-19, 897, 2005, 2041
Porter, Cole **739**
Porter, Quincy **1492**
Powell, John **24, 44, 219, 247,**
1589, 2014
Presley, Elvis **781**
Price, Florence **1622**
Price, John E. **632**
Protest music **63-64, 85, 659, 670**
Psalmody **856, 867, 870, 878, 880,**
888, 890, 920, 924, 929, 938,
953, 963, 1068, 1072. *See also*
Hymnody
Purvis, Richard **254**

Ragtime **21, 790, 1574**

Reich, Steve **256**
Reinagle, Alexander **211, 261,**
423, 624, 2161
Revivals and music **844, 848, 878,**
938, 943
Revolutionary War, music of **597,**
667, 1353
Reynolds, Isham E. **951**
Rice, Edward E. **727**
Rice, Thomas Dartmouth **2144**
Rich, Buddy **769**
Riegger, Wallingford **248, 252,**
455, 634, 1420, 1436, 1619
Rippon, John **979**
Roach, Max **769**
Robinson, D. G. **2098**
Rochberg, George **327, 1434,**
1489, 1583, 1606
Rock and roll **13, 770, 772, 781,**
801, 810, 821, 897, 2030-31
Rodgers, Richard **376, 719,**
737-38, 758
Rogers, James Hotchkiss **344, 364**
Rome, Harold **724**
Roosevelt, Theodore **100**
Root, George Frederick **372, 649**
Rorem, Ned **222, 270, 320, 392,**
1623
Rose, Billy **735**
Rosenfeld, Paul **1994**
Ross, Walter **1515**
Rózsa, Miklós **288**
Rubinstein, Artur **24**
Rudhyar, Dane **369**
Ruger, Morris Hutchins **1106**
Ruggles, Carl **414, 1541, 1616**
Ryan, Duane Chester **528**
Ryder, Noah Francis **1113**

Sacred music **110, 232, 265, 285,**
305, 331, 393, 402, 424, 438,
825-1091, 1487, 1575

Taubman, Howard **1995**
Taylor, Raynor **253, 834, 1555**
Theophane, M. **999**
Thomas, Alfred Jack **1114**
Thomas, Charles John **395**
Thomas, Jean **1811**
Thomas, Theodore **471**
Thompson, Daniel **168**
Thompson, Randall **346, 401, 422,
    671, 1413, 1479, 1487, 1522,
    1564, 1597**
Thomson, Virgil **700, 1572, 1988,
    2001**
Timrod, Henry **110**
Titcomb, Everett **1483**
Trombone music **612, 1059, 1501,
    1515, 1980**
Trumpet music **806, 815, 1388,
    1401, 1605, 1610, 1972**
Tubb, Ernest **1951**
Tufts, John **929**
Tullidge, John Elliott **242**
Tunebooks **645, 652-53, 862,
    864-65, 874, 879, 884, 911, 921,
    929, 934, 937, 952, 1042, 1044,
    1328, 2082.** *See also* Hymnody

Ussachevsky, Vladimir **322, 388**

Van Hulse, Camil **1483**
Van Vactor, David **398**
Varèse, Edgard **322, 384, 593, 1440,
    1518, 1591, 1609, 1621, 1630**
Vaudeville **723, 730, 743-44, 748,
    750, 752, 2361**
Vietnam War music **55**
Viola music **1496**
Violin music **218, 390, 411, 626,
    630-31, 808, 1378, 1457, 1658,
    1923, 1939-44**

Violoncello music **1373, 1387,
    1427, 1555, 1596**
Vocal music **4, 200, 239, 290-91,
    299, 419, 438, 857, 862, 905,
    1147, 1242, 1316, 1573, 1575.**
    See also Anthems; Songs

Wainwright, John W. **1119**
Wald, George **1382**
Walker, George **632**
Walker, William **921**
Walter, Thomas **929**
Ward, Robert **630, 1524**
Warren, George William **896**
Warriner, Solomon **874**
Washington, George **108**
Watt, Douglas **1995**
Weber, Ben **630**
Weber, Louis **221**
Webster, Joseph Philbrick **214**
Weill, Kurt **734, 739, 1572**
Weisgall, Hugo **452**
Wetmore, Truman S. **953**
White, Benjamin Franklin **1590**
White, Clarence Cameron **274**
White, Minnie **1649**
Whitman, Walt **105**
Whittier, John Greenleaf **946**
Wilder, Alec **1593**
Williams, Anthony **824**
Williams, Clifton **635**
Williams, N. L. **949**
Wills, Bob **1956**
Willson, Meredith **1422**
Wilson, Teddy **763**
Winner, Septimus (Alice Hawthorne)
    24, 383
Wolff, Christian **322**
Wolpe, Stefan **430**
Woodbridge, William Channing
    1132, 1328